Thinker, Learner, Dreamer, Doer: Inn Pedagogies for Cultivating Every Student's Potential

This book is brilliant. It is astonishingly practical and insightful. We create the conditions for each child's brilliance to manifest by a strengths-based approach in a culture of true caring. We may know these truths but have been too casual in practicing them. Today's world demands unfamiliar levels of courage and commitment to implement these practices wherever we can. It's now or never. A truly remarkable work!

Margaret J. Wheatley, Ed.D,
author of 10 books, from *Leadership and the New Science* to *Who Do We Choose to Be?*

Gamwell and Daly have done it again. With *Thinker, Learner, Dreamer, Doer,* they provide parents, children, teachers, administrators, and anyone else interested in schooling with an antidote to narrow-minded thinking and stifling technocracy. Key takeaways and practical ideas you can run with end each chapter. If you're tired of testing mandates and one-size-fits-all curricula, start earmarking your favorite pages of this book now. Mine already looks like an accordion.

Joel Westheimer,
University Research Chair in Democracy and Education at the University of Ottawa, Education columnist for CBC Radio

Peter Gamwell and Jane Daly challenge our understanding of what resiliency can mean. They introduce us to educators and other leaders who are succeeding (or creatively failing) as they seek to allow resiliency to flourish. Read this book: you will gain valuable tools to bolster your own skills and growth. You will be given insight in educating and engaging others towards their better lives.

Kate White,
Executive Emeritus,
United Nations Association in Canada

This is an indispensable work for anyone deeply committed to an education system that will inform not only students' minds but also their hearts. Education innovation really flourishes at the magical fusion of top-down strategies and bottom-up initiatives. Educators will find a practical framework to implement and create a support base for their innovation strategy or practice.

Piet Grymonprez,
Cofounder and Managing Director of MyMachine Global Foundation,
Brussels, Belgium

This book is both compelling and informative, filled with invaluable nuggets that resonate. The links to the videos punctuate the text with a creative and personal dimension that offers a kinaesthetic engagement for the reader. At a time when education is faced with an undeniable need for change, this book is a must-read for everyone—teacher, parent, and student!

Peter Gamwell and Jane Daly use powerful and moving stories to lay out what schools can do to help students fully develop their potential and become the dreamers, doers, learners, and thinkers we need. This book provides specific actions educators can take to create a better educational environment where students can grow their potential and follow their passion. It is a book education needs in the effort to rethink and reimagine a better future for all children.

This is a new kind of book—one that invites us to perceive the innovation capacities within us all. Its bold goal is to inspire environments that enable our inherent brilliance. Read it—as it will help you emerge spaces that enable leadership, engagement, and thriving futures in the Age of Complexity.

This book is outstanding. Its unique perspectives are stimulating, thought-provoking, inspiring, challenging, and enlightening. I recommend this book to fellow scholars who are interested in innovation education, as well as teachers, trainers, and anyone curious about innovative pedagogies for cultivating every student's potential.

Peter is a creative leader and educator who speaks and leads from the heart. He is a proven nurturer of the seeds of brilliance in others. He is a curator and a cheerleader of the innovative practices of educators. All of this comes alive in the book *Thinker, Learner, Dreamer, Doer*. As leaders and educators, we want to ensure the active engagement and development of each student and each adult with whom we work. Peter and Jane inspire and offer insight on to how we can do this better.

Through charming recounts of authentic experiences inside and outside of the classroom, *Thinker, Learner, Dreamer, Doer* weaves together lessons to be learned in the dynamic intersection of leadership, learning, and living . . . and it does so brilliantly! The book's voice is its greatest strength! The stories, shared with grace and humour, description and detail, and tact and tension (at times!), make it an intriguing read from start to end. The book's relevancy is as clear as can be: the creation of conditions for stakeholders to flourish in the systems they inhabit!

Pino Buffone
Director of Education Renfrew County District School Board
Pembroke, Ontario, Canada

Gamwell and Daly's approach gets back to the types of learning at the hopeful center of all our work. Each vignette is wonderful and attainable in some way as a model. The authors' strength-based approach to innovation is informed by research, grounded practice, conversations, and common sense. It rings refreshingly clear in these uncertain times. The work should inform and support teams across the world.

Peter Dillon
Superintendent of Schools
Berkshire Hill Regional School District Stockbridge, Massachusetts

This book focuses on the elements necessary to create a culture in which every child's particular brilliance is enabled and enhanced. The video clips are extremely compelling and illustrate the points perfectly. Peter Gamwell and Jane Daly, consummate storytellers, have written another gem of a book that shows us the conditions necessary to grow creativity that is present in each child. In so doing, their brilliance shines.

Dr. Betty J. Sternberg
CT Commissioner, Director, Teacher Leader Fellowship Program
Central Connecticut State University

This book is a WINNER!!! An important read for those who truly believe that every person has unique brilliance. I LOVE the student video interviews! The TRY THIS sections and the authentic stories of schools are powerful and effective and will help committed educators begin the conversations necessary for change and transformation. The opportunity is NOW as we leverage complexity and chaos to envision things differently . . . because we can and because we must.

Lynn Macan, Retired Superintendent
Cobleskill-Richmondville CSD
Bluffton, South Carolina

Thinker, Learner, Dreamer, Doer

For my granddaughters, Leah, Dylan, and Grace
Love, Grandpa

For my Mom, Who taught me a love of books,
and for whom nature-based learning and camping
always came naturally.
Jane

Thinker, Learner, Dreamer, Doer

Innovative Pedagogies for Cultivating Every Student's Potential

Peter Gamwell

Jane Daly

Foreword by Yong Zhao

For information:

Corwin

A SAGE Company

2455 Teller Road

Thousand Oaks, California 91320

(800) 233-9936

www.corwin.com

SAGE Publications Ltd.

1 Oliver's Yard

55 City Road

London EC1Y 1SP

United Kingdom

SAGE Publications India Pvt. Ltd.

B 1/I 1 Mohan Cooperative Industrial Area

Mathura Road, New Delhi 110 044

India

SAGE Publications Asia-Pacific Pte. Ltd.

18 Cross Street #10-10/11/12

China Square Central

Singapore 048423

President: Mike Soules

Associate Vice President and
Editorial Director: Monica Eckman

Senior Acquisitions Editors: Ariel Curry &
Tanya Ghans

Senior Content Development Editor:
Desiree A. Bartlett

Editorial Assistants: Caroline Timmings &
Nyle De Leon

Production Editor: Astha Jaiswal

Copy Editor: Patrice J. Sutton

Typesetter: C&M Digitals (P) Ltd.

Cover Designer: Rose Storey

Marketing Manager: Margaret O'Connor

Printed in Canada

Library of Congress Cataloging-in-Publication Data

Names: Gamwell, Peter, author. | Daly, Jane, author.

Title: Thinker, learner, dreamer, doer : innovative pedagogies for cultivating every student's potential / Peter Gamwell, Ph.D. and Jane Daly.

Identifiers: LCCN 2021053915 | ISBN 9781071837221 (Paperback : acid-free paper) | ISBN 9781071837214 (ePub) | ISBN 9781071837207 (ePub) | ISBN 9781071837191 (PDF)

Subjects: LCSH: Educational leadership. | Creative thinking. | Organizational change.

Classification: LCC LB2806 .G2895 2022 | DDC 371.2/011—dc23/eng/20220215
LC record available at https://lccn.loc.gov/2021053915

This book is printed on acid-free paper.

22 23 24 25 26 10 9 8 7 6 5 4 3 2 1

Contents

Videos may also be accessed at
www.corwin.com/ThinkerListofVideos

List of Videos

· ·

Note From the Publisher: The authors have provided video and web content throughout the book that is available to you through QR (quick response) codes. To read a QR code, you must have a smartphone or tablet with a camera. We recommend that you download a QR code reader app that is made specifically for your phone or tablet brand.

Videos may also be accessed at **www.corwin.com/ThinkerListofVideos**

Acknowledgments

The early stages of writing this book coincided with the passing of someone who had a profound influence on my life, both personally and professionally. I was fortunate to have known Sir Ken Robinson for some thirty years. He was a mentor to me and a dear friend, as he was to so many. I first met him in the early 1990s at a Toronto conference regarding the arts in education. It was at that conference that I first felt compelled by his unique vision, which resonated with so many people around the globe.

It wasn't just his vision. He also provided a structure to help us make that vision a reality; he shared a lexicon to express this vision in our own way. And he created an urgency in his call to action—action that would transform the lives of students, families, communities, and educators.

For twelve years, I led a creativity movement with a school district in Ottawa, Ontario, Canada. We wanted to foster learning cultures founded on the belief that in every person, adults and children alike, there lies a seed of brilliance—and that our primary focus should be to create the environmental, leadership, and cultural conditions that allow those seeds to flourish. Sir Ken was incredibly helpful in guiding and advising me on that journey, and on several occasions he gave keynote speeches and workshops at events we called Lead the Way. He was generous with his time and in the way he personalized the experience for everyone with whom he interacted. He immersed himself in the process and often put in twelve-hour days. His humanity always stood out—and his humor. He was never more than a semitone away from a one-liner.

So I felt it important to express my acknowledgment and to express my gratitude for his vision, his courage, and his mentorship and friendship. I really am not sure that without his influence and encouragement, I would be writing this book. Thank you, Sir Ken.

Another person who was very generous with her time, who helped guide us during the initial planning of this book, including how to present our stories coherently in print, was Margaret J. Wheatley. Meg, thank you for sharing your rich insights on organizational behavior and living systems, and for your warmth, wit, and encouragement.

The publication of our first book, *The Wonder Wall: Leading Creative Schools and Organizations in an Age of Complexity,* also coincided with the birth of our first two granddaughters, Leah and Dylan. They were just in time for the book launch, though they tell me they don't remember it.

Leah and Dylan

They were joined a year later by their cousin, Grace. I was delighted to watch their seeds of brilliance come to life, following the path of the three foundational imperatives of healthy and innovative learning environments that we explored in *The Wonder Wall*. And thanks to their amazing parents, family, and their grandma, Lele, the girls have bridged their inspiring environments to shine light on the characteristics of leadership we've explored here in *Thinker, Learner, Dreamer, Doer*: curiosity, the challenging of assumptions (and the assumptions on which they are based), and yes, their vibrant collision of ideas, alive in such young minds. All has brought a joyful lens and invigoration to the writing of this book.

Many years ago, I started to document and videotape the stories I came across. Now, whenever I'm asked to work with a class, a group of educators, or a school or community group, I bring the role of the ethnographer. I'm as eager to learn from their stories as I am to share my ideas. I've collected hundreds of such interviews, and many of the stories are told here. I'm so grateful to those who opened up to me and allowed me to share their journeys through the videos on these pages—people from age six to ninety-six. It's one thing to read these stories in a book; it's quite another to experience the telling of the story in the moment. Through sharing their experiences, they help us to determine how to reimagine learning cultures and the conditions that will foster our seeds of brilliance.

Thanks also for those who contemplated and answered the question that Jane and I have been asking for many years: If you were given a blank slate, a magic wand, and the opportunity to reimagine and redesign a culture of learning, what would be some of your unshakable, foundational characteristics? The answers to this question, and others, helped us to shape and hone our own ideas. And it enabled us to craft, in our last chapter, a somewhat different approach to the assessment of creativity, shifting the focus from assessing the learner to assessing the learning culture.

Every now and again the stars align, and we meet someone who has a deep impact on our lives. I am fortunate this has happened often in my life. In 2012, when I was looking for someone to tell the story that traced our school board journey and research findings on fostering cultures of creativity, the search led me to Jane Daly. Since that time, Jane and I have coauthored a book and several articles together. This current book is told through my voice. But I want to make it clear that the ideas in the book are a result of two minds exchanging ideas, playing with ideas, and continually seeking new and novel ways to think things through.

Curiously, it came to me that the underpinning characteristics that we reveal in this book, pertaining to the growing of cultures of brilliance, capture precisely the dynamic of our thinking and writing. We are both insatiably curious; we often challenge each other's assumptions and the assumptions on which they are based; and yes, we collide. And through that collision emerge new pathways and new possibilities. This is a genuinely collaborative effort, and the book simply would not work without it. Thank you, Jane, for your brilliance, insight, and beautiful writing.

Publisher's Acknowledgments

Corwin gratefully acknowledges the contributions of the following reviewers:

Pino Buffone, Director
Renfrew County District School Board
Pembroke, Ontario CANADA

Peter Dillon, Superintendent of Schools
Berkshire Hill Regional School District
Stockbridge, MA

Jill Gildea, Superintendent
Fremont School District 79
Mundelein, IL

Kandace Jordan, Deputy Superintendent of Schools, Director of International Programs

Golden Hills School Division
Calgary, Alberta CANADA

Lynn Lisy-Macan, Retired Superintendent
Learner-Centered Initiatives
New York City, NY

Betty Sternberg, Project Director
Teacher Leader Fellowship Program
Central Connecticut State University
New Britain, CT

Karen Tichy, Assistant Professor
Saint Louis University
St. Louis, MO

Yong Zhao, Foundation Distinguished Professor
University of Kansas
Lawrence, KS

About the Authors

Peter Gamwell

Born in Liverpool, England, Peter is the co-author, with Jane Daly, of *The Wonder Wall: Leading Creative Schools and Organizations in an Age of Complexity*, 2017, Corwin, foreword by Sir Ken Robinson; and *Thinker, Learner, Dreamer, Doer: Innovative Pedagogies for Cultivating Every Student's Potential*, April, 2022, Corwin, foreword by Yong Zhao.

An insightful, entertaining, and knowledgeable speaker, presenter, and consultant, Peter brings decades of academic research, experience, and insightful knowledge, gleaned from his award-winning career as a teacher and administrator at all levels of the education system. Through his presentations, workshops, books, YouTube channel, and website, he explores learning, leadership, and innovation and their impact on individual and organizational health and culture. Peter has worked across Canada and throughout many parts of the world, showing students, educators, administrators, schools, districts, companies, and policy makers how to foster that vibrancy in their own organizations.

Through the course of his work and research, Peter has captured the voices of hundreds of students and adults alike, video clips that provide unique and insightful glimpses into the lived world of our classrooms, schools, and organizations. These clips also provide critical insight as to how we might imagine our learning cultures in a way that reawakens the brilliance that lies in all of us, with a central focus on individual, group, and organizational well-being.

An adjunct professor with the University of Ottawa, Peter has been the recipient of many awards throughout his forty-year career. In 2013, he was awarded the Distinguished Leadership Award by the Ontario Public Supervisory Officers' Association for the work he led in

Learning, Leadership and Creativity with the Ottawa-Carleton District School Board. In 2015, he was awarded the Global Distinguished Leadership Award by the Alberta Teachers' Association.

In 2020, he cofounded the Canadian Network for Imagination and Creativity, @CNIC, which holds monthly *IdeaJams* on a wide range of topics—and which evoke lots of lively interactive conversation.

Jane Daly

Although Jane's career took her into the marketing and communications world, she was always fascinated by the field of education and the seeds of potential in every individual—especially when one of her own sons had difficulty reading and thus became "a problem to be solved." She has worked on numerous communications projects for educational institutions and has taught at the college level. She has often observed the challenges and opportunities that both educational organizations and businesses share when it comes to organizational learning.

Jane was happy to join Peter Gamwell as coauthor for *The Wonder Wall: Leading Creative Schools and Organizations in an Age of Complexity* and again with *Thinker, Learner, Dreamer, Doer: Innovative Pedagogies for Cultivating Every Student's Potential.*

Jane freelances as a communications strategist and commercial writer by day and enjoys fiction writing by night, as well as spending time with her husband John, and their kids and grandkids, at the small MacLaren's Landing beach community outside of Ottawa, Ontario, Canada.

Foreword

Yong Zhao
University of Kansas
University of Melbourne

This is a time when we need to dream. The COVID-19 pandemic resulted in millions of loved ones gone, tremendous disruptions to our normal life, and an unpredictable future. To move forward we must look to and dream of a better world. Hope lies in what we can imagine and what we can create for tomorrow.

Children are natural-born dreamers but beyond dreaming of passing exams and receiving college acceptance letters, we want our children to dream of a world that is more prosperous and peaceful for everyone. This requires an education that guides students in asking questions about how humans can live peacefully together, and how we can respect differences and share our prosperity rather than wasting resources on creating divisions and fighting with one another.

We need schools that can prepare our children to become pragmatic dreamers who strive for justice, equality, and peace for all. But dreams are not enough. We need doers. We need to nurture students who can dream *and* take action.

This requires preparing them with the abilities and knowledge they will need to accomplish their goals. Instead of relying on the skills and knowledge requirements of the past, educators need to make rich connections between students' strengths, passions, and the skills and knowledge they will need to apply their individual strengths to their particular passions. A homogenous curriculum will not work. Our increasingly diverse world needs new and emerging talents – often students are our best guides as to what those talents are.

As we design the curricula of tomorrow, we need to do so knowing that what students learn during their K-12 education will not serve them for their entire life. The world is constantly changing, and the changes can be fast and significant. We need to prepare students to become self-motivated learners who will continue to seek out additional skills and knowledge throughout their entire lives. When faced with novel possibilities and challenges, someone with a learner mindset can quickly respond with timely learned and invented approaches. We need to stop limiting teaching to a few domains of knowledge and skills, instead, schools must prepare students to become lifelong learners who can seek out the learning they need when they need it in an infinite range of domains.

A dreamer, a doer, and a learner has also to be a thinker: an independent and critical thinker. The world is filled with misinformation as well as biased and manipulated messages. The world is also filled with mysteries, unknown places, and uncertainties. Beyond our planet is a vast space of unknown. We need our students to develop their capacity as thinkers so they can make sound judgments and reach for heretofore unimagined scientific discoveries.

To prepare dreamers, doers, learners, and thinkers requires innovations in education. In *Thinker, Learner, Dreamer, Doer: Innovative Pedagogies for Cultivating Every Student's Potential,* Dr. Peter Gamwell and Jane Daly use powerful and moving stories to lay out what schools can do to help each and every student fully develop their potential to become the dreamers, doers, learners, and thinkers we need in the Age of Complexity. This book does more than chart a frontier in education. It provides specific actions educators can take to create a better educational environment in which students can grow their potential and can follow their passion. It is a book education needs in the effort to rethink and reimagine a better future for all children.

CHAPTER 1

THINKER, LEARNER, DREAMER, DOER

INNOVATIVE PEDAGOGIES FOR CULTIVATING EVERY STUDENT'S POTENTIAL

"We need to help students adapt to the strong winds of change more like a resilient palm tree, rather than a strong oak."

—Peter Gamwell

In our first book, *The Wonder Wall: Leading Creative Schools and Organizations in a World of Complexity* (Gamwell & Daly, 2017), Jane Daly and I proposed that our modern society has entered a new era, one which we called the *Age of Complexity*.

That was in 2017, and while we thought we were living in complex times then, little did we know that our world was about to get significantly more complicated.

In the fall of 2019, we received an invitation from our publisher, Corwin, to submit a proposal for our next book, *Thinker, Learner, Dreamer, Doer: Innovative Pedagogies for Cultivating Every Student's Potential*. We carefully did our research and conducted interviews and busily plotted chapter outlines—all based on what we perceived to be our world's reality in that moment. We submitted the proposal just before Christmas.

And then COVID-19 hit, and everything changed.

We weren't alone, of course. Those four words, *And then COVID hit*, became a defining phrase for us in the years 2020 and 2021, as we listened to so many of our friends, colleagues and family members describe how their best-laid plans had gone awry. Weddings, graduation ceremonies, and long-awaited family vacations and reunions were canceled. Those who had been setting off to college or university stayed home. Schools and day cares closed, and our neighborhood parks and playgrounds were silent.

All of us were thrust into learning new ways of doing things. The way we shop changed dramatically. Companies, especially small, local businesses, scrambled to find and set up new ways to serve their customers and keep the lights on. Businesses of all sizes saw their supply chains disrupted as they struggled to stay afloat and remain relevant in an increasingly turbulent global market. Too many sank beneath the surface, and job layoffs and losses followed.

Many of those who were able to keep their jobs began to work remotely, an especially challenging experience for those trying to juggle jobs and children. Once sedate and dignified business meetings became riddled with toddlers in full tantrum mode, barking dogs, bleary eyes, and yes, the odd participant caught in the buff.

Others, from first responders and health care workers to truck drivers and retail clerks, risked their own health and lives to keep the world going. Among those heroes were teachers and educators who, even if they were not physically in a classroom, pulled out all the stops to try to keep some semblance of normalcy and stability for their students, in a rapidly changing world no one had ever experienced before.

Many people, especially those who lived alone, became socially isolated, cut off physically from their friends, co-workers and loved ones. With hospitals closed to visitors, too many lost loved ones to the disease without even having the chance to say goodbye.

Our once busy roads trickled to a few cars and empty city buses rumbling by. As workplaces, restaurants, movie theatres and other social gathering spots were shuttered, friendly chats over the back fence disappeared. Without planes overhead, even the skies were quieted, save for the rather incongruously cheerful chirping of birds.

Welcome to the Age of Complexity

Strangely enough, Jane and I had actually predicted a global pandemic in *The Wonder Wall* as one example of how, when living in an Age of Complexity, even the best-laid plans can change forever in an instant. The COVID-19 pandemic was having an impact on nearly every conceivable aspect of our lives, and we were filled with the uncertainty of not knowing how long the situation would last and how bad (or not so bad) things were going to get.

We learned our book proposal had been accepted in early June of 2020, with a publishing date set for the spring of 2022. As we began writing out *Thinker, Learner, Dreamer, Doer* in earnest, in the midst of the pandemic and the ongoing unrest for George Floyd's senseless death, we had no idea what was going to happen next, how the world was about to change, or whether the content of our book would even be relevant in nearly two years' time.

As we now draw closer to finishing our first draft of *Thinker, Learner, Dreamer, Doer*, here in April of 2021, the changes in our lives continue to astound us. While Jane and I met at least weekly in person while working on *The Wonder Wall*, we've not seen each other face-to-face in well over a year. This has made co-authoring a book together a much different kind of exercise. We've faced a lot more challenges and have sometimes felt like we were flying blind.

But through the process, one thing became crystal clear to both of us. Despite the ongoing uncertainty in the world, *Thinker, Learner, Dreamer, Doer: Innovative Pedagogies for Cultivating Every Student's Potential*, has never been more relevant. The more things change, the more chaotic and unpredictable things become, the more we need to bring out the seeds of brilliance that are lying dormant in our students—the thinkers, learners, dreamers, and doers of today and tomorrow. We need to arm our people with the innovative skills, resilience, and compassion it will take to not only bring us through these challenging times but also enable us to find, embrace, and build new opportunities for healthy learning and working environments and true cultures of belonging for students, teachers, parents, and communities.

> *The more things change, the more chaotic and unpredictable things become, the more we need to bring out the seeds of brilliance that are lying dormant in our students—the thinkers, learners, dreamers, and doers of today and tomorrow.*

Thinker, Learner, Dreamer, Doer builds on some ideas introduced in *The Wonder Wall*, but don't worry if you haven't read it or if you need a refresher. There are only two things you need to know about, which we've briefly summarized here: the impacts of living in an Age of Complexity, and the three imperatives and four supporting conditions for building healthy, innovative learning environments.

Adapting to an increasingly complex world

In times past, eras typically began or ended in a very linear fashion, due to some significant social upheaval such as war, political changes, cultural revolutions, or innovation or when the "Next Big Thing" came along. And yes, when a pandemic occurred.

But with today's much faster rate of change and scope of complexity, eras are no longer politely waiting for a former era to leave the stage before emerging from the wings. Instead, we're seeing hundreds of eras take the stage simultaneously across all spheres of society: educational, political, spiritual, economic, social, technological, medical, scientific, environmental, and more. There are no longer beginnings or endings but rather a blurred, continuous confluence of changes, upheavals, down-heavals, round-and-round heavals, and influences.

Our current Age of Complexity is a time in which we're pulled in dozens of different directions and influenced by multiple competing factors at once, to the extent that it's no longer clear or sometimes even possible to determine the right courses of action to take. You could see this phenomenon during COVID-19, in which measures taken to protect the public's health could plunge people into poverty, while measures to protect the economy could risk people's lives. Issues can no longer be viewed in strictly good or bad, right or wrong, terms.

Thinking about a jigsaw puzzle can help you envision what living in an Age of Complexity is like. A jigsaw puzzle can be both messy and neat—its pieces scattered randomly across a table, or arranged into one coherent piece, matching what we expect it to look like from the picture on the box. But imagine if that picture on the box was different from the finished puzzle; or if there were not only some puzzle pieces missing but pieces from other puzzles added in. And what if some puzzle pieces changed their images, colors, or dimensions? Or after you'd correctly put some pieces together, they later changed shape and no longer fit?

Such is life in the Age of Complexity.

Although COVID-19 was certainly far-reaching in its complexity, complexities are increasingly ubiquitous, ranging from the environment to the economy to social media to family structure to science. This Age of Complexity will likely be with us for generations to come.

Unprecedented impacts on our world

This state of complexity impacts our world in three unprecedented ways.

1. **Changes push and pull us in all directions at once.** Ages were once perceived as evolutionary stages of progress, each building on the lessons and developments of the previous in a

linear fashion. In states of complexity, however, we are evolving, devolving, and revolving, and advances that push one sphere of society forward such as resource extraction may have a direct and negative impact on another, such as the environment. For example, electric vehicles, which reduce emissions, also cause significant pollution from lithium mining to manufacture car batteries.

2. **There is less consensus on what "progress" looks like.** The internet and social media have given us the ability to instantly communicate and refute opinions, facing off multiple stakeholder groups with opposing viewpoints. This can make it harder to find solutions a majority can agree on, or even figure out which direction we should be pulling together.

3. **This complexity makes future trends more difficult to predict.** Within the mathematical concept of chaos theory, complex systems are highly sensitive to changes in conditions, so even small alterations can result in disproportionate consequences. It's important to bear in mind that these results aren't always negative, however. Even a single teacher making a single positive change can have a domino effect more quickly than ever before.

The impacts this complexity is having on our traditional methods of teaching and leading employees are profound and introduce a messiness and uncertainty that we must embrace if we are to reimagine the future. It's human nature to strive for equilibrium and balance; today's Age of Complexity means we must instead adapt to the idea that balance may no longer be attainable and re-engineer our education systems to build a better, more innovative future for all, regardless. We need to help students adapt to the strong winds of change more like a resilient palm tree, rather than a strong oak. We need to help them not only survive in the Age of Complexity but to *thrive* through innovative thinking.

How we react to times of inbetweenity

In times of complexity, people are often forced to get creative and come up with new ways of doing things if they're going to survive. The late Dr. Bobby Moore introduced us to the concept of inbetweenity—times in between times when one era is on its way out and another has yet to emerge (Gamwell & Daly, 2017). He believed there are three main ways people typically handle this state of flux.

1. Some attempt to stay rooted in the past, holding on to the status quo for dear life. For this group, change is a source of great anxiety, and they try to cling to the old ways of doing things.

2. Others take a more hybrid approach, trying to deal with the uncertainty by projecting past or current trends in the future. They say they're okay with change, as long as it's predictable and stays obediently within known parameters.

3. A third group, by contrast, embraces the developing uncertainties, employing a faculty of vision. Less threatened by change, they believe any negative impacts can be overcome through innovation and that there are always opportunities to be grasped. They lead others by fostering environments that harness imagination in pursuit of solutions; they don't try to control or to predict the future but to *invent* it. These practical visionaries have the ability to construct worlds that are not yet but can be.

The confluence of so many changes and variables makes it hard for people to even know where to begin sorting it all out, so many of them get the urge to try to *control* the complexity, nail it down, put it into a plan and contrive ways to monitor it, manage it, measure it, and mitigate it. We tend to become more rigid and inflexible as we try to control the complexity, attempting to micromanage things within our spheres of influence.

However, when things are changing so quickly and in so many different directions, attempting to find the *one right answer*, or even determine the *one wrong thing*, may be futile; it may be more advantageous to research a variety of flexible and nimble solutions, back up resources, and make contingency plans.

> *We need to move beyond teaching students to answer the questions and teach them to question the answers.*

That means that in our classrooms, we need to move beyond teaching students to answer the questions and teach them to question the answers, as well as to question assumptions and the assumptions on which the assumptions are based.

The Three Imperatives and Four Conditions

So how do we get students and others to become more innovative? Exploring these ideas led Jane and me to a confounding conundrum. If innovative thinking is a skill that only a lucky few possess, how do we explain those situations in which students, individuals, and entire teams suddenly and inexplicably become brilliant, displaying innovation, insight, and leadership capabilities significantly beyond what they have ever demonstrated before?

And more importantly, what is the elusive formula that can allow teachers and other leaders to consistently replicate this "blossoming brilliance" in classrooms, boardrooms, and living rooms alike?

Building on our own experiences in education and business, as well as a decade of research and input from more than a thousand leaders across education and a range of other industry sectors, we uncovered some surprising truths about innovation and leadership. Our most crucial lesson learned is that innovation and leadership are not things we can effectively teach to individuals or teams. What we really need to do is change our learning and working environments in such a way that it allows the natural brilliance—brilliance that lies untapped in each and every one of us—to shine through.

To show how that could be done in *The Wonder Wall*, we identified three crucial imperatives and four supporting conditions for healthy and innovative learning environments. Once embedded, these imperatives and conditions enable teachers and leaders to reimagine and reshape individual and organizational learning environments to increase innovation, leadership, well-being, enhanced learning, and more.

These are the three imperatives:

1. **Recognize that there is a seed of brilliance in everyone.** Believe this, value it, and find ways to tap into this potential.

2. **Think and act from a strength-based perspective.** For example, instead of approaching budget meetings as figuring where we can cut programs, pose questions such as, "What are the amazing possibilities that we want to achieve? How will we make that happen? Who can we partner with?" Avoid deficit thinking that views everything, including struggling students, as "problems to be solved."

3. **Foster a culture of belonging.** This isn't just "nice to have." Brain science is proving that emotions play a crucial role in our ability to think, learn, and retain information.

Four conditions support these imperatives:

1. **Storytelling and listening.** The brain is hardwired to learn through storytelling. Tell your stories. Encourage others to share theirs. Listen with intention. When we encourage people to tell their stories and practice active listening, we build stronger relationships.

2. **Moving beyond diversity to true inclusivity.** We must recognize that every person, of all levels and backgrounds, has important ideas, experiences, and talents to share. Encourage the kind of inclusivity that drives real innovative change.

3. **Making it personal.** We need to make learning deeply personal to allow learning to be embraced. Connect the subject being taught to something that is deeply personal for the learner.

4. **Recognizing that celebration is an attitude.** We need to understand that celebrating isn't an event; it's a way of life. We must foster a sense of joy and novelty with the sheer wonder of learning, knowing that stretching the imagination will lead to tangible results.

How to Get the Most Out of This Book

We don't have all the answers or a one-size-fits-all solution for trans-forming our learning systems. We're always looking for new ideas and insights. So we reached out to classrooms, schools, districts, and orga-nizations in various parts of the world to find inspiring examples for building environments that spawn innovation, leadership, education, humanity, community, and the interconnectedness of it that binds us together.

We were overwhelmed by the positive response, and many schools and organizations invited me to come speak to, lead, or participate in their own quests for innovative environments. I traveled to several loca-tions to work hand in hand on large projects with these partners, who are reimagining what learning environments can be. Eight detailed case studies from these experiences form the basis for this book, and you'll find key themes throughout:

Learn from powerful examples

As you read through *Thinker, Learner, Dreamer, Doer*, you'll find you can "learn by example," as you're invited to view the inner workings of classrooms, school boards, and districts that are using the three imper-atives to enable engagement, innovation, and the unique brilliance of both students and teachers to shine through. You'll also see how this growing brilliance didn't remain in the classroom or confine itself to a few individuals—it sparked a resonance that took the brilliance beyond the classroom and indeed grew throughout the entire community and beyond.

Hear directly from students themselves

In this book, the students become the teachers. One voice that's rarely heard in discussions about educational transformation is the voice of the student. During my many visits to the schools I've been involved with, I've not only talked to the teachers, principals, and parents but also to the students. I've developed an extensive collection of face-to-face, vide-otaped interviews with them to gain a better appreciation of what's hap-pening "on the ground" and to learn from their lived experiences. Many of the stories told here are accompanied by a quick response (QR) code that you can use to access full interviews with students and teachers, as well as other resources.

[*Note:* To read a QR code, you must have a smartphone or tablet with a camera. We recom-mend that you download a QR code reader app that is made specifically for your phone or tablet brand.]

Review main ideas with the Key Takeaways

The end of each chapter includes key takeaways, so you can quickly recap the main points. Think of this as your cheat sheet.

Gain insight for your next steps through Reflective Questions

You'll also find reflective questions you can ask yourself, your colleagues, and even your students to help inform and guide your thinking and next steps to create a truly healthy and innovative learning environment.

Get ideas for related lesson plans with TRY THIS!

Through our own spheres of influence, we can make an enormous difference for those around us by implementing conditions that foster creative learning environments, with practical, simple suggestions. You'll find the book is packed with actionable tips and ideas, and at the end of each chapter, there's a TRY THIS! mini-lesson plan you can try out in your own classroom, school, or community.

Leverage insights about learning in an Age of Complexity

To succeed in an Age of Complexity, Jane and I have learned that students, and everyone else, must be allowed to question assumptions and the assumptions on which the assumptions are based. Deep change is never easy, and there is always pushback. In *Thinker, Learner, Dreamer, Doer,* you can explore deeply ingrained assumptions that our society, and thus our schools and organizations, must challenge if we are to strive for a more optimistic and harmonious world in our new Age of Complexity. Teaching students (and adults) how to untangle and challenge these assumptions and engage in productive discussion provides the tools they need to be more resilient and compassionate, and to think critically and innovatively. Although focused on schools, the insight, ideas, and methods included in *Thinker, Learner, Dreamer, Doer* can be applied in virtually any environment, whether it's a classroom, business, family, organization, or community.

You may want to read this book twice

Thinker, Learner, Dreamer, Doer is for people who want to create environments that foster and support innovation, leadership, and engagement. It's for people who believe that everybody has unique creative capacities, and in this age of incredible complexity, they want to find ways of fostering cultures that tap into that brilliance and uniqueness that lie within everyone. It's an intricate and interconnected process, with no easy answers and some overlap. We hope you find great joy and inspiration in this book, and to understand the full nuance, we encourage you to read it twice.

CHAPTER 1

Key Takeaways

- We're living in an Age of Complexity: The speed of changes taking place across all spheres of life and the increasing number of competing agendas means it's no longer possible to determine the "one right answer" or the "one wrong problem," and we must find new ways to communicate and innovate.

- Times of Inbetweenity: People tend to react in one of three ways when facing times of uncertainty—strive to hold onto the status quo; attempt to move forward by using tools and knowledge from the past; or embrace the uncertainty and invent the future through a faculty of vision.

- Every person has seeds of brilliance, which flourish through healthy learning environments: The three imperatives and four conditions that create those environments and drive innovation will help you in creating your own healthy environments.

Reflective Questions

1. How can we, as teachers and leaders, model and shape the learning culture to be sensitive to students' stages of inbetweenity and transitions? What would happen if we talked to our students about our own times of inbetweenity and what we did to cope?

2. Even day-to-day transitions throughout the school day can become times of inbetweenity. Some students might experience anxiety moving from class to class, and we probably all remember the dread of wondering if we'd find anyone to sit with at lunch. How can we create a caring culture of support for everyone to ease these daily transitions at school?

3. How do we consider the broader community each child comes from and the times of inbetweenity they're experiencing outside school? What can we do on a day-to-day basis to help students articulate their experiences and approaches to coping with inbetweenity?

4. How do we create this supportive environment for our teachers? How do we help new teachers or teachers who are new to the school or a specific grade?

Try This!

Make a Plan for Your School's Times of Inbetweenity

This chapter discussed the three main ways people react to times of inbetweenity. We experience the anxiety—or hope and excitement—at times of inbetweenity that take place throughout our lives: graduations, marriage (or divorce), starting a new job (or losing one), switching careers, moving to a new city, becoming a parent, retirement, and many other of life's milestones.

Children are impacted by the inbetweenities of the adults in their lives, but they grapple with their own as well, from welcoming a new sibling and the first day of school to the death of a grandparent and applying for colleges or first jobs.

Host an Inbetweenity Workshop

Hold a workshop to introduce the concept of inbetweenity to your colleagues and teachers.

- For a true diversity of ideas, invite some students to join the workshop as well. Invited students should not be only the high achievers but students from all levels, including those who struggle.

- Build a list of the daily, weekly, or seasonal times of inbetweenity staff and students may experience. Invite an open discussion on how these times make people feel, and how it impacts learning and well-being.

(Continued)

(Continued)

- Choose three to five of the most disruptive or opportunistic times of inbetweenity to work on.

- Break into groups, ensuring that each group has a good mixture of administration, teachers, and students. Ask them to think deeply about how to be sensitive to staff and students' own times of inbetweenity, and how to help individuals and groups cope with and embrace these momentous milestones and changes.

- Each team can be assigned to tackle one of the chosen inbetweenities, or you may want to have the teams work around the room clockwise, so all have a crack at coming up with solutions for each inbetweenity.

- Share the results with the school community and invite more solutions from across the district.

Be sure to take a strength-based approach. Get creative! Rather than viewing these times as problems to be solved, explore how these events might bring about positive experiences and exciting opportunities. For example, if ninth-grade students experience the first day of high school as a nerve-racking time of inbetweenity, perhaps each could be assigned a senior student to greet them at the door, take them to their locker, tour them around the school, and get them to their first class—helping not only to ease the anxiety of the younger students but building a mentorship opportunity between different-aged peers as well.

CHAPTER 2
THE UNCOMFORTABLE CHAPTER

"We must be able to question assumptions and the assumptions
on which the assumptions are based."

—Peter Gamwell

Jane and I call this *The Uncomfortable Chapter* because, well, it might make some people a bit uncomfortable. In fact, we struggled over whether or not to include it, because we really don't like creating awkward moments.

So if you'd rather, feel free to skip over this chapter and continue on with the rest of the book. You can always come back to it later if you get curious. And in the meantime, you'll still get to explore eight inspiring stories where teachers, school boards, businesses, and communities are working together to spark innovation and bring out the seeds of brilliance in their people.

However, we believe that if you bear with us and read this chapter to the very end, you'll find getting there is well worth it. We believe you'll be able to reframe your thinking in such a way that you'll feel calmer, stronger, and more capable of dealing with the constant trials and turbulence we face in this ever-changing Age of Complexity. Best of all, you'll be better able to equip your students with the resilience they need to do the same.

This chapter will show you how you can question the assumptions and the assumptions on which the assumptions are based. The ability to do that is, after all, the very foundation of innovative thinking: If our cave-dwelling forebears had accepted the status quo without questioning it, we would never have reached a point where we could walk on the moon, cure disease, build artificial intelligence, or buy a Chia Pet in the shape of Baby Yoda. Your students will need abundant curiosity and the courage to fearlessly question the status quo throughout their lives. And we need to prepare them for that and give them the tools and the permission to do so.

As always, we don't pretend to have all the answers, so please email us at peter@petergamwell.com with your own questions, insights, and ideas. If you're still with us, let's take a deep breath, and off we go!

There's a New Monster Under Our Beds: Cognitive Dissonance on Steroids

We've all heard of cognitive dissonance, but in our Age of Complexity, it's evolved into something new. It's become cognitive dissonance that's on steroids. . . . in a blender . . . set to pulse—with the lid off. It's become the new monster hiding under our beds and in the dark corners of our minds, actively stifling innovation for ourselves and our students. Here's an example.

Misconceptions and Comfort Zones

Jane was once asked by a small marketing group to proofread a short paper. This marketing team was the new kid on the block, and was looking to find a niche with bankers, establishing themselves as intelligent, innovative thought leaders with fresh ideas. The plan was to distribute the paper to banking professionals, with recommendations on which segments of the population they should target for online banking services, which was just starting to grow.

Now at the time, there was a rather deeply ingrained belief that young adults had a natural, almost wizard-like ability to use digital technology. The thinking was that this cohort had grown up with technology, whereas those born earlier struggled to learn and adapt to this new way of doing things—not just because it was novel, but because they actually *feared* this new technology.

True to the mindset just described, the paper Jane was asked to proofread concluded the most promising market for online banking was the younger crowd. Older cohorts would be a waste of time, due to their fear of online technology.

That pervasive assumption gnawed at Jane. After all, while the younger generation was adept at using the internet, it was their parents' generation who had *invented* it. Why would older generations, who had built their own ham radios and go-karts and flown airplanes over a war zone and put a person on the moon—have a fear of online banking?

To satisfy her own curiosity, Jane decided to question the assumptions and the assumptions on which the assumptions were based. She went to the original research to see how it had been conducted. And that's where she discovered a key fact that turned the paper's premise on its head: Every one of the research participants, young and old alike, were selected from a group that was *already* banking online. The researchers had simply taken aggregate statistics of online banking services and correlated it to the ages of users. When it found older users used fewer online banking services than younger ones, the assumption was it was due to their fear of technology. Jane realized the more likely reason is that retired people are less likely to have the need to pay student loans, mortgages, registered education plans, or retirement saving plans—online or otherwise.

Back Jane went to her clients with her findings, suggesting they could include this exciting senior market as well as the younger set. She thought they would be happy. They decidedly were not. "They said it was common knowledge older people were afraid of technology, and they would lose credibility if they said otherwise."

(Continued)

(Continued)

The funny thing, Jane noted, was that she was bringing them *good* news, the chance to develop a lucrative new market with opportunities for growth. And there was a lovely, warm, and fuzzy feel to it—an opportunity to help seniors do their banking from the comfort of their home.

But accepting the research's results would have required each individual to question their assumptions and change their ingrained perception about older adults and technology. Accepting the survey's results meant embracing a new way of thinking that was outside of the comfort zone. And so, they rejected it outright.

You've just seen how cognitive dissonance could negatively influence decision-making and innovation. But we believe such levels of cognitive dissonance have become even more extreme within the context of *today's state of complexity*. Understanding that is critical to setting up your students for innovative success.

Here's why. Ordinary cognitive dissonance is the uncomfortable feeling, or psychological distress, you get when you hold two or more beliefs or values that are at odds with each other. We believe, however, that in this Age of Complexity, we're being exposed to far more conflicting ideas and beliefs than ever before. Since our natural instinct during such chaotic times is to control whatever we think we can, we've moved beyond being uncomfortable with conflicting ideas within ourselves— and now seek to *control the ideas of others* that conflict with our own. This urge to control stifles innovation not only within ourselves but also within others, especially those (including our students) who fear speaking up or questioning the status quo.

This urge to control stifles innovation not only within ourselves but also within others, especially those (including our students) who fear speaking up or questioning the status quo.

Cognitive dissonance isn't necessarily a bad thing. It can provide the motivation to improve ourselves, particularly when the cognitive dissonance comes from the sense that we're not reaching our full potential.

But cognitive dissonance is a double-edged sword. Especially in today's Age of Complexity, unchecked cognitive dissonance has become a blocker for innovation.

Blame It on Our Left Frontal Cortex

You can lay part of the blame on our left frontal cortex, an area of the brain that's involved in all kinds of things, from decision-making to anger to cognitive dissonance (Harmon-Jones, 2004). While we can't get into all the deep mysteries of this particular lump of grey matter here, it does influence cognitive dissonance in two key ways. In other words, cognitive dissonance isn't simply about having uncomfortable feelings—it's actually biological.

First, researchers (Sharot et al., 2019) have found that when you and a fellow human agree on some point, this part of the brain lights up and becomes very active as the person explains the reasons behind their thinking. But if someone disagrees with you on an issue, it becomes *less* sensitive to the counterarguments. Your brain simply won't absorb or process the points made as effectively (Kappes & Sharot, 2019).

Add this to our Age of Complexity and the urge to control, and achieving agreement seems to be growing evermore difficult. We believe there are three main reasons why.

Why Has Reaching Agreement Become Ever More Elusive?

1. **Fallacies of the *one right answer* and the *one wrong problem***

We not only fall for the fallacy of the "one right answer," we're now caught up in the fallacy of the "one wrong problem." In this Age of Complexity, competing interests and agendas, a myriad of issues, fast-paced changes, and seemingly insurmountable challenges—as well as unprecedented opportunities—are rising up to face the world from all angles, all at once.

Humankind has always sought refuge from cognitive dissonance by seeking out like-minded souls and kindred spirits who generally share our opinions, values, and ideas. Brain science shows we're hardwired to do so (University of Kentucky, 2016). Our fight or flight response encourages us to flee to those who we feel will protect us (or at least not attack us), because we're of like mind.

But today's overwhelming complexity brings on a state of anxiety, chaos, and confusion for many people, putting our discomfort with cognitive dissonance into monster-truck overdrive. We crave, more than ever, the stability and peace that comes from surrounding ourselves with those who think the same as we do. And let's face it—it really is easier to be with people who agree with us, rather than challenge our ideas. Sometimes debating or defending our beliefs requires emotional energy that's already in short supply. It's comforting to find our tribe and share criticisms, memes, and jokes about the things that the *other* side is doing, the things that scare us most in this uncertain new world.

It's easy to see how this way of thinking blocks innovation. Diversity, of backgrounds and of thought, is the lifeblood of creativity and imagination—as well as the ability to talk civilly about new and different ideas. Unless we can do the hard work of putting ourselves into the

(Continued)

(Continued)

shoes of people from all walks of life and persuasions, we'll never move beyond a fixed mindset and grow.

When we believe there's only one right solution to a problem, we stop considering other viewpoints or solutions. This prevents us from finding better methods or engaging in continuous improvement.

When we come upon a problem, we need to do the time-consuming, tough tasks of figuring out all the underlying issues and nuances that might contribute to the problem. Jumping on the first answer or blaming a scapegoat means the issue never gets fully solved, and the energy and resources expended far outweigh what it would have cost us if we had embraced the complexity in the first place.

2. **Avoiding cognitive dissonance has become an addiction**

Cognitive dissonance has always been with us, but something's changed. Why is cognitive dissonance, evolved to be a healthy response, such a powerful force in our lives today?

To find the answer, we need to look again at the left frontal cortex and other parts of the brain involved with rewards, such as shots of dopamine. As we already know, it feels good to find out we're right about something. Research shows that at the moment we realize we're right, hormones are released that literally give us a sense of mental and physical well-being (Weinschenk & Wise, 2012).

Conversely, when we're told that we're wrong about a belief we hold, by being downvoted, for example, or come across evidence or arguments that make us question our beliefs, this induces stress and our brain releases a shot of cortisol, a hormone that can cause feelings of confusion, anxiety, and depression. Research has shown that giving up Facebook can reduce these levels of cortisol (Nield, 2018).

It's not hard to see that it's far more pleasant, both mentally and physically, to believe that we're right! It makes evolutionary sense, as survival meant coming to an agreement on just what needed to be done to survive. But in times past, the world was a simpler place— not easier by any means, but far less complicated from a decision-making standpoint. Fight or flight were the two primary choices of our ancient forebears, and the consequences were clear, even if they were sometimes brutal.

Moreover, in times past, we had fewer people in our lives, fewer choices, and far less complexity in a world that consisted almost entirely of our close family and neighbors. Issues were typically confined to our own small rural area or community. If we disagreed with someone, the cognitive dissonance might still sting, but it was a blow that was contained within our small social footprint, with predictable consequences that were relatively short-lived.

Today, our ability to view news and strangers' opinions from around the world almost instantaneously and to communicate in real time with millions of people through social media, means that the intimate, relatively low-stakes disagreement of yesteryear now has the potential to go viral, with risks including death threats, job loss, and shunning. Seeking out people whom we know will agree with us looks more and more like the safer bet!

Significantly, as we saw in the 2020 documentary *The Social Dilemma*, there's evidence that each upvote our posts or tweets receive, each comment agreeing with us, gives us that same shot of feel-good hormones we get when we're told that we're right—and each post or tweet that challenges our increasingly entrenched views releases the barking hounds of cortisol (Orlowski et al., 2020).

It's no wonder so many flock to this wellspring of good feelings. But with Generation Z spending an average of eight to ten hours per day online, depending on which source you look at, I have to wonder if we've reached a tipping point not only in terms of innovation but also in human connection and empathy.

It's important to look at how we communicate and discuss issues in our world today. It seems email, texting, and phone calls are often considered the easier way to deliver bad news these days, rather than face-to-face. It's much easier to avoid the discomfort of cognitive dissonance when you communicate through social media. You can sort out your thoughts, ask a third party for advice, or walk away for a bit instead of responding immediately. And if you don't like a person's opinions, you can simply block or ghost them.

Our purpose here isn't to argue the pros and cons of one type of communication over another. But as far as innovation is concerned, the ability to cocoon ourselves from frank—and sometimes uncomfortable—discussions means you place yourself in a world of singularity, without diversity of thought. Instead of solving problems together, we simply avoid them, or we magically think they'll cease to exist if only we can force everyone else "on the other side" to stop talking about them.

When people shy away from face-to-face communication, it becomes harder to empathize with the other person. Research has shown that empathy among college students fell 40 percent between 1979 and 2009 (University of Michigan, 2010). Online, we don't see the whole person, both literally and figuratively speaking. We can't see body language or facial expressions, or we see a perfected photo-shopped image. Nuance gets lost in an email or a text. Sometimes, the medium truly is the message.

(Continued)

(Continued)

3. We've returned to burning people at the stake

One of the imperatives for healthy and innovative environments is to create cultures of belonging. At first glance, it seems as though we have. We live in a world where we can instantly find hundreds, even millions, of people with whom we share ideas in common.

This can be a wondrous thing, when we gather with others to further positive goals and expand our thinking on certain topics. It fosters a growth mindset within the group. The challenge arises when we use it as an escape to avoid the collision of ideas, discussion, and debate, as well as critical thinking and self-reflection. Once we do that, we force ourselves into a fixed mindset, believing there's no longer a need to explore ideas any further.

We may no longer turn into angry mobs that go after people with pitchforks and torches, but we too often punish people for having a different opinion than we do. Consider our youth, who are well aware that "the internet is forever," and just imagine the fear they must have of saying the wrong thing or something others don't agree with.

Because we no longer have to consider or explore different ideas, we're increasingly encouraged to see things in a starkly *right or wrong* world. We pounce on small errors, setting expectations for perfection. We don't see the whole story of a situation or a person, but from behind our online personas and masks, we make judgements, often harshly.

This has created a deep fear about expressing opinions that go against the current bubble you're in. This isn't to say that there aren't some opinions that should change. We do need to eradicate issues such as bigotry, sexism, and ageism, for example. But real change doesn't grow out of fear or not communicating, but through learning. Every disagreement is a teachable moment for both sides, and a chance to change opinions and learn new things.

After all, if we can't be open to new ideas, if we can't discuss differing opinions, if we stop expressing ourselves for fear of online retaliation, then we lose one of the most important parts of our humanity.

Ten Insights About Learning in an Age of Complexity

Jane and I believe no one ever changed their values or opinions because someone fought with them, shamed them, or silenced them. We believe the only way to change a person's mind, and subsequently their behavior, is to first open our own minds and consider what they have to say through active listening—sometimes they may well be right, or at least have some valid points, and we're the ones who change our ways of thinking or decide to look for a compromise. Then we can walk beside them and see what they're going through. In other words, we use a strength-based approach to help them see a different world and "what could be."

I believe students and adults respond best by having hope (through a strength-based perspective); having someone see the good in them (knowing they have seeds of brilliance); and creating a culture of belonging where they, too, are welcomed and feel they have something important to contribute.

> *The only way to change a person's mind . . . is to first open our own minds and consider what they have to say through active listening— sometimes they may well be right . . . and we're the ones who change our ways of thinking or decide to look for a compromise.*

Deep change is never easy, and there is always pushback, especially when cognitive dissonance has become the powerful influence it is today. We've observed the effect of deeply ingrained assumptions of our society and know our schools and organizations must challenge these if we're to strive for a more optimistic and harmonious world in our new Age of Complexity. Teaching students (and adults) how to untangle and challenge these assumptions arms them with the tools they need to be more resilient and compassionate, and above all, gives them more power to think critically and innovatively.

We need to prepare our students and our colleagues for this unprecedented time that's so tumultuous, fast paced, and multifaceted that it's hard to determine the best course of action. The impact can be seen in our students (and adults), in the dramatic increases in depression, anxiety, suicide, and other mental health issues (Bloomberg School of Public Health Staff Report, 2020).

The following are ten key insights we believe teachers, parents, and other leaders can consider to help students and adults in overcoming pervasive cognitive dissonance. These ten principles can also give us a sense of control over what is now deemed uncontrollable.

Ten Insights About Learning in an Age of Complexity

1. **See schools and educators as positive forces of change.** Our society currently believes change happens from the top down: from government down to the public, from adults to children, from the top brass to the shop-floor employees, from politicians to constituents. But we can embed and build the three imperatives from the top down and the ground up in our classrooms and boardrooms, as well as horizontally

(Continued)

(Continued)

and vertically. Children who learn to live by the three imperatives (recognize that there is a seed of brilliance in everyone, think and act from a strength-based perspective, foster a culture of belonging) will naturally be more innovative and will take that creativity with them out into their companies and communities.

We must also understand that learning doesn't just take place in schools, but in businesses, organizations and broader society. Schools don't exist in a vacuum—they're part of a symbiotic system that extends into the community, and the community should extend into the school. We need to see negative events as teachable moments, taking a strength-based approach.

2. **Consider the interconnectedness of our world**, instead of trying to address every situation that needs fixing with a seesaw approach: that is, if one side is up, then another must be down, and the sole way to address this is to take some from one side and put it on the other until it balances out.

    The problem with this zero-sum approach is that it not only traps us into thinking that the resources and solutions we have available are finite, but it also prevents us from seeing that perhaps both sides are down or that we could work to get both sides up. The seesaw is unsustainable and eventually just substitutes a new problem for the old. With a strength-based approach, we may see that both or multiple groups need things to thrive, that they have things to offer each other, that they can work together, and that we can reimagine better solutions to benefit us all.

3. **Build partnerships and connections everywhere.** Partnerships are essential because they not only enable synergy but also interconnect us as a community. If families don't thrive, then schools won't have healthy, engaged students, and in turn businesses will not have the motivated, educated workforce they need to succeed in the global marketplace and build thriving communities. We must nurture the symbiotic relationship between schools, businesses, governments, communities, and individuals and groups. We can only benefit from improved bonds, relationships, and shared knowledge, resources, insights, and kindness.

    Teach your students about living systems and the interconnection of things. Point out during the daily goings-on in the classroom how things are connected and depend upon each other. Ask the students for their observations as well.

    Introduce real-life learning experiences. Partner up with companies, organizations, charities, another school, or governments in the area or internationally and ask them to describe to your students some of the things they're trying to solve or build. Let your students work on finding solutions and have them present them to the "client."

4. **Look at the unique needs of each individual, classroom, organization, and community.** A student might view himself as an average student, teenage father, artist, brother, employee, and hockey player. Each segment is a part of who he is—if we ignore the father while focusing on his average marks, or the musician while ignoring the artist, we may miss key ways in which to engage and inspire him. Similarly, we can't make the assumption that all people of a certain group have the same needs or desires. Bringing out the seed of brilliance in everyone recognizes their uniqueness. We need to learn how to compromise and work toward solutions. Model the behavior you want to see. Inspire and motivate. Demonstrate genuine concern for everyone's needs and feelings. Challenge our small thinkers, learners, dreamers, and doers to be innovative, to reach higher levels of performance, to bring out their very best efforts.

5. **Set a good example.** We tell students that bullying and cyberbullying will not be tolerated. Yet we too often provide the example that it is cool for adults to bully, mock, meme, humiliate, and name-call people we disagree with online, or even physically assault them in person, simply because their ideas differ from ours.

    How many of our children witnessed adults making fun of Trump's alleged orange skin tone? Or referring to him as a Cheeto? Consider that children (and adults) can develop an orange skin tone when battling cancer or various liver, kidney, and blood diseases. How did they feel when they heard the adults in their lives deriding someone for the color of their skin? When Joe Biden stumbled going up the stairs of Air Force One, how did children square the fact that some adults were laughing at his misfortune?

    If we are ever to weed out the problem of bullying, then we must become the leaders that we want our children to be. We need to teach them to debate ideas without demeaning people or individuals. We all need to practice empathy, regardless of our personal feelings about someone who disagrees with our values.

6. **Explore how to properly research and analyze conflicting viewpoints.** This is especially true when it comes to consuming news. In our Age of Complexity, we can no longer depend on hearing only one side of a story if we are to find solutions that benefit everyone in our communities. This has important implications for how we rethink, reimagine, and restructure our cultures of learning and our cultures of belonging.

    Teach students to question assumptions and the assumptions on which the assumptions are based. Show them multiple sides of the same issue or news story. Practice "what if." Try to come up with multiple solutions to one problem. Try to come up with multiple possible causes for that

(Continued)

(Continued)

problem. Find a problem in your classroom, school, or community for them to resolve. Play detective. Play negotiator or mediator between two or more opposing sides.

7. **Embrace the things that hold us together, and nurture diversity while moving to a culture of inclusivity.** While we need to look at and address the unique needs of groups for the whole to thrive, we must also explore the many characteristics and goals we have in common. The more we collaborate, the more synergy, inspiration, and momentum we'll gain to reach goals we could never achieve alone. As educators, we will be able to model and ignite this synergy and understanding. Often overlooked, we need to address the bullies' or scapegoaters' concerns, too. Bullies often hurt others because they're emotionally troubled. We've seen amazing examples of how bullies or "problem" students are turned around when caring adults help them find their own seeds of brilliance.

8. **Expand beyond math and language to other subjects to explore.** Students must be able to make connections between many different subjects and competing issues if they're to succeed. For example, teaching empathy can help with reading skills. Teaching music helps with math. Teaching leadership provides the soft skills businesses say are their number-one need.

   As so many teachers already know, teaching to standardized tests only enables children to memorize language and math skills and then regurgitate them back. But a student who aces a spelling test can grow no further, unless they can innovate and take the leap from spelling words to creating books, speeches, and documentaries that change the world.

9. **See the challenges the world faces as interconnected, changing systems.** Discrimination; world hunger; war; the economy: These are all complex interconnected systems. We can't tackle them by dealing with each one individually. By the same token, we can work toward solving complex problems only as a team: acceptance, creative solutions to food production and distribution, peace, building a stronger economy through better education, and more.

10. **Think big, even while we start small.** Students need to understand that we can plan for the short-term, medium-term, and long-term, knowing that each small step builds a foundation for the next step. What we do today impacts not just the present but also the future and in some ways even the past—we are changing how we view history and learning new things as we look back at certain events with fresh eyes.

CHAPTER

2

Key Takeaways

▸ The urge to avoid cognitive dissonance has become much more powerful of late: With the constant flux of changes and contradictory interests in our Age of Complexity, we yearn to be with like-minded people in a comfort-zone bubble.

▸ This increasing discomfort with cognitive dissonance has made us less tolerant of those with different opinions and ideas. We mistakenly believe there is only one right answer or belief system (or one wrong problem); we've become addicted to the dopamine hits of "likes" and others' agreement with our ideas; and we've returned to "burning people at the stake" online if we don't agree with their beliefs. This aversion to different ideas kills innovation and prevents us from finding better solutions.

▸ Ten insights to live and learn in an Age of Complexity: Ten ways to cope with and calm cognitive dissonance are discussed, enabling us to listen to, consider, and even embrace differing viewpoints with a goal to find more innovative solutions that make a better world for all.

Reflective Questions

1. As a leader, how do you feel when someone disagrees with you? Do you allow people to question assumptions and the assumptions on which they are based?

2. How do you react when you strongly disagree with someone else? Are you able to model active listening and empathy? Do you see it as a teachable moment for both of you, or do you try to shut the other person down?

3. Are you comfortable with conflict? How is conflict managed in your school or district, with teachers, students, parents, or other community members?

Try This!

Ask Me Three Questions

Ask Me Three Questions

1. What do you see as the biggest problems in your world, and which one matters most to you?

2. What are the biggest opportunities you can see, and which one matters the most to you?

3. How would you reimagine that problem or that opportunity if you could?

Play a different kind of Ask Me Three Questions with your staff or students. Allow them to think deeply about their answers, to come up with solutions, and to realize they have the power to change things.

CHAPTER 3
WHAT IS BRILLIANCE?

"Potential is never set in stone; our capacity for curiosity and our thirst for knowledge and new skills should continue until our last day on Earth."

—Peter Gamwell

When Boyan Slat went scuba diving during a vacation in Greece, he was surprised to see more plastic bags floating in the ocean than fish. Curious, he dug deeper into the issue of plastics pollution in our seas and found nobody was doing much about it—because there was an assumption that cleaning something as large as the ocean was impossible. The few ideas that had been floated would be prohibitively expensive, cause considerable ecological damage, and take thousands of years to complete (Theoceancleanup.com/milestones, 2021).

So Boyan questioned the assumptions and the assumptions on which the assumptions are based and designed the world's first ocean plastics cleanup system. Soon after, he founded and became CEO of The Ocean Cleanup, a Dutch nonprofit foundation that develops advanced systems to rid the world's oceans of plastics.

Seeing his innovation come to life has been a long journey, but a decade later, Boyan is indeed on his way to achieving what was once considered impossible. It took 273 models, six prototypes, several rounds of trial and error, and a team of scientists and engineers, but the U-shaped System 001, wryly called "Wilson," was launched off the coast of San Francisco in 2018 (Morjaria, 2019).

Today, Boyan leads a team of ninety that continues to work on the foundation's innovations, such as the Interceptor, and has also developed sunglasses made with recovered ocean plastic from the Great Pacific Garbage Patch. All proceeds from the designer shades are invested back into ocean-cleaning operations. It's estimated that an area the size of twenty-four football fields in the Great Pacific Garbage Patch can be cleaned from the proceeds of just one pair.

Boyan Slat on the Interceptor.

Photo used with permission of ©The Ocean Cleanup.

Although Boyan Slat isn't yet the household name it deserves to be, you may have heard of his work. But what you probably didn't know is that when Boyan began this initiative he was just 16 years old, and it started as a high school science project where he was allowed to pursue something of personal interest to him. Now, his technology aims to remove 90 percent of floating ocean plastic by 2040, a boon for us all.

What Is Brilliance? And How Do We Know It When We See it?

The world has long been fascinated by individuals who are considered brilliant. Yet we've never been very good at pinning down how people become brilliant, how we recognize it, or even the best way to guide "giftedness" once we think we've figured out who has it.

No doubt we can all agree that Boyan Slat is a brilliant young man. He was also pursuing postsecondary education in aerospace engineering when he decided to devote himself fully to The Ocean Cleanup project. It's easy to point to him and say, "Yes, that's what brilliance looks like."

And there are other students whose brilliance shines through from a much earlier age. A recent example is Alena Analeigh. In 2021, Alena completed high school at the age of twelve and was accepted into Arizona State University, with a double major in astronomical and planetary science and chemistry. She's pursuing her dream of getting an engineering job with NASA to build rovers—something she became passionate about when she started playing with LEGO blocks as a preschooler (ABC7 Eyewitness News, 2021).

At the same time, Alena founded The Brown STEM Girl (www.thebrownstemgirl.com), a nonprofit organization to support and educate girls of color around the world about the importance of science, technology, engineering, and math (STEM) and how to excel in it. In July of 2020, she even created an initiative to Send a Girl to College on her Facebook page, with a goal to raise ten thousand dollars for scholarships in ten days (facebook.com/thebrownstemgirl, 2021).

But brilliance is rarely so manifest or easy to spot during early childhood and the school years. This is especially true when, with so many competing priorities, teachers feel there are simply not enough hours in the day to truly get to know each individual student on a deep level.

And then, there are so many mysteries and anomalies surrounding human potential that it's simply not possible to predict who will succeed

Alena Analeigh, headed off to college at age 12. Photo credit: D Lacy Photography.

or who won't with any real accuracy. This isn't due to a lack of effort, as studies have been conducted on the subject of human potential for centuries. The goal, we're told, is so that we can more effectively funnel resources toward nurturing a student's gifts or "fixing" them, as we think the case may be.

A person's "intelligence quotient" (IQ) and their brilliance are two vastly different things. Moreover, our current methods of trying to predict one's potential through testing can inadvertently stifle it instead.

In our opinion, this is not only unfair to students and society, but it puts an unfair burden on educators as well, as there isn't a single method to test human potential that isn't fraught with risks and errors.

Jane and I have been questioning some assumptions, and we've come to believe that a person's "intelligence quotient" (IQ) and their brilliance are two vastly different things. Moreover, our current methods of trying to predict one's potential through testing can inadvertently stifle it instead.

IQ Tests Don't Capture the Full Story

Brilliant people are often great at being innovative, at coming up with inventions and novel ideas. But we believe brilliance also shows up in less recognizable ways, as people become leaders, healers, or nurturers, for example. And we need to evoke that "brilliance" in every person, because when an individual is able to reveal their brilliance, the whole community benefits. We vehemently affirm throughout this book that you can have great brilliance no matter your IQ.

In schools, we currently seem to define *brilliance* as being intellectually gifted (those who score in the top 2 percent on IQ tests). It is true that those who achieve high scores on IQ tests have the potential to excel in learning in general. When it comes to helping gifted students get the resources they need, we're all for it.

Where IQ tests fail us is that they're far less likely to predict the future potential or success of those who score below that 98 percent level. This is practically all of us, of course. Even Binet recognized how his IQ test couldn't recognize creativity, for example (Gadye, 2021).

▶ **We can't be one and done.** In some school boards, students are administered a single, standard IQ test in fourth grade. While this can help teachers see where more resources are needed, our opinion is that this single snapshot is too heavily relied upon to stream children into programming options. They can also influence how a student is perceived, starting at the tender age of nine. This is especially problematic when we consider that things like poverty, war, discrimination, and other environmental factors can have an impact on results (Oommen, 2014).

▶ **Two is not enough.** School IQ tests often measure only two things: language and math. Students whose gifts fall outside of these two subjects are often overlooked and their brilliance undervalued.

▶ **Too many seeds of brilliance never get the chance to flourish.** Consider that in Mozart's time, there would have been fifteen million people with genius-level IQs (those who would have scored within the top 2 percent on an IQ test). We know of Mozart's work (he was considered to have an extremely high IQ), but what of the millions of others who didn't have nurturing environments or the opportunity to pursue their dreams and be recognized for it?

Even Wolfgang Mozart's sister, Maria Anna Mozart, a gifted musician and composer in her own right, wasn't properly encouraged or recognized for her gifts due to her gender. Tragically, the music that she composed has since been lost to the world (Michon, 2018).

Jane and I have no doubt that at this very moment, there are vast numbers of innovative, imaginative, and passionate youngsters and adults in this world who aren't studying or working in the area where their true brilliance shines, because they were filtered out at an early age or never had the opportunity. And that's a great loss not only to them but also to the advancement of our entire civilization.

Maria Anna Mozart was a gifted composer, but she did not get the recognition she deserved due to her gender. Unfortunately, her music was lost to the world.

Source: powerofforever/istock.com

▶ **Students are more than just a number.** There are simply too many variables to human potential to nail down a student's life at a young age. We too often approach these test results as if we're born with a certain level of intelligence, nothing will change it, and therefore, we're slotted into a band of life and career choices within a hierarchical range. Yet there are countless examples of individuals who received low test scores in school and succeeded despite all odds.

Then there are those who accomplished great things much later in life. Julia Child didn't release her first cookbook until she was fifty. Rodney Dangerfield didn't get his acting career off the ground until he was forty-six. After Vera Wang's dream of becoming an Olympic figure skater was crushed, she took up fashion at the age of forty. Donald Fisher was forty years old with zero experience in the retail industry when he opened his first Gap store (Murphy, 2015).

There are situations in which everyone within a group seems to get swept up into a project, and each individual suddenly displays skills, talents, and growth that had not been evident before. We'll talk more about that in the next chapter.

We could go on, but our point is that few of these successes could have been predicted by an IQ test at the age of nine. This isn't to say that every person can learn to be anything they want to be. Learning our own limits, wisely changing our choices, and setting new courses is a lifelong rite of passage to wisdom as we grow. Teaching students how to meet setbacks with resilience and to continuously update and revise plans on their unique journey is a gift that will last them a lifetime.

▶ **Who gets to determine what success looks like?** We also need to question the assumption that there's a one-size-fits-all definition of what success looks like. Success is unique to each person. Not everyone aspires to be at the top of a corporate ladder. Abilities that enable people to pursue dreams of being a good cook, a good listener, one who is kind to others, who can build things with their hands, start a business, make people laugh, garden, innovate, or create thought-provoking artistry are just as valuable. IQ tests can no longer be the gold standard for determining potential.

We Propose a New Way to Look at Human Potential: Brilliance

An individual's potential is extremely complex, stemming not only from a mixture of nature and nurture but also from external factors that one may have little to no control over, such as being born into a prosperous community or one impacted by poverty. There's no doubt some have either far more barriers to overcome or more opportunities to get themselves aloft on their personal path to success. There's also something within a person's heart, a passion that often benefits from being nurtured and cultivated by someone influential to the individual. Without that positive influence, or even discouragement, that passion may fail to flourish. And Jane and I believe that potential is never set in stone; our capacity for curiosity and our thirst for knowledge and new skills should continue until our last day on Earth, making the availability of lifelong learning for all essential. So rather than put so much focus on IQ scores and test results, Jane and I propose we focus more on what we call "brilliance."

Our definition of brilliance

We've crafted the following definition and three requirements for *brilliance*, which mirror our imperatives for healthy and innovative learning environments. (Although we'd love to hear your ideas, too!)

Brilliance is . . .

1. a unique passion or ability, too often hidden or stifled, that every individual possesses: when allowed to engage in their passion, people experience an intense sense of engagement, of "being in the zone" or "flow";

2. that which takes a strength-based, innovative approach: an individual's brilliance is driven by curiosity and creativity, with the focus on furthering knowledge or imagining "what could be" instead of "what is";

3. what draws others in and invites the collaboration and sharing of different passions and abilities rather than filtering others out based on ability level or differing sets of knowledge or interests. Brilliance welcomes everybody and has a positive impact or influence on those involved.

Figure 3.1   How Brilliance Differs From IQ

IQ	Brilliance
2% of the population is considered to have "high IQ."	Brilliance is possessed by every person.
IQ is determined and measured through a standardized test.	Does not require measurement, since everyone possesses it. The focus is on nurturing the seeds of brilliance within each person.
	While we can't measure brilliance, we can see its impact when it's been allowed to flourish in the environment.

(Continued)

(Continued)

IQ	Brilliance
	We can measure conditions in the environment that nurture people's seeds of brilliance. This is explained in Chapter 12: The But, But, But, But Chapter: Evaluation and Assessment. There is evidence that students who are engaged in healthy learning environments have better outcomes on average, including on standardized tests.
Is considered to be relatively fixed from birth. Encourages a fixed mindset.	Is considered to be influenced by numerous factors throughout life. Encourages a growth mindset.
Typically focuses on two primary abilities, language and math. The subject itself typically becomes the basis for the lesson plan. This creates a hierarchy in which math and language are viewed as more important than other subjects and are accordingly allotted more teaching time during the school day.	Recognizes infinite possibilities in all realms and subject matters. The student's passion or curiosity becomes the basis for the learning, and the curriculum is "baked into" real-life projects designed to pursue these interests. This creates a more fluid and flattened hierarchy of learning. While math and language are still considered to be key subjects, they are taught through interconnections with all subjects.
IQ scores put the potential of most students in a box: average scores lead to average expectations. Scores are objective and "fixed"; there's less encouragement or motivation to "go outside the lines."	Brilliance sees success as the ability to grow and pursue one's own area(s) of brilliance, with the ability to make choices and change direction along the journey.
Is at risk for inaccuracies. For example, students who have learning disabilities, who are having an off day, or are grappling with external factors may not test to their true ability.	Looks at the bigger picture of not only the student, but also their interconnectedness with the school, their parents, and the community over a significant period of time.
Scores help to determine which children could use more resources or more help.	Concept currently needs more acceptance to secure the resources and leadership buy-in needed to embed the conditions for healthy and innovative learning environments.
Scores are easy to analyze, making it an effective tool for aggregate data over time.	Is often hidden and difficult to measure or analyze; must overcome leadership reluctance to implement.

We took a page from gemology

When we were trying to understand and demystify exactly what brilliance means to us, Jane and I came across an interesting metaphor from the science of gemology, which uses both the terms *brilliant* and *brilliance*.

In gemologists' vocabulary, a *brilliant* is not an adjective, but a noun—it's what they call a gemstone, particularly a diamond. Diamonds are considered to be very rare, just like the top 2 percent of the population who are defined as gifted (Clark & Shang, 2021).

But gemology also uses the term *brilliance*, which describes how a gemstone *shines* and *illuminates*. Since recognizing that every person has a seed of brilliance is the first imperative to building a healthy, innovative learning environment, we believe that helping every student discover their own brilliance—how they shine and illuminate for those within their spheres of influence—is a path to success and well-being, and to making the world a better place for all of us.

We all possess seeds of brilliance; the question is, how do we help students bring out the brilliance that lies within? To help every student and staff member find their passion and reach their true potential? To do that, we need to reimagine how we perceive and develop potential in all children and adults. Tests play a role, but they're simply not *enough* to help us understand and grow the true, full potential of a student. We need more, and our students deserve more.

It's okay that brilliance can't be measured

We live in a world that's enamored with measuring pretty much everything, from student test scores to how many people read an online story, to bottom-line profits. This is understandable in some ways. With increasingly limited budgets and demands for higher accountability and precise decision-making, we need to know which of our initiatives is having an impact and which aren't. This is why standardized testing is popular in so many parts of the world.

"Brilliance," by its very nature, can't be measured. An individual's seed of brilliance is not a test of something already learned but the potential for future growth that can have powerful influences if nurtured under the right conditions. The result is potentially infinite.

> *"Brilliance," by its very nature, can't be measured. An individual's seed of brilliance is not a test of something already learned but the potential for future growth that can have powerful influences if nurtured under the right conditions. The result is potentially infinite.*

If we must measure something, our efforts would be better placed in assessing whether the three imperatives and four conditions of innovation are present in the environment, as well as the three characteristics of leadership, and to what degree. A high ranking should correlate well to increased innovation and well-being for teachers and students alike.

Chapter 12 provides an assessment tool for how to recognize whether the imperatives, conditions, and leadership characteristics that support brilliance have been allowed to flourish in the environment. If you have students who are comfortable questioning the answers rather than just answering the questions, you probably are well on your way to a healthy, brilliance-nurturing environment.

Sympathetic resonance:
The rippling beauty of brilliance

There's a harmonic phenomenon called sympathetic resonance, or sympathetic vibration, in which a passive string on a musical instrument will start to vibrate when it picks up external vibrations from a string that is singing a harmonic likeness (Dawson & Medler, 2010). As both a musician and an educator, what fascinates me is that every object on Earth has a natural vibration frequency, a frequency at which it will start to vibrate in sympathy with the vibrations around it.

This metaphorical phenomenon comes to life in our interconnected systems, of which our educational system is but one. We can't expect a child's school experience to begin and end within our classroom walls; to start at age five and finish at age eighteen. Our students' experiences, and our own workday experiences for that matter, will resonate outward into our families and communities, and forward in time, as students go out into the world as adults. In other words, seeds of brilliance that are nurtured and allowed to flourish tend to "jump the garden"; what we do in our classrooms today will create an influence miles away and decades from now.

Each resonation can have a profound impact on these families, friends, and other groups, and in turn, the vibrations of those impacts will resonate even further afield, to other individuals and groups within these secondary spheres of influence, impacting more and more people, for better or for worse, as the ripples fan out.

We often hear the adage that we can't change the world, but we can change the life of one person. And considering sympathetic resonance, changing the life of one person can in turn change the world, or at least the lives of a lot more people than we initially realize. As teachers, we need to realize the power we hold within our hands, of the amazing, reverberating impacts we can have by bringing out the seed of brilliance in just one student. We have no way of controlling how far or how fast our own resonances will travel, but we can influence whether the sympathetic resonances we produce will give our students a voice and the harmony they need to soar.

You'll Discover Beautiful Examples of Brilliance

We need to recognize there is that seed of brilliance in everyone; just because we can't initially see it doesn't mean it's not there. We can't see a seed hidden in the ground, but we know that with enough water and sunlight it has the potential to turn into a thriving, fruitful tree.

It breaks my heart, for both the teacher and the parent, when parents have to say to a teacher, "You always look at what's wrong with our child and what he's not doing right. But at home, we see a different side of him. We see the brilliance in him. Why don't you see those things?" It's not that the teacher doesn't dearly want to do just that, but the constrictions of time allotments and other set priorities too often prevent them from doing so.

We seek to change that. In the following chapters, you'll see some intriguing examples that shine a brighter light on how we perceive and nurture brilliance. This is our chance to start seeing those seeds of brilliance, those grains of magic in each and every one of our students and each of our employees, family members, and our community members.

Key Takeaways

CHAPTER 3

▶ We need to reimagine how we define, recognize, and nurture human potential: Replacing our heavy reliance on IQ tests with the concepts of "brilliance" and "seeds of brilliance" allows us to foster healthy learning environments where innovation, leadership, and new skills can emerge.

▶ Our definition of brilliance includes three primary characteristics: (1) Every person has seeds of brilliance, although they can often be hidden or lie dormant due to an environment that prohibits them from flourishing. (2) A person's brilliance may lie in any type of subject matter or ability, beyond what is usually assessed in traditional school structures. (3) A person's brilliance cannot be tested or measured.

▶ As teachers, we have the power to transform a child (or colleague) and in turn transform the world: Using the three imperatives and four conditions, we can create learning environments in which a child's seed of brilliance can emerge and create a sympathetic resonance and ripple effect that spreads out into the community and beyond.

Reflective Questions

1. As a leader, what is your seed of brilliance? How do you recognize the seeds of brilliance within your staff and your colleagues?

2. How will you start a conversation about seeds of brilliance and bring the concept to life with your students, staff, parents, and the broader community?

3. After reading this chapter, how will you engage staff in an active exploration to discover the seeds of brilliance, hidden talents, and interests of every individual in your organization?

Try This!

Discover Seeds of Brilliance with a New Kind of Wonder Wall

Revealing seeds of brilliance is a beautiful and transformative step to transforming your learning culture. But when adults and children start to think about discovering their own seeds of brilliance, they often don't even know where to begin. Here's how to get started:

- Talk about seeds of brilliance and how we all have them. Take on a spirit of celebration by announcing a quest where everyone will discover and reveal their seeds of brilliance over the next semester or school year.

- Create a Wonder Wall outside of every classroom, as well as the staff room, custodians' room, administrators' office, and others. Every person in the building should be included. You can even put one up for parents and visitors.

  To make each Wonder Wall, mark off a large area of the wall with painter's tape (or use a very large piece of paper), as illustrated in Figure 3.2 where we imagined a school that had members of the custodial staff named Jody, Asher, and Padi. Include each person's name on the left-hand side and then columns to record each person's wonderings, curiosities, interests, and passions with sticky notes. Feel free to make your own columns for your unique school situation.

Figure 3.2   A Wonder Wall from the Custodial Staff

Wonder Wall

Name	I sometimes wonder . . .	I'm curious/ passionate about . . .	I'd love to learn more about . . .	One thing you may not know about me (because I never do it at school) . . .	Ideas that I have . . .
Jody	If students should be taught how a building works, such as electrical wiring, plumbing, etc.	Birds and aviation.	How to grow heritage vegetables.	I play the banjo.	Custodians could make a presentation on how a building works. We should start a school garden.
Asher	How many medicinal benefits of plants have yet to be discovered.	Creating documentaries.	Making a soundtrack for a documentary.	I do stand-up comedy on weekends.	We should plant a garden. I would like to make a documentary about the new garden.
Padi	How to create a cleanser that's less harmful to the environment.	The environment, wildlife, and camping.	Chemistry and public speaking.	I volunteer to make birthday cakes for seniors at the retirement home.	I can teach others how to bake and we could have a bake sale. The custodians and the chemistry students could work together on a new cleanser project.

▶ Once your Wonder Walls are even partially filled out, they'll provide a rich assortment of ideas for passions, projects, and the opportunity for each individual to start discovering their seeds of brilliance. Make it a living document, allowing sticky notes to be added or taken away as the individuals grow.

▶ Make time, perhaps four to eight hours each week, for people to nurture their seeds of brilliance. Find ways of making the extraordinary happen. Now that you know these skills and talents, partner people up and enable them to learn from each other or collaborate in a large team project.

▶ This will take some coordination and preparation work, but the transformation in your culture and your people will be well worth it. As a leader, you'll need to show support and allow people to take risks and learn from mistakes for the learning culture to transform.

CHAPTER 4
SEEDS OF YESTERYEAR
JESUS CHRIST SUPERSTAR

"I remember feeling so little on that stage, but there were people in the wings, it felt like I had these arms around me. I felt the responsibility to do my personal best and more, because I have my *Jesus Christ Superstar* family counting on me."

—Traci Foley

In the last chapter, I discussed sympathetic resonance and how, as teachers, we have the awesome power to nurture a student's seed of brilliance, creating a rippling wave of positivity that can span out into the community and through time. This is a story regarding what I learned about seeds of brilliance, strength-based approaches, and cultures of belonging through producing musicals and rock operas early in my career. Most notably was the first one—a high school production of *Jesus Christ Superstar* (Rice et al., 1972), which I helped produce as a young teacher almost forty years ago.

It was during this experience that I first began to realize how innovation and a passion for learning didn't manifest in students because someone had taught them how to be creative and curious, but because an environment had been created where each individual's seeds of brilliance naturally emerged and flourished. I recently learned that an active Facebook group had been formed by students to reminisce about their experiences putting on *Jesus Christ Superstar*, almost four decades after it happened!

The idea that this group of former students had come together on Facebook certainly brought a smile to my face, although I admit I was a bit curious as to why they'd be talking about something that happened so long ago.

How Far Do Seeds of Brilliance Travel After the Last Bell Has Rung?

I've since learned that it's because the healthy learning environments educators create in the classroom today—those that recognize students' seeds of brilliance, build cultures of belonging, and take strength-based approaches—are indeed transportable through time and place. These environments don't just impact students' lives for a semester or a school year; like seeds carried on the wind, students take that environment with them and transplant it wherever they go in life.

We decided to follow up with some of these "kids," as I continued to call them (Jane keeps reminding me that some of them are grandparents now!), and see what insights we could learn from them. We connected with six of them while drafting this book, and we hope to connect with more.

These reconnections with my former students are deeply personal and very emotional for me. And as it turns out, it was very emotional for some of my former students as well. I'd already had a taste of just how moving it was to talk to these students in April of 2018, when I received an unexpected email from Billy McGrath, asking if I was the same Peter Gamwell who had taught in the town of Gander, Newfoundland and Labrador.

Billy wrote, "I was watching *Jesus Christ Superstar* (on TV) this evening and thought of you and all the amazing work you did at the school. I don't know if you remember me, but you made a huge impact on me and really helped me back then, so thank you, and as long ago as it was you are still remembered as a great teacher and great person."

Of course I remembered Billy! It was incredibly touching to hear from him, although I'd like to make it clear that there were many, many people who made our production of *Jesus Christ Superstar* a success, including the students themselves!

Something magical unfolded during that high school production. It deeply affected not just students, but everyone involved, including the faculty, the parents, and the entire community of that small town. I believe the story needs to be told for three reasons.

First, the story illustrates what is meant by brilliance—how it sparks, what it looks like as it's unfolding, its characteristics, and the do's and don'ts of how to foster its continued growth without inadvertently stamping out the flame. This will also help you recognize examples of brilliance as you delve into the other chapters. Secondly, telling the full story documents the steps and initiatives taken that helped the students, teachers, external partners, and the broader community bring out this brilliance and allow every participant to flourish.

Finally, the story comes with a unique perspective, as we've reached out to some of the former students to get their perceptions and glean some insight about the power of healthy learning environments on students' futures. The *Jesus Christ Superstar* production didn't just impact the students. It completely transformed the way I look at learning and education.

In this chapter, we'll

- briefly describe what happened during the *Jesus Christ Superstar* production to gather insights on cultivating brilliance that you might like to try in your own classroom;

- explore how you can interweave the arts into any subject you wish to engage and teach—and why brain science says you should;

- share some of the remarkable perspectives we gained from reconnecting with the former students, now in their fifties, who were involved in *Jesus Christ Superstar*.

As you read the other chapters in this book, you'll notice that the importance of cultures of belonging and a strength-based approach play out over and over again in enabling seeds of brilliance to flourish.

How *Jesus Christ Superstar* Forever Changed My Ideas on Learning

I made the jump over the pond from my birthplace of Liverpool to what Canadians affectionately call "The Rock," or the province of

Newfoundland and Labrador, in 1977. I'd accepted an advertised position for a female music teacher. They forgave me for being the wrong gender, but going from a city of six million to a fishing village of barely a few thousand was a huge culture shock. I vividly remember wandering around the town for the first few days, wondering what the hell I had done.

But I soon learned the raw power of small communities to make extraordinary things happen. When you reach out to the people in small towns like Wesleyville, where I spent my first two and a half years, and later Gander, they won't hesitate to help. Masters of self-reliance, they're warmhearted and innovative to their very core, having learned over generations to improvise and grapple together to forge ahead. It didn't surprise me that several years after I'd moved away, in September 2001, the people of Gander made the extraordinary happen by hosting some 6,500 stranded airplane passengers from around the world, including putting them up in their own homes.

And these good-humored people are well versed at creating cultures of belonging, convincing first-time visitors to kiss a cod fish on the lips in order to become an honorary Newfoundlander.

I soon felt at home.

I was later hired by a school whose staff wanted their learning culture brought alive through the arts. And they gave me the time and flexibility to make it happen. One day, a fellow teacher, Paul O'Reilly, asked me, "Would you be interested in putting on a musical opera?" And through that conversation, we came up with the idea of doing *Jesus Christ Superstar*. Paul was a remarkable person who soon became a mentor to me (although I don't think I ever told him that).

We were taking a risk, as this was at a Catholic high school in a rather polite community. I had also never produced anything in my entire life, and this project was huge, to say the least. But again, the administration supported us and gave us the go-ahead.

I'll admit I was scared. What if it didn't work out? The production loomed before me like a massive, multidimensional jigsaw puzzle. But I finally realized that when putting together a jigsaw, some of the pieces will always fit together. In a pinch, you can even *make* some of the pieces work. So we took the approach that we would all be learning as we went along, and this built a kind of connectivity and community among us.

We had many questions:

▶ Did we have kids who could play the roles?

▶ Would any of the kids audition?

▶ Would the church let us do it? (It was a Catholic school, after all.)

▶ Could we garner the interest required to get the support we needed?

▶ Did we have musicians who could play music of this complexity?

- ▶ Would we have a set?

- ▶ How would we map out the scenes?

Some of the decisions were easier to make than others. From the very beginning, we understood that if we were going to do this, we wanted it to be much more than simply a high school production. We went to the Arts and Culture Centre, where it would be performed, and we imagined the people walking out of the center after the performance, saying, "That was amazing."

Not "That was amazing—for a Grade 7 to 12 school production," but, "That was amazing." Period.

Manifesto: Bring out the best in people

My personal unwritten manifesto is that if you want to bring the best out of people, set the task, preferably in a collaborative manner, put in place reasonable accountability processes, and then, get out of the way.

Let go of the control.

People are incredibly creative, yet our default is to make people conform. Our structures and organizations are set to keep people confined. But life's too complex for that now. Our current realities are going to require every ounce and drop of creative juice that lies within all of us to help us forge pathways to our futures.

We need to awaken possibilities, not stifle potential; to fire enthusiasm, not dampen spirits; to reveal magic, not settle for mediocrity.

Flip the learning experience

I've noticed how eager students become when we flip the learning experience upside down. Instead of teachers leading the way to learning—deciding the curriculum and the lesson plans, teachers can set things up so the students are empowered to take the lead, driven by their own natural curiosity. The result is engagement, imagination, innovation, and learning.

So, working with many people, we mapped the journey for the production, but only so much. We trusted people to know the balance between certainty and uncertainty, and to embrace it.

We also decided that anyone who wanted to be in the play was in the play. There were no auditions, except for the lead roles. If a kid wanted to be in the chorus, they were in the chorus—whether they knew how to sing or not. Or if they wanted to get into the woodworking or the lighting, the backstage workings, the costuming, or the make-up, they were in.

It was an entirely open approach, and in retrospect, that was one of the most powerful pieces of magic, because it drew in people based on their particular interests and allowed them to try something they were curious about. And they were welcomed whether or not they had any background experience in the subject.

You may notice I'm referring to people and not to students, and that's because participation in the production soon went way beyond the kids. The adults who got involved were not just school faculty and parents, but people from across the community. As more and more people heard about what was going on, the momentum snowballed.

One morning, I got a phone call from a woman who said, "We've heard you're doing a production. Would you like us to make the costumes?"

I was thrilled and gratefully accepted her generous offer. I asked her the name of her group, and she replied, "Oh, we're with the Gander Stitch 'n Bitch society. We've already talked about it, and we'd be happy to make the costumes."

And so they made *all* the costumes for us.

There was a military base in Gander, and one day a commander connected with me and mentioned there was a military scene in the film production of the musical. He then offered to send some soldiers over to train the kids in the precision of military movement.

This community involvement introduced the students to expertise they wouldn't have received otherwise, but I think the community got much enjoyment out of it, too!

Teachers and other members of our school staff stepped up to become engaged in all manner of things, from stage construction to ticket sales. They taught students the intricacies of how to work behind the scenes and to master the absolute silence required to move things on and off the stage—which might sound so simple, but it's not.

It was rich, multifaceted hands-on learning and engagement across all subjects. With the music, they were learning patterns and anticipation. With the construction of the sets, they were learning math, project planning, engineering, and art. Good communication skills were critical throughout everything we did, from the choreography to the lighting to the cues to go on and off stage.

And as each individual's seeds of brilliance emerged, they blossomed right before our eyes. We saw skills, talents, leadership, and innovative ideas in abundance, often from those who had never displayed such characteristics before. Cliques collapsed and new friendships formed throughout the group, and the sense of connectivity and community was tangible.

As one of the former students I've reconnected with explains, "The experience with the production didn't just change the way I felt about myself; it changed the way I felt about my classmates."

From a Teacher's Perspective

I recently reconnected with Paul O'Reilly, the teacher with whom I collaborated, and asked him for his insights on what made the production so magical.

"Our collaboration grew out of many facets," Paul said. "We each understood the other's take on teaching and schooling. We encouraged questions from our students and created discussions to foster the academic aspect of their work. However, we both knew intrinsically that academia was secondary to the people we were teaching. We cared greatly about them as individuals: their growth, their love of life, their happiness, and everything that a young person would need to be their best self at this time in their lives. We saw this as the real crux of education. In short, academia and other school experiences fell under the umbrella of people and life for us, and that's how we went about our workdays with students."

Building trust is crucial

Paul continued, "Students knew we meant what we said. If we promised to do something a certain way, we would. We also needed to trust our students. I had a healthy belief in the abilities of the youth, but you surpassed my perceptions at times, so much so that you scared me. You entrusted students at a level I thought was over their heads. Yet they could reach these limits you saw readily, after our suggestions of what was needed from them. You weren't being naive, because you also knew the level at which they would fail in the task. That pushing of the envelope was what allowed this performance to reach the level it did.

"We also needed to trust each other. We divided the tasks between us and never looked back to see if the other was getting things done. We both carried the big picture with us all the time.

Organization is critical

"Ironically, artistic types aren't perceived as being organized, but I'll tell you why creative people actually have an advantage here, because it's the basis for innovation," Paul said. "We were juggling incredible and varied amounts at any given moment for a long time to get this play to performance. But a production of this magnitude is fluid every day. We were both on task but also totally open to changes. When we wrote the rock opera, *Leaps and Bombs*, you composed something, and each time you revisited it, it became something else, and a new composition arose. We had to record your composing while writing, because the piece was quite different a half hour later, and the words no longer fit. Each time I designed a piece and came back to it, I saw it another way. So, when you accept the *necessity* of change, you have to work knowing that yesterday's accomplishments had to sometimes be left behind to accommodate the new visions that you, I, some student, or contributing adult brought to our attention today.

We must embrace the unknown

"We had so much to learn, but that never stopped us one bit. It just meant we had to find it and do it. We had to believe we and the group could make it happen even though we never had the skill sets in place ourselves. A good example of that was when we knew we needed a choreographer. We found a teller at a local bank who had trained in dancing, but due to her time constraints, we set it up so that I'd learn from her and teach it to the students.

"Admitting to our limits was an asset; I think it was a great experience for the students to watch us learn along with them," Paul summed up. "Too often, teachers feel they're supposed to know everything. The destruction of that thinking yielded us a greater respect from the students and a learning environment that consisted of all teachers. One of the truest statements I took away from my teaching years is that I learned a hell of a lot more from my students than they learned from me."

Challenges add to the drama

This isn't to say that Paul and I didn't have challenges, Given our inexperience, there were new challenges every day, but we always worked together to figure out a solution, each person contributing their own knowledge and skills.

A major challenge was that only a few of our young musicians could read music, so we learned to play it all by ear. At first, some of these young people were doubtful they could do this, but they stretched themselves and learned the part, which still amazes me to this day.

Another challenge was that, despite all of the enthusiasm of most everyone else, there was one group that wasn't so eager to jump on the Superstar bandwagon—the older sixteen or seventeen-year-old boys. So every recess, I would fill up my coffee mug and wander the halls, targeting the biggest hockey players, boys who were considered leaders, and harass them to join the production.

I was honest with them: I said we needed more guys in the play, and if even one of them joined, others might follow. I was more right than I would have thought possible. Once two or three accepted, the flood gates opened, and with our rule that no one would be turned away, Jesus ended up having thirteen disciples instead of twelve. We could hardly fire one, after all the work we'd done to recruit them! Luckily, no one in the audiences appeared to notice.

But other than initially having to get the older boys into the spirit of things, there was no requirement for motivation, not for the students, the staff, or the parents. We often hear complaints that kids don't want to go to school, but we couldn't get them to go home! At 6:30 p.m. they would still be there, pleading for just a little more time to keep working on the musical.

We had expected to host two performances, but we ended up having to extend it due to the high demand. The auditorium held 500 people, and we sold out five times over, for a total of 2,500 attendees in a small town. Some people came back to see it more than once. And as per the goal that we first set, everyone leaving indeed said, "That was absolutely amazing," and "That was truly magical."

Create More Environments Where Brilliance Emerges Naturally

Most of us have had the pleasure of seeing a student break out of their shell and undergo a transformative change. It's much rarer, however, to see every individual in an entire classroom, school, or organization burst forth with abilities and innovative ideas far beyond what they ever showed us before, such as in our production of *Jesus Christ Superstar*.

Jane and I have long been curious about this phenomenon of a burgeoning of group brilliance. How we can replicate it in the classroom and in business settings? Looking back, I realized that during *Jesus Christ Superstar,* our Gander school community didn't teach our students how to be brilliant and leaders and innovative through the rock opera project. It was the other way around: the rock opera created an environment, founded on the three imperatives and four conditions for innovative environments, which enabled the students' natural brilliance, leadership, and unique abilities to germinate and push through.

Weave the Arts Across the Curriculum

I've also learned since then that the arts are a highly effective way to engage and teach students across any subject imaginable, from math and science to literature and history. Which makes it an even bigger pity that the arts are currently banished to the bottom of the teaching hierarchy in most school districts, considered simply a "nice to have if we run out of more important things to do."

If you don't believe that arts have such a low status in schools, consider the following challenge that somone once posed to me. A quick Google search will yield you dozens of research papers and articles trying to justify expanding the arts in the school curriculum because of the positive impact they have on math and language scores. But can you find even one article attempting to justify the expansion of math and language in the curriculum due to their positive impact on the arts?

And yet studies have indeed shown that the arts improve test scores not only on math but also on language, problem solving, and soft skills such as empathy. A 2006 study by Christopher Johnson, professor of music education and music therapy at the University of Kansas, found that elementary schools with superior music programs had students that scored not only 20 percent higher in math on standardized tests but also 22 percent higher in English, compared to schools with low-quality music programs. This held true even after socioeconomic disparities among the schools were accounted for (Johnson & Memmott, 2006; see also NAMM Foundation, 2007).

A study by the University of Sydney, the Australian Government, and Australia Council also shows drama to have a positive effect on learning, and other research has shown drama's effects on learning is especially valuable in teaching children from impoverished communities (see *Arts Participation and Students' Academic Outcomes*, 2014, on YouTube). And yet another study that compared lower socioeconomic students who received music lessons in Grades 8 to 12 with those who did not saw math, reading, history, and geography scores increase by as much as 40 percent (Gardner et al., 1996).

Use arts as a catalyst for learning

I became so curious about the astounding results of our musical—and our subsequent productions—that I wanted to figure out how to make class learning a similar experience. And so in 2002, as part of my PhD, I conducted an action research project with an eighth-grade English class, using the arts as a catalyst for their learning.

The first two weeks involved creating a culture of trust, which is how I believe every learning culture ought to start. This involved having the students engage in a range of activities that stretched them. Dance, lots of conversation, dramatic interpretation, and a focus on allowing them to explore their learning in ways they had never done before.

Next, I engaged the students in a project I called musical soundtrack stories. I asked them to choose a piece of classical music about three or four minutes long. For the first week I just wanted them to listen to the music over and over, so they came to know it by heart. Then I explained I wanted them to interpret that music in a way that made sense to them, and in a way that mattered to them.

Of course, initially there was a chorus of boos and statements like, "I have no idea what you're talking about, sir."

So I told them, "Close your eyes and listen to your piece of music again. This time, allow your mind to create images of what the music represents to you. What does it make you think of? How does it make you feel? Then think of how you could represent those ideas. Maybe a story, or a piece of art, or a dance, or a sculpture, or a video."

I then set a series of dates when the kids would bring in the artifacts of their learning over the next two weeks.

What occurred was a blossoming of creative ideas in all shapes and sizes. A couple of the kids produced a skateboarding video. Two students designed and presented a puppet show. One young man created a video montage to the music of *Fanfare for the Common Man* (Copland, 1942), a series of taped television segments which, together, in his words, showed the contrasting passions and failures of humanity.

This was backward to the conventional approach, where a composer writes music to capture the action of a movie, for example. In this case,

I asked the students to interpret the music in any way they wanted to, to explore it in their own ways, and to go through the creative process of interpretation. I was attempting to emulate the openness and the opportunity for exploration through personal interest that was so characteristic of rock operas and musicals.

Explore the power of community

I also wanted to explore the power of community that develops when working in such a mutually dependent and collaborative way as *Jesus Christ Superstar*. I believe that the success of large and complex endeavors rests on the collaboration, timeliness, and commitment of all involved.

It reminds me of the definition of *living systems theory* I once came across: The health of any system is entirely dependent on the delicate and intricate balance of the subsystems within the system overall. Once one subsystem goes out of kilter, pathology occurs throughout the whole system. For example, if the prop person forgets a crucial prop, it can throw the whole scene out of balance. Everyone matters, no matter whether they're the lead actor or the lighting person. Through this need to depend upon one another, a community of family emerges, where learning and well-being are synchronous. The whole becomes greater than the sum of the parts.

Weave emotional and personal connection to the learning

While in many instances it was up to the students as to whether they worked alone, in pairs, or in groups, collaboration emerged as a recurring theme, even to those working alone. Whether it was through conversations with me, their peers, other educators, or their friends, parents, and family, their ideas were shaped by social interaction.

Make it personal

Possibly the most crucial aspect of any learning culture is to prioritize personalized learning. Learning must be sparked by curiosity, driven by purpose, and brought alive by the continual thirst to know more.

If we're to make learning matter, we must personalize learning and embrace choice as an underpinning of the learning process. We can do this by studying which conditions best foster cultures that unleash potential, curiosity, and the creative capacities that lie in everyone.

How Is Meaning Created by Students Through Arts Experiences?

I later asked the students to express how they felt about their learning experiences through journaling. It soon became clear that learning through the arts provided six broad themes or learning catalysts for the students: active engagement and focused attention; emotional engage-ment; contextual memory; commitment to problem-solving; social con-struction of meaning; and personal choice and control (Gamwell, 2002).

Active engagement:

Arts activities provide novelty and were a key element in focusing the students' engagement. Active involvement through the arts provided a catalyst for creativity, which led them to explore various approaches in the construction of their meaning making.

One thing that has always puzzled me is the lack of opportunity for students to engage in, and explore fully, the learning process. Tasks are often completed in a context divorced from active engagement, even while research in the field of neuroscience and psychology is uncover-ing connections between cognition and emotion. The implications of this connection for learning are profound.

The students enjoyed playing with ideas, and this helped them get to know one another, to know how their partners worked, and to under-stand their strengths and weaknesses.

While observing them, I could predict problems that would arise and give advice or guidance without providing specific solutions. Best of all, I could be there when a group had a breakthrough, the moment when they discovered a direction or an idea worth pursuing. It was empowering for the students to share these moments of discovery and receive immediate feedback, to hear a teacher say, "Oh yes, I really think you're onto some-thing there," or, "Tell me how you came up with that."

Emotional engagement:

I noticed that there was a connection between active involvement and emotional engagement to the students' construction of personal meaning. Students said their emotional engagement to the material greatly impacted their interest in learning more about the subject. For example, an enact-ment of *Julius Caesar* provided a glimpse into such a moment, far more memorable and meaningful than what can be learned from a book. "It was like being a Roman citizen," some students explained.

Of course, you don't have to put on an entire musical or play to get this effect. Simple classroom role-playing is a multifaceted, interactive teaching technique in which students can imagine and experience a situ-ation as "the next best thing to being there." This can help children empa-thetically figure out how others might feel in a certain scenario, as well as develop deeper self-awareness about how they themselves might react.

Contextual memory:

Several students believed they would be more likely to remember the material that they had experienced through the arts activities. Ellen Langer concluded that varying the target of our attention, whether a visual target or an idea, can improve memory of it. Making art, in whatever form, is all about the weaving together of ideas into a unified, coherent creation, working the individual parts.

Commitment to problem-solving:

The students' emotional connection to the material and the problem-solving process had an impact on construction and personal meaning. All of the groups faced challenges and difficulties throughout this problem-solving process, and brainstorming ended up being a continuous process, with new ideas coming to mind right up until and even through the final presentation. After certain decisions were made, they would take ownership for finding and carrying out a solution, as they had choice in determining what would happen next.

Social construction of meaning:

Social interaction played an important role in the meaning-making process, as projects required an enormous amount of collaboration over a long period of time. The students made decisions regarding the nature of their projects, actively engaging in the processes of interaction: they discussed, agreed, disagreed, argued, negotiated, and laughed.

They also communicated between groups, to gain access to expertise not available in their own group. When groups became stuck, the characteristics of individuals, and the interaction of these characteristics within the groups, guided how they worked together.

> *The students made decisions regarding the nature of their projects, actively engaging in the processes of interaction: they discussed, agreed, disagreed, argued, negotiated, and laughed.*

Personal choice and control:

The arts projects were designed to grant the students the flexibility and freedom to control their own learning experiences and to personalize their meaning making. The personal relevance of the material appeared to be the driving force behind, and the reason for, the strong commitment for engaging in their projects.

Then and Now: *Jesus Christ Superstar* Revisited

As we'll discover through many examples over the next several chapters, innovative learning environments can transform the lives of students over the short and medium term. But what about long term? Can the healthy learning cultures we create for our students in the here and now have a sympathetic resonance and positive influence that spreads across decades? Can they even influence the decisions these future adults make and how they raise the next generation? And just what are the most common aspects of a learning environment that "stick" in the minds of students as they go forward in life?

Imagine the public commitment that could follow, to allow and enable educators to take the time and resources they need to reimagine learning cultures and embed the imperatives and conditions for healthy learning environments today, to help build a better tomorrow for us all.

With our curiosity piqued about these questions and others, Jane and I caught up on Zoom with six students who were involved in the 1984 production of *Jesus Christ Superstar* at St. Paul's School in Gander, Newfoundland and Labrador. We asked them, based on their experiences in the musical, what worked back then, how did it affect them, and how can we set the conditions today to draw out the seeds of brilliance that lie in every student. Here are some glimpses into these revealing conversations.

Lesley Ann Andrews and Kelly Moorcroft, flutist and cast

Sisters Lesley Ann Andrews and Kelly Moorcroft were both in the production. Lesley played flute in the band, and Kelly was in the cast. For both of them, the building of a culture of belonging stood out.

Kelly explains, "It was a culture of equality that you created. That we were all equal, and just allowing kids in."

Says Lesley Ann, "From a large group aspect, it really was a culture of belonging. It was a small rural school for Grades 7 to 12, and I don't know how you had the balls to do what you did. Your attitude was, let's just do it! But it was truly a culture of belonging because it brought all grades, everybody, together. And not only the students but the staff, and our parents, and other people in the community as well. It went way beyond those four walls of the school.

"So that's what stood out for me, the connections we had with other people. And when we pulled it together, it was the most beautiful thing. When I was playing flute. . . . I get goosebumps thinking about it even now. I toss out everything. But the fact that I still have this (she shows her music sheets from the production on-screen), and I will not let this go, until my last breath, says a whole lot. I still have my pencil notes in this music, and it means so much to me."

"Despite all the privilege of having private lessons, it didn't mean there weren't some excellent musicians sitting right beside me that I was unaware of. That so many people did have skills, and someone just needed to show them it was there." –Kelly Moorcroft

As a teacher, Lesley Ann was also asked to do a musical at her school, for which she had no experience. And her response was, sure, let's do it! "And we just learned as we went," she says.

Lesley Ann also says the experience influenced some of the life decisions she made, such as becoming a music teacher herself. "The seeds of that all started there. It will stick with me forever."

Kelly agrees. "It definitely influenced me. It gave me the confidence to do things I otherwise might not have done. To go outside that box. Peter always challenged us."

Interestingly, Kelly says being within that culture of belonging didn't just influence the way she thought about herself, "it influenced the way I felt about other people around me. Despite all the privilege of having private lessons, it didn't mean there weren't some excellent musicians sitting right beside me that I was unaware of. That so many people did have skills, and someone just needed to show them it was there."

Jeff Scott, guitarist

Jeff went over to St. Paul's School one evening because he'd heard that a girl he liked was taking judo lessons there. He actually went to a different high school, but we'd met when I was his teacher in junior high. He didn't find the girl, but he ran into me, and when I heard he was now playing guitar, I asked him if he wanted to be in the *Jesus Christ Superstar* production.

"I was flattered you asked me, because I'd just started playing guitar. I didn't even understand what a bar chord was, but you showed me. I had a record of *Jesus Christ Superstar,* and I just started plugging away at it," says Jeff. "What a learning experience that was for me! I'll always look at *Superstar* as the quintessential launching period of me as a guitar player."

He wasn't kidding, because as Jane and I chatted with Jeff on the Zoom call, we could see all kinds of different guitars in the background.

"After, I learned the chords, I'll never forget, Peter Gamwell looked at me and said, 'Jeff, you're going to be one hell of a guitar player.'"

Like the other former students we talked to, Jeff says he found magic in the theater, which has defined him as a person and an educator. "My students talk about the theater bug, and it's just that magic and that spirit when all those people are working for the same cause. Something grows inside of them and between them and everyone becomes a family. I'm sure it happens in sports or any great experience where you share that common bond, but I think it's very strong in theater and music.

"I think for every kid and adult that was in *Superstar*, it was something different. Gander was a small town with not much going on, so I don't think anybody expected it to be that magical, because nobody had ever done anything like that before. You know the lights go down, and it was like my heart is pounding, it was magical, it was beautiful, and I don't think people knew what to expect. It did change their lives, you better believe it. They'll never forget it, that's for damn sure."

And just as Lesley Ann saved her music notes from the production, Jeff still has, among the many beautiful guitars in his collection, the original guitar he played in the production.

"You want to know something, even though this guitar cost $125, if the house is on fire I'd grab this one first, because this is the guitar I learned on, when I played *Superstar* with this."

Traci Foley, cast

Traci Foley, who played Mary Magdalene, was just twelve years old during the *Jesus Christ Superstar* production. Like Kelly and Lesley Ann, the culture of belonging had a lasting impact on her.

"In high school you had geeks, you had jocks, you had preps, you had the popular ones, but in our world today, inclusive is such a huge word," she says. "It was like this was a high school that already had a community within it that was all inclusive. There were no lines. It was like an all-inclusive club that was like high society, but you didn't have to be high society. You could be anybody that went to the high school to be in it. Everybody felt safe and supported. All of them. From the actors in crowd scenes to people doing the behind stage work.

"I remember feeling so little on that stage, but there were people in the wings, like the Grade 12 apostles who were coming on next, or kids for a dance scene, and I remember even though I felt small, it felt like I had these arms around me—the people were all there to support me. I felt the responsibility to do my personal best and more, because I have my *Jesus Christ Superstar* family counting on me.

"I'd gone through blood, sweat, and tears with these people, and I remember thinking that if I don't do my best, if I don't work my ass off, if I don't get rid of these stupid nerves . . . the audience is still going to clap and people are still going to be proud of me. But I know if I gave it my everything, then that applause might not be any louder, it might not be a standing ovation, but it's a different experience. And that's what it became."

Billy McGrath, stagehand

Billy McGrath lives in Nova Scotia today with his wife and four children, along with a family owned business of a few restaurants. He reached out to me via email after watching *Jesus Christ Superstar* on TV.

In part, his second email explains the strength of believing there is a seed of brilliance in everyone and the power of positivity:

"I thought about how you gave me a purpose, to realize I needed to stay on track in school, and as difficult as I could be at times, you had faith in me to do a job at a young age. I often think of how positive you were with everyone and how you could motivate a group of kids to do great things. I have coached my kids in many sports and often tried to make sure I was positive and supportive as I remember how it helped me. I felt the need last night to reach out and let you know, and thanks to our modern tech and the internet, I found you."

During our Zoom call later on, Billy spoke about how the musical production gave all of the students a purpose.

"For me, I was a kid getting into a little bit of trouble. I was fighting at school and whatnot. You and I had a conversation at one point where I had to follow the rules or make a decision. And that was good for me because it really gave me a purpose and enjoyment. It gave me confidence, it gave me a sense of direction and commitment.

"I transferred that over to sports and I ended up having a long rugby career. It taught me you had to commit to what you were doing to make it work. It all stemmed from back then. You included everybody; you weren't selective in who you supported. I didn't know a lot about music, and I didn't know anything about theatre. It rounded me out as an individual because now I enjoy the arts as well."

Martin Kelly, cast

During these conversations with my former students, there was another student's name which was brought up unprompted by every single person, and that student's name was Martin Kelly. Although Martin was only in ninth grade at the time, he played the role of Judas, a complex and difficult musical piece. Yet his performance was, in a word, stunning. Absolutely captivating. It didn't surprise me that his classmates were still reminiscing about his moving and memorable performance all these years later. In fact, a major reason that some people saw the show more than once was because they wanted to hear Martin sing again.

Martin was born with music in his blood. His father, he told me, played the accordion without ever having taken a lesson. In addition to his singing ability, Martin also played in a band and played the tuba.

"Now music was introduced to me at a very early age," says Martin. "That's one thing we don't see now in the school system is music. As soon as you see somebody picking up a spoon and beating it on the floor that person is musically talented."

But when he initially transferred to our school from St. Joseph's, there was no music program.

"So when we went to St. Paul's," he told Jane and me on our Zoom chat, "all of us who were musically inclined from Saint Joseph's were lost. We had nowhere and then you came and found us. So when you came there we had a purpose to be there again. Once you've got the music in you, it doesn't leave, does it?"

It certainly doesn't!

Like everyone else, Martin says the culture of belonging was important to him. "It was how everybody was watching for everybody. They were feeding off everybody. When it came to the rehearsals, it was the first time a lot of us were doing something like this.

"I'd always performed with a crowd or at the back, such as the church choir at St. Joseph's. I never had to look at anybody and nobody had to see me. But right there, Peter put me front stage center."

Martin talked about how the culture of mutual support was such a powerful motivator for him. "I had a lot of fun. I'm picturing it now. I remember I said, 'We can do this.'"

"When we were in music there was no age. Like I was 14 or 15, and others were probably 16 or 17. There were some people who were 13 and 14. And there was no age. We were all the same category. We were in it together. I remember the camaraderie was awesome."

Not long afterward, Martin won the Musician of the Year Award for our school.

"I know that music was what disciplined me the most in school," says Martin. "More than any other subject, music was the one that kept me calm. I loved it."

As our conversation neared to a close, Martin said to me, "I don't want to say this but I'll be going home with regrets if I don't, so I'll say it anyway. I wish I could have had something that would have shown you that what you did was good back then. But the memories that are in my head, the lasting memories are awesome. Like I don't think I have to show you I've done anything in music or had to go anywhere to show you how much I appreciate you."

Martin has overcome tribulations in his life, but I don't think he recognizes the triumphs he has had, the lasting impact he has had on me and so many other people. It's not only because of his unforgettable presence in *Jesus Christ Superstar*, both on and off the stage, but also because of the positive influence he offers today—a presence that simply makes people feel good to be around him.

When I spoke to Traci Foley, I think she summed it up best. "I see Martin at the grocery store maybe once a year and I light up and he lights up and it's because of *Jesus Christ Superstar*. The last time this happened, after we had a conversation about JCS among a few other things, I said, 'Martin, can I give you a hug?' And he looked at me in disbelief and said, 'Traci Foley, you want to hug me?' And I said 'Yeah, Martin, I do want to hug you,' and we hugged and we both had tears."

CHAPTER 4

Key Takeaways

▶ The impact we have on our students is much bigger and broader than we think: As teachers and educational leaders, we literally have the opportunity to transform lives.

▶ By creating opportunities to develop deep connections, those connections impact in ways we can never fully imagine: The emotional bonds that were formed by the students still exist today, some forty years after the final curtain fell.

▶ Allow seeds of brilliance to flourish in everyone by enabling people to gravitate toward and try out things that they are curious about or have a passion for. Don't underestimate what individuals are capable of if given the opportunity to show their brilliance.

Reflective Questions

1. One of the reasons the *Jesus Christ Superstar* production was so successful was that students and adults were able to pursue and learn about their areas of interest, rather than being given an assigned task. How often are students and staff in your district assigned or told what to do, versus having choice or input? How can you enable more teacher-led initiatives and innovation in the way the learning takes place? How do you ensure the learning culture provides a diverse variety of individual and group work?

2. How comfortable are you with allowing individuals to participate in projects or take on roles in which they have no prior experience? What parameters and safety nets could you put in place to allow more curiosity and exploration to take place?

3. Partnerships were another key success factor in the production. How do you initiate, build, and sustain partnerships with parents, companies, and other community members continuously—not just when you need something from them? How do you make the partnerships mutually beneficial?

Try This!

Improv Your Next Conference

You don't have to put on a full-scale production like *Jesus Christ Superstar* to enable your teams to pursue their passions and learn new things. When you think about it, most education and business conferences are set up just like a production—with an agenda or script laying out what will happen, everyone cast in their usual roles, and often no shortage of monologues!

(Continued)

(Continued)

Have a conference where you reimagine your learning and working culture.

- Start with no agenda. Have the first activity of the conference be a discussion where you ask the participants what they would like to do for the day; then, spend about thirty minutes creating an agenda from the several main themes that arose.

- Write the main themes on large charts placed around the room, where people can gather, discuss, debate, collide, and explore ideas.

- Individuals can then gravitate to whichever themes they are drawn to. Have participants record their collective ideas on the charts.

- Use a small bell to prompt people to move to another topic, or people can switch to other groups as they wish.

- At the end of the day, your charts will be packed with rich ideas and initiatives that your teams actually care about.

CHAPTER 5

FINDING FERTILE GROUND

FIONA'S STORY

"Diamonds don't sparkle in the dark. You need to shine a light for their true brilliance to emerge."

—Peter Gamwell

Fiona Milligan has faced her challenges with dyslexia head-on and is now helping others do the same.

Photo courtesy of Kelli Milligan

"No friends, no track and field, no life. It sucks, and I'd like to kill me."

—Fiona Milligan, sixth grade, 2011

That was the message Fiona Milligan wrote for a class assignment more than a decade ago. At the tender age of eleven, she'd all but given up on herself in school. Outside the classroom, Fiona thrived—she was a gifted athlete who enjoyed a variety of sports, had lots of friends, and loved being in the outdoors. But having struggled for years with dyslexia, she saw no academic potential in herself, no seed of brilliance, and, surrounded by the loneliness of not fitting in to the expected student mold, no hope for the future. Her despair was not only swallowing her whole but also resonating outward to impact her parents and siblings.

But that was then, and this is now. Today, I'm delighted to tell you that Fiona graduated from high school; earned a diploma in sports management with a background in business; started her own business to help other children and families coping with dyslexia; writes a blog; plays for a women's hockey team (having also played at an elite level during her teens); and enjoys having good friends, a long-term boyfriend, and a close-knit family.

Most significantly, she has hope and big dreams for the future she's working toward. That includes her vision of traveling internationally with her company, Downright Dyslexic, sharing her story to help and inspire others with learning disabilities. She wants them to see they can be successful and achieve any goal they set out to—because they each have a seed of brilliance inside of them—just like Fiona.

So what changed for Fiona? How does a child transform from the depths of despair, too uncomfortable with her communication skills to even present projects in front of her grade-school class (as she relates in her video *Dyslexic Daisy*, Milligan, 2017), to a bright, thriving, articulate young woman of twenty-one, whose mission is to give technology, entertainment, design (TED) talks around the world? We thought the best way to find out was to ask Fiona herself!

As we explore Fiona's story here, it becomes abundantly clear that stifling her seeds of brilliance in her formative years came at a steep price—to herself, to her parents, to her sister and brother, and surely to many of the teachers who tried to help on her behalf.

And as Fiona and her supporters agree, it didn't have to be that way.

> *"Maybe if we stopped forcing kids into a circular mold and just let them be the squares, we could have a lot more people contributing great things to our world. As a society we have to do better."*
>
> —Fiona Milligan, founder and owner
> of Downright Dyslexic

The bulk of her transformation, of course, is thanks to Fiona's own hard work over the course of many years. It's also due to her parents, who never gave up their struggle with the school system to get the things Fiona needed, even when it seemed like they were getting nowhere. And it was supported by Fiona's sister and brother, who received less attention due to the focus on Fiona's dyslexia.

Teachers Who Take a Different Approach

I first met Fiona in 2015, when I was invited to attend a Celebration of Learning in Rebecca Chambers' classroom. A teacher in Ottawa, Canada, Rebecca had been an active contributor to our school board's very successful Lead the Way program.

Rebecca has a very different way of teaching. As a high school social-studies teacher, she never used textbooks, didn't believe in exams or tests, and had developed a very interesting and novel approach for her students. (We explore Rebecca's methods in more detail in Chapter 6.) Being a fan of innovative thinking myself, I was very curious to see her classroom's first Celebration of Learning.

But first, I have to back up nine months to the beginning of the school year in 2014, just for a moment, so you can understand just what learning was being celebrated, and how you might want to replicate it in your own classrooms.

It was in September that Rebecca had asked her students to identify topics that really mattered to them: things that were personally intriguing and ideas they wanted to explore. Through that exploration, they needed to show how their project made a difference in the lives of people, not only for the lives of the students themselves but also for the people within their community. They were to think of themselves as change makers.

Rebecca also challenged her students to present their learning in a way that was as engaging and as creative as the learning process itself had been. This was an exciting aspect of the project as the students needed to come up with novel ways that would help them teach what they had learned to other students and community members. As the end of the school year was nearing, I was excited to see what they'd come up with during this nearly year-long learning adventure.

When I walked into the school library for the Celebration of Learning, it was abuzz with activity. Over in one spot were students with guitars, while in another corner, students were tinkering with car parts. There were students with bikes and one student who had built himself a cardboard jail—to which he was handcuffed and seated inside. I wondered what that was all about! There was also an array of interesting artifacts that served as metaphors for the quest the students had been on.

At events such as these, I always video record any students who are willing, for my own documentation and learning. Hearing unique perspectives in students' own voices has enabled me to expand my own ideas about learning. Students' perceptions often surprise me, being very innovative and different from my own.

One of the first students I interviewed at that celebration was Fiona, who was eighteen years old by this time. She had decided to do a self-reflection of her own rather tumultuous journey through the school system. Her artifacts consisted of two documents—one written when she was in fourth grade and one from sixth grade. As Fiona explained, her mom had kept these notes because she "thought there was something strange about them."

The first document was a self-awareness worksheet. Figure 5.1 summarizes what it says and, just as importantly, what it doesn't say. Note that under the heading, "I am strong in these areas," Fiona left it blank. At nine years of age, some five or six years into her education journey, she had yet to experience the feeling or knowledge that she was talented or good at something, not even a single thing. She had absolutely no idea that she had strengths, and inspiring things to contribute to her spheres of influence.

However, Fiona was all too able to come up with areas of struggle. She lists four: reading, spelling, math, and talking. Not surprisingly, these are the foundational subjects in the school hierarchy and what we measure through standardized testing. Other responses in the note build upon and illustrate these struggles, as she finds reading and doing her work stressful, and says she's "not good at school." Her reading difficulties are evident, as she's unable to answer one of the questions.

Figure 5.1 Fourth-Grade Self-Awareness Worksheet

Self-Awareness Worksheet	
Prompt	**Response**
I am strong in these areas:	(Left blank)
I struggle with:	Reading, spelling, maths x – +, talking
Here's what the teachers I feel most comfortable with do to make that happen:	(response is illegible)
The most stressful part of my school day is:	Doing my work, reading
I'd like some help with:	School—I am not good at it
When I need help, I'm comfortable asking for it in the following ways	Talk to my mom

In her note from the sixth grade (Figure 5.2) Fiona writes:

"Fiona: No friends, no track and field, no life. It sucks and (I'd) like to kill me."

Figure 5.2 Sixth-Grade Note

I found her notes to be so desperately sad, so I asked her to please describe the school experiences that led to them. We explore her summarized answers here, but to view videos capturing Fiona's insights, aim your phone's camera at the QR codes here and then click on the link that pops up.

Video 5.1

Fiona: The Meaning Behind Notes

Hear from Fiona what her notes about school really meant, and how things are different today.

To read a QR code, you must have a smartphone or tablet with a camera. We recommend that you download a QR code reader app that is made specifically for your phone or tablet brand.

Video 5.2

Fiona: When Kids Don't Fit in the Line

Fiona provides an interesting insight into what happens when some kids simply don't learn the same way others do.

"In fourth grade, I felt like I wasn't strong with anything in school. So I wasn't smart; I didn't feel smart—as you can see, the things I struggled with. I'm dyslexic, so I have a hard time with reading, spelling, math, talking. And a few other things.

"Clearly, when I was that age, I didn't know anything about the school system. But now that I'm older and I've learned a lot more, I can tell that the school system has clearly failed me. And that with Ms. Chambers, I appreciate so much what she is doing, because she makes me feel smart. She makes me remember there are different types of learning. And that book-smart, sitting at your desk and writing an essay, and handing it in on time, isn't the only 'smart' there is in the world."

Regarding the second document, written in sixth grade, Fiona told me:

"I felt like, Grade 6 is a big year, but I didn't have any friends, and I didn't make the track and field team but I'm over that now. I felt like

I had no life. And again, the spelling is bad, but it says, 'it sucks, and I'd like to kill me.'"

I asked Fiona to describe the impact this experience had on her, and she responded without hesitation:

"It sucks thinking that you're not smart. Because there's a line, and if you don't fit in that line, then it sucks for you. And the truth is there are so many kids out there that don't fit that line. And that's why we need to change the system. Because instead of making it so we have to fit in that line, why don't we make it so that there is no line? And understand that everyone is smart in their own way?"

Fiona's response was so personal, clear—and ironic. Here is a young lady, with an obviously bright, reflective, empathetic, and caring mind, who spent most of her school life in a system that had branded her as "not smart"—at anything. Until she reached Rebecca's class and began to see that she had something to contribute after all. And the sad thing is the reality Fiona identifies herself with: She's not alone. There are indeed many, many youngsters who "don't fit the line."

Fiona and many other students that day granted me permission to share their very revealing stories with others. And over the next several months, I played Fiona's and other students' video clips at different keynote events and presentations I was doing. I asked people what they thought about Fiona's story, and of course, most people were visibly moved. But what was really interesting was how many people said Fiona's story reminded them of their own school experiences, or that of someone close to them.

As a former school principal and superintendent, these were some of the hardest conversations and questions to address. Parents and guardians, especially those dealing with children with challenges, would often say to me that when they observed their child at home, they saw all sorts of potential and intelligence and beauty and creativity. But whenever they received a phone call from their child's school, it was invariably to point out some negative aspect or failing of their child. They wondered why the people who were with their child for hours each day couldn't see the magic, the wonder—that beautiful seed of brilliance within them.

As we're living in an Age of Complexity, I think there can be no simple or singular right answer to these questions. Nor can we attribute the situation to one particular issue. As Jane and I have always said, we don't have all the answers ourselves, but I do know this: It is not the fault of teachers and educators. It is not the fault of parents or the children themselves. It is not even the fault of our greater society.

The solution is complicated and complex, but I truly believe the root of this enigma is that our education system has been stuck for several decades. We know the status quo of education is working well for some students, but it could be working so much better for countless others. We're enmeshed in a system that we're afraid to let go of.

Our education system has been stuck for several decades. We know the status quo of education is working well for some students, but it could be working so much better for countless others. We're enmeshed in a system that we're afraid to let go of.

When it comes to education and how we prepare our youth and lifelong learners for the future, we—educators, parents, business leaders—are afraid to question the assumptions and the assumptions on which those assumptions are based. But only by doing so can we change the rigid mindset of our system and move forward.

The students I talk to, like Fiona, are already questioning those assumptions, and by allowing ourselves to learn from their experiences, we can fundamentally transform our education system and break free of our self-imposed sentence of endless stagnation. After all, educational systems should evolve along with the changing world, yet our system has remained relatively the same since the Industrial Age.

In Chapter 1, we described the three imperatives that need to be present for healthy organizations to flourish, and one of these is to flip from deficit thinking, which tends to be our default, to strength-based thinking. We need to seek out and reimagine new possibilities and opportunities instead of accepting and resigning ourselves to the status quo. We need to look for and see the potential in people rather than defining them by what we perceive are their problems and trying to "fix" them. Because when that is a child's experience, not just for a day, or a week, or a year, it can have devastating and lasting emotional impacts, not just on the child, but on the classroom, the family, and the broader community, as children will almost invariably live down to the low expectations people set for them.

The Ripple Effect: Fiona's Mom Gives a Parent's Perspective

As Fiona talked to me about her parents, I became curious about their perspective. What had the reality of Fiona's journey been like for her mom and dad, and the family? How had they experienced it? A few months later, I had a chance to find out when Kelli Milligan agreed to meet with Rebecca and me. I asked Kelli how she felt when she saw those two notes Fiona had written in fourth and sixth grades.

Kelli explained that these weren't the first instances in which they'd been made painfully aware of the struggles their daughter was enduring they'd been experiencing the pain of going to school, alongside Fiona, ever since she was in kindergarten.

One poignant example Kelli gave was that Fiona's personality would perk up as weekends, summer, and school holidays grew nearer and then return to anxiety and depression as the times to return to school neared.

"There was the personality change that would take place on a Sunday night, because school was the next morning," she says. "When school ended in June, I always used to joke with my husband and say, 'Look, our kid's back.' And we had her for July, and we had her for August, and then maybe two weeks before school started, you'd start to see a change in her."

However, upon seeing Fiona's note from fourth grade, Kelli realized Fiona was starting to grow. "It was cathartic, because I felt like, okay, she's recognizing this as opposed to only us recognizing some of what she's gone through. And she's not just recognizing it, she's starting to overcome it, and to self-advocate, and she's beginning to take over."

Things came to a head for Fiona in sixth grade. "In her elementary school, the learning-support teacher was amazing. We had an advocate, somebody who was very supportive of us," Kelli explains. "But things changed when she went to middle school. And I learned very quickly how to become an advocate and how you have to go in, you have to demand things. You have to be the squeaky wheel. You have to be 'that parent.' As I was coming in from the parking lot I could just feel the administration looking like, 'Oh god, here she comes.' Which I didn't like being, but you have to be."

About halfway through sixth grade, Fiona's parents realized they were getting nowhere. "That's when we pulled her out and put her into private school, because we were just banging our heads against the wall. You can see how, when you bring up Grade 6 . . ." At this point in our meeting, Kelli began to weep.

One of the questions I ask, most everywhere I go, is this: If you were given a blank slate to reimagine a learning space so the seeds of brilliance that lie within every person could be unleashed, what would be your top one or two priorities? I posed this question to Kelli, in light of Fiona's experiences.

"I remember when Fiona was very young, she would say within the first couple of months after joining a classroom, 'Mom, the teacher doesn't get me, the teacher doesn't get me.' So I think first and foremost is having teachers be open to differences and to 'getting' the child. That not every child can sit, stare at the board, read notes, write notes. I think that would be first and foremost one of the greatest things that could be done."

You can watch the full videos with Kelli by pointing your camera phone at the Video 5.3 QR code.

Video 5.3

Kelli: Schooling From a Mom's Perspective

Kelli, Fiona's mom, talks about how her daughter's personality would change as the start of school neared.

Trying a New Recipe for Success: The Vegetable Soup Book Report

A second priority for Kelli would be allowing lessons to be personalized to the student. She explained that before moving to the private school, Fiona had never done a book report. But her new teacher gave her the option of doing a traditional book report or presenting her learning in a novel, personalized way. The teacher said to Fiona, "I want you to do the report with food."

The results were nothing short of extraordinary. And not just because Fiona was able to provide a completed project involving books and language arts but because making the project personal (one of the four conditions of healthy learning environments) enabled Fiona to reveal her seed of brilliance and show that she was indeed an intelligent, insightful, and extremely bright child.

Kelli explained how the project unfolded.

"We read the book for the report, but we threw out the writing component. The new approach tapped into her creativity, and the things this kid came up with! She made a menu and gave every kid in the class a serving of vegetable soup. She explained the reason for the vegetable soup was because the main character has all these emotions and turmoil, much like the vegetable soup, with the carrots and the peas and the potatoes. So obviously there was brilliance there, and she was able to illustrate it. She didn't have to try to write it out to show that she understood the book."

Fiona further created a nontraditional "plot graph," where the milder parts of the story were represented with bland food; then, more exciting parts, such as the climax, were represented with something spicy, which she served to her classmates as she explained it to them.

"It always gets better in the end and if it's not better, it's not the end."
–Kelli Milligan, Fiona's mom

"As a parent, I thought, why can't everybody do projects this way?" says Kelli. "I look at my other two children, who could write a book report no problem, and they were actually kind of jealous, thinking 'that's a cool book report!' This was great for Fiona; she took pride in her work. It made school fun, it motivated her, it made her feel accepted. There were so many positive things."

Teacher Rebecca, who admits she was also unengaged in school, says there are too many youngsters who find their school experiences extraordinarily difficult, which is a powerful motivator for her to foster more learning opportunities that are personalized to the individual.

Video 5.4

Kelli Fights for Her Daughter

Kelli, Fiona's mom, explains the frustration of trying to advocate for her daughter in the school system.

Video 5.5

Kelli Reimagines Learning

Fiona's mom, Kelli, describes the key characteristics of what she would like to see in a learning culture, which would have allowed her daughter to thrive at a much earlier age.

The Student's Perspective

I asked Fiona the same question I asked her mom: What are some of the fundamental things she would change if given the chance to reimagine our education system?

Fiona's response was immediate. "I would get rid of the literacy tests and all standardized testing. Just because one kid can do well on tests doesn't mean that the kids who can't are not smart. It's just one test, and yet it sort of predicts your future."

She'd also get rid of exams and do more project-based work instead. "That opens the boundaries for anyone to show how they learn, how they excel in their own way. I think it's more work for the teacher, but I think it's something that has to be done."

Reach Beyond the Classroom Through Collaborative Thinking

Fiona made a connection between what the traditional curriculum taught her versus what she needs to know—beyond the classroom and beyond university. She gave a few examples.

"I may know how to write an essay now, but I have no idea how to do taxes or pay my bills," she said. "In Ms. Chambers' class, you learn a lot about connecting with others, and the importance of collaborative thinking. But in a lot of classes, you're on your own. So how do you learn to interact with others when you're not learning it in school?

"Having a lot more group work would improve this situation," says Fiona, "But I don't mean people sitting around working on questions. I mean groups of young people getting together and going out and working in the community and learning. So it might be a food bank or a seniors' home or something like that where you're reacting and interacting with people in a lot of different ways. I think you would grow a lot from that."

Fiona, Age 21

A few years later, I became curious to hear Fiona's thoughts and reflections, in hindsight, of her school experience. So in December of 2019, we met up at a local coffee shop in Ottawa, Canada.

As you read what Fiona had to say about her school experience in retrospect and her life today, I'd like you to consider just how precisely the three imperatives for healthy learning environments enabled Fiona to thrive—and how she has in fact embedded the imperatives into her own life.

1. **Recognize that every person has a seed of brilliance.** With the help of Rebecca, her parents, and family, Fiona has come to recognize her own seed of brilliance—and quite brilliantly, it stems from her dyslexia itself and her decision to "own it."

2. **Flip your mindset from deficit thinking to a strength-based approach.** Much of Fiona's school experience focused on what was "wrong" with her and figuring out how to "fix it." As you'll see below, once she was able to flip that mindset and cultivate the seed of brilliance within herself, she built on that positivity to start a company that can help others deal with what she calls the "mental side" of dyslexia. What was once considered her weakness has now become her strength.

3. **Build cultures of belonging.** With her seed of brilliance, her strength-based approach, and her first-hand knowledge of how isolating having a learning disability can be, Fiona is building a powerful culture of belonging—not only for those with learning disabilities but for those who love them as well.

At the coffee shop that snowy December day, Fiona reiterated the incredible challenges that school had presented for her, as a person with dyslexia. She described her experiences as "trying to get a kid in a wheelchair to climb stairs."

She also described how lonely it was. "A lot of fellow dyslexics have grown up with the same feeling. They're very quiet and in the dark about it, and for a long time, I was, too. I was an outsider. I didn't appreciate or like what I had because I never fit in.

"Every day, I was pulled out of classes to work on my reading and writing, when all the other kids got to stay in class together and hang out. I always had to do extra work to try and make up for what I was lacking. I was really quiet, and I didn't express what it was like until it got to a point where it was like, this is who I am. I have dyslexia; there's no changing it, so I have to deal with it."

But before Fiona got to that point, she recognized the impact of her school experiences on her family.

"It took a toll on my whole family because a lot of times, when my mom would be helping me, I would have a tantrum because I didn't want to do it. I didn't understand why it wasn't working for me."

Fiona understood that the time spent with her detracted from her parents' time with her brother and sister, and to this day, that bothers her. As does the amount of money her parents spent for such things as computer software, tutoring, and endless programs.

"Any program you can think of, I've probably done it or tried it. That cost money and that puts a big toll on me, because all my friends who don't have learning disabilities, their parents never had to pay that extra out of their pocket."

The cumulative impact of these experiences motivated Fiona to take action and to try to help others struggling with the same challenges. In 2018, she created her company, Downright Dyslexic (downrightdyslexic.com.)

Fiona emphasized to me that it's not just the individual who's impacted by having a learning disability; there are compound effects on family and friendships. She created Downright Dyslexic to provide emotional support and awareness for "the mental side of things" of dyslexia, focusing on how to help children and families cope with the profound complexities of life with a learning disability.

Family Blogs Reveal the Impact on the Family

To help her understand the impact her dyslexia had on her family, Fiona asked her family members to write blogs on the subject. These reflections provide a glimpse into the way a student's experience has a ripple effect that goes far beyond the classroom walls. Her mother, Kelli, and her sister, Michaela, have been generous in sharing their blogs with us here.

Kelli's blog
Fiona's mother

"Whenever faced with a new challenge, the first place I go to get information is to books. I've always loved reading (again, I know, ironic). Off I went to the local Chapters store to the parenting section because my gut told me there is something here (going on with Fiona), and I was going to figure it out.

"This brings us to that moment on my lifeline that stands out in my mind. I can see myself clear as day, standing in the store, reaching for a book called *The Secret Life of the Dyslexic Child* by Robert Frank and Kathryn E. Livingston (2002). I see myself beginning to read through the book and I start crying. Right there in the middle of Chapters I was crying. I was crying because I had found what I was looking for. This author was describing my child and the challenges we'd been having. I suddenly understood the reason for the tantrums and the struggles with reading.

"I was crying because I was happy that I now knew what we were dealing with. You can't solve a problem if you don't know what the problem is. I was crying because I was afraid of what this meant for the future. I was crying because I was mourning the loss of a carefree childhood for my daughter, but most of all I was crying because I realized the struggles that lay ahead for her.

"I think that moment stands out so strongly for me because it marks the beginning of a journey. Although it has been Fiona's journey of growing up with the challenges of dyslexia, we have all been along for the ride. It has affected everyone in the family. We've grown together, we've learned together, we've screamed at each other, we've felt left out, and we've cried together (I think that was mostly me). I know that things could be far worse. I knew back then that dyslexia wasn't something that would take my child away from me or end her life, but it was a challenge on many levels and it would continue to be a challenge for a very long time.

"When Fiona asked me to write a blog post for her, I asked her to give me an idea of what she wanted me to cover. Her exact text to me said: *I wanna know how it effects u and dads relationship, mentally, health, money and family time, straight up dealing with me.*

"My text back to her said: *'That's a lot for one post. I'll see what I can do.'*"

Since starting Downright Dyslexic, Fiona says she's received a lot of questions about how dyslexia impacted her family. She asked her sister, Michaela, to help provide some insight on her experiences of growing up with a dyslexic sibling.

"You're going to read all about the good, the bad, and the ugly," Fiona told me, referring to her sister's blog below. "A lot of the things my sister mentioned I would have to agree with. Growing up with dyslexia has been hard for me, but it's also been very hard on my family. There were many times where arguments and frustrations could've been avoided.

"If I had known more about how my mind worked, if there had been more education on dyslexia, and if I received the support I deserved in school, I don't think I would've been angry all the time. Downright Dyslexic was created to not only help other dyslexics, but to guide families through the dyslexia diagnosis. It wasn't easy but we made it. I don't think my family would be the same without everything we've been through. What didn't kill us made us stronger."

Michaela's blog

Fiona's sister

> *"Siblings: your only enemy you can't live without."*
>
> –Anonymous

"To summarize it in one word, growing up with Fiona was a challenge.

"Being a sibling of someone with a learning disability includes a few key responsibilities. You are a support system. You are constantly explaining what dyslexia means, and then, you have to go over the definition again when they ask, 'Is that when the words dance around the page?' No.

"The next responsibility is acting as an interpreter. Growing up with Fiona I learned how to speak her language. I could easily follow her seemingly insane thought patterns (which is thanks to my ADHD [attention deficit/hyperactivity disorder]). When everyone else would be lost following her conversation, I would interject with what she 'actually' meant. I was and am still a translator, fluent in English and Dyslexic. Even our own mother would often turn to me and ask if I knew what the hell Fiona was talking about. And I always did. Even just the other day we were having a heated political discussion, and Fiona had one of those moments that needed to be unraveled."

Fiona: "You know that guy that gave the speech . . . Michael something."

Me: "You mean Martin Luther King."

Fiona: "Yeah!"

Me: "Just say MLK. It's easier."

Fiona: "Isn't that in Las Vegas?"

Me: "No. MGM Grand."

Fiona: "Oh."

(Continued)

(Continued)

"Those conversations happen on a regular basis. When Fiona started dating her boyfriend, Liam, we were often receiving texts from him because he had no idea what she was talking about. After spending four years together he is now fluent in Dyslexic, though he may call for backup every so often."

Liam: "I'll pick you up at 7. Sounds good?"

Fiona: "Yup! 4 10!"

Liam: "No. 7 p.m."

Fiona: "Yeah I know. 4 10."

"At first glance, it seems Fiona is confused about the time for her date. But to a sibling fluent in Dyslexic, you know she's referencing the popular radio communication 10-4, meaning 'understood.'

"Fiona's dyslexia is probably the reason my brother loves trivia and *Jeopardy*. Fiona presents us with an obscure definition, and we have to figure out what on Earth she is talking about. Alex Trebek would have had a field day with Fi (Fiona).

"Growing up with a sibling with a disability came with its challenges. From the minute she started talking, we could tell there was always something 'up' with Fiona. She called me, Adda (real name is Michaela) and Cameron (our neighbor up the street), DumDum. It wasn't until Grade 1 when a child is *normally* supposed to learn how to read that my parents thought to get her tested.

"Dyslexia took up a lot of real estate in our lives. From the minute she was diagnosed it was a constant battle that Fi and my parents fought. Most of the battles were with the education system, which is not equipped to deal with people that don't learn traditionally. My parents were always fighting to get her the support she needed. The school system in our area didn't know how to deal with someone with dyslexia.

"My parents were always in meetings with the school board or with her teachers, advocating for my sister and her dyslexia. She went to tutors, psychologists, teacher's houses in the summertime, and this one lady that taught her to use clay to try and visualize words.

"Fiona's dyslexia consumed the dinner table discussions, filled homework time, and it was the root of most of the arguments in our house. Fiona would get angry because she couldn't read and nothing seemed to be working, my parents would get frustrated because they weren't able to help my sister with what appears to be such an easy task, and I would get angry because I had my own problems and it felt like no one cared. My parents spent so much time on the dyslexia and Fiona, I constantly felt left out. My issues didn't seem as important. I didn't think I added value to anyone else's life. I can remember hundreds of times where I was told, 'Can you just wait—I have to deal with this with your sister,' or 'I have to do this for Fiona, I just don't have time for that right now.'

"These feelings of being on the outside, forced me to be more independent and accomplish things on my own (which I now can see value in, but it still hurt). As a young teen you need the support of your parents, and I never felt like I was getting my 'time' with them.

"I grew up feeling less than.

"I was all on my own for a while when it came to assignments, responsibilities, and personal issues. I'm not used to getting support. I don't like it. To this day I get defensive when people try to help me. I had never received any support in the past, so why all of a sudden are they trying to help me now? Have I failed? Do they think I can't do it on my own?

"I have ADHD; I was diagnosed around the age of 13. My parents thought to get me tested because my mother (as a pharmaceutical sales representative) started representing an ADHD medication. When I received my diagnosis, I was relieved. I finally had a reason for how I function. I wasn't stupid, useless, or lazy. (All real things teachers and classmates called me growing up.) I have ADHD. Even with my new-found diagnosis, it wasn't enough to warrant me more attention from my parents or the school.

"As I got older, I became heavily involved in creative areas. I am very artistic and good at almost everything creative that I pick up. I love theatre, and I genuinely believe that the reason I was so heavily involved was because it forced people to pay attention to me. A single spotlight and a sparkly dress is not something you can ignore.

"I blamed Fiona for my lack of attention—which isn't fair. As children, you're always competing for the love and affection of your parents, and it felt like Fiona was always winning. I resented her for it and viewed her as a rival, which is probably why we fought so much as kids. It really wasn't until I left home, to go off to university in Toronto, that Fiona and I started to get along. We were on our own, doing different things, and I didn't feel the need to compete with her.

"I am thankful for her, and at the end of the day I am thankful for her dyslexia. Fi without her dyslexia just wouldn't be Fi. I don't blame my parents for the amount of real estate that dyslexia took up, that wouldn't be fair to them, and it just wouldn't be true. They did the best they could. That's a lie. They did even better than anyone could ever imagine."

Fiona agrees with her sister's assessment. "Regardless of disability, being a parent or sibling isn't easy. That is what family means: no one gets left behind. My Dad is dyslexic, I am dyslexic, my sister has ADHD, and honestly the jury is still out on my brother, Corey. So we might be three for three for children with disabilities. And my mom, well, she's perfect but really short. We all have our own things and that's what makes us the Milligans."

She adds, "Families are like fudge: mostly sweet, with a few nuts."

What We Can Learn From Fiona's Story

So why did we include such intricate details about the experiences of one student? Because although she is just one, Fiona represents nearly "every student." Her story is not atypical. I've been in education for four decades and counting, as a teacher, a school administrator, a superintendent, and as a university professor. And right from my very first day of teaching, I remember coming across young people just like Fiona—thousands and thousands of them, throughout my career. Kids who suffered with the belief that they were somehow lacking, judged by a system of hierarchies that perpetuate the status quo. Here are some of those hierarchies.

- **Intelligence.** Our current structures are grounded in the belief that human intelligence is hierarchical, with language and mathematics at the top, the arts begrudgingly included at the bottom, and other subjects sprinkled in between. This hierarchy is reinforced when we focus more time and attention on the subjects at the top. This discounts and devalues intelligence and brilliance that lies outside the "top subjects," failing to recognize the brilliance of students like Fiona. What we need to strive for are learning cultures that support the seeds of brilliance in everyone, adults and children alike, through imperatives and conditions that allow each person's potential to blossom.

- **Creativity.** We've ranked different subjects and occupations on a scale of creativity, even though innovation can and should be embedded in all subjects, all occupations, and all walks of life. We consider the arts to be the most creative (ironically showing how little we value creativity by placing arts at the bottom of the hierarchy of school subjects and time allotments); followed by perhaps science and scientist/inventors. We perceive other subjects to have little creative involvement. We often consider mathematics to be the least creative subject, for example, since there's only "one right answer," when in fact, the creativity of mathematical theories, including discovering new ones, and the creative applications of math are bursting with innovation that draws in children's natural curiosity.

- **Leadership.** Much of our understanding and practice of leadership in our education systems (and indeed, in other organizations) assumes that the positional hierarchy is best practice, with those at the top making the decisions and cascading them down the chain of command to the bottom. Yet in the most successful, dynamic, and caring organizations, the formal leaders (usually modeled by the senior leader), create spaces where people feel comfortable expressing their ideas and their creative innovations. There's a vision of possibilities in a culture of openness and trust. The critical driving force for the innovative energy of the organization is the informal leadership that exists at all levels.

What's Next for Fiona

Fiona plans to start writing a book about dyslexia, something she couldn't imagine doing in her elementary school years.

"This isn't going to be a book about numbers, statistics, or the science behind how the dyslexic brain works," she says. "It's going to be a behind-the-scenes personal account of growing up with dyslexia in today's society."

She also wants to use her experiences to support children and families who are on a similar journey, as the voice of someone who understands what they're going through and can help with strategies gleaned from lived experience.

To do that, as described on her website, she has made it her mission to begin public speaking to elementary schools, "where I can begin to build my network of people, to open up more opportunities for myself, and connect with young kids and families who may be just finding out about their learning disabilities. As well, I plan to provide a social media platform in which students, teachers, and parents can view my videos that spread knowledge on learning disabilities. This will be where people can ask me questions, book workshops, and book public speaking events."

Some may think that Fiona is an anomaly, an intelligent young woman who wouldn't let her dyslexia define her and came out the other side through her own effort and sheer luck. But if we're going to respect Fiona's struggle and success, then we must respect her own accounting of how she made it through. And on her own company website, under the tab for mentors, she credits her mom—and her teacher, Rebecca Chambers.

I can practically guarantee you that every teacher will have at least one Fiona in their class this year. They may not be struggling with dyslexia. They may be struggling with another learning disability, or poverty, or challenges at home, depression or anxiety, shyness, or simply the belief that they are not smart and have nothing to contribute.

And every teacher and educator reading this book will have the opportunity to help them turn that around.

But the solution, despite our gut urges to do so, cannot be to try to "fix them" or to try to solve all of society's troubles, far above and beyond what we are required to do by policy. In our current world and Age of

We can . . . help the students in our care to discover their own seed of brilliance, to take a strength-based approach, and to create cultures of belonging, both for themselves and others.
–Peter Gamwell

Complexity, teachers and school boards are already stretched to the limit. We simply don't have the resources or the time to handle such monumental tasks alone, and those who attempt it can soon end up stressed and burned-out.

But if we follow Rebecca's lead, we can use the three imperatives to create a healthy and innovative learning environment. We can become that first sympathetic resonance, to help the students in our care to discover their own seed of brilliance, to take a strength-based approach, and to create cultures of belonging, both for themselves and others.

CHAPTER 5

Key Takeaways

▶ Our learning cultures can be enriched by flattening hierarchies that currently define traditional learning structures: (1) Math and language are at the top of the subject hierarchy, taking the lion's share of time allotments. (2) The arts and possibly science are at the top of the creativity hierarchy. (3) Formal leaders are at the top of the leadership hierarchy.

▶ Embrace the idea that seeds of brilliance, innovation, and leadership capacities lie in every individual, regardless of their test scores in the top hierarchical subject areas.

▶ Consider the effect the student's school life has on the family and the broader community. The experience doesn't just stay with the student.

Reflective Questions

1. Fiona's mother, Kelli, said teachers need to be open to differences and to "getting" or understanding the child. How do you model the vital importance of ensuring your teams are able to "get" the unique differences in every child? What tools, resources, and time can you provide?

2. Every teacher is also unique, each with their own seeds of brilliance. In what ways do you try to "get" each teacher and team member in your organization?

3. What's the communication style at your organization? How do school leaders model to teachers that they look for and see the magic in them—rather than focus only on where they need to improve? How do you encourage teachers to talk about the student to their parents, not only about their seeds of brilliance but whether they like to come to school?

Try This!

Alternative and Novel Ways to Demonstrate Learning

Kelli, Fiona's mom, told the story of how Fiona was allowed to use food to demonstrate her learning of a book the class had studied rather than write the traditional book report. The result was an inspiring vegetable soup analogy that shone a light on Fiona's brilliance.

Have a brainstorming session to come up with other novel ways to demonstrate learning. Read the story of the vegetable soup report. Then invite your teams to list ways to demonstrate learning. Don't forget to ask students for their ideas, too.

CHAPTER 6

THE COURAGE TO DO THINGS DIFFERENTLY

REBECCA'S STORY

"Part of this transformation was a gradual letting go of what I knew school to be. I gained the confidence to do it by seeing other educators who were doing things differently."

—Rebecca Chambers

Now that we've seen transformative learning cultures through a student's eyes in the last chapter with Fiona, let's explore it through the eyes of a teacher.

When I've discussed Fiona's remarkable transformation during my keynote presentations, educators and other guests become intensely curious about how her teacher, Rebecca Chambers, creates such a healthy, innovative learning environment in her high school social-studies classroom.

They have all kinds of questions about how she cultivates those seeds of brilliance in her students and makes the extraordinary happen. What curriculum and lesson plans does she follow? How does she format her tests? How often does she test? How is the classroom set up? What is her seating arrangement?

A Classroom With No Walls

Those who have the good fortune to see Rebecca's classroom in action at the beginning of the school year can feel a little disoriented and even taken aback. After all, there are no desks in the room. In some ways, there are no walls because Rebecca believes in taking her students out of the classroom as much as possible. And there are no textbooks, no tests, no exams. She lives by the imperatives and conditions set out in *The Wonder Wall* by flipping the concept of learning on its head.

The seemingly unstructured setting at the beginning of the school year is intentional. Rebecca wants to set her young learners on a path of uncertainty, giving them permission to see things through different lenses and perspectives and to question all manner of assumptions. During the first several weeks, she focuses her time on figuring out with her students what their individual interests are, what drives them, what they're passionate about, and what changes they'd like to see in their communities and the world. Through this intensive process, she helps them discover their own seeds of brilliance, and she begins to nurture them by choosing one project per semester that intrigues and fascinates them. And then, the students immerse themselves.

Rebecca first set upon this method as a teacher at the Ottawa-Carleton District School Board (OCDSB), where I also worked as a superintendent. She was interested in the creativity, innovation, and leadership work we were doing, and wondered how she might reimagine her own teaching to inspire and unleash the potential of her students—to engage them in meaningful work that really mattered to them.

It is not easy to step outside the norm and try something new, but Rebecca took courage from other educators who were also trying to break the mold.

"I had an epiphany," Rebecca explained to me. "Part of this transformation was a gradual letting go of what I knew school to be, and what I was expected to do in the classroom. I gained the confidence to do it by seeing lots of different examples throughout North America and the world, other educators who were doing things differently."

Rebecca's motivation for the change was the students in her classroom. "Our (traditional) education system is doing a disservice to three-quarters of our student population. I think about a quarter of the kids thrive and get a lot out of it but most don't. They're doing what they have to do to move on to the next goal, whether it be postsecondary or just getting out of here. It needs to change so that the students are engaged rather than just being compliant."

We Need to Reimagine Our Learning Environments

Like Rebecca, it's become increasingly clear to me that we need to reimagine, reshape, and redesign our learning environments to put human potential, possibility, and innovation as the central priorities. We must embrace the idea that within every child and adult lie the seeds of potential and brilliance and the need to foster the conditions for them to flourish.

In many jurisdictions, students spend as much as 65 percent of their school day on math and language, leaving little room for exploring other areas of their potential. As a result, a surprisingly large number of students don't know themselves, what their passions or capabilities are, even as they're graduating high school.

> "Our (traditional) education system is doing a disservice to three-quarters of our student population. I think about a quarter of the kids thrive and get a lot out of it, but most don't. They're doing what they have to do to move on to the next goal, whether it be post-secondary or just getting out of here. It needs to change so that the students are engaged rather than just being compliant."
> –Rebecca Chambers

According to a 2019 study by Ellucian, *Course Correction: Helping Students Find and Follow a Path to Success,* the problem is getting worse not only for colleges but also for the well-being of students. The research report states, "Today's college students struggle with choosing a career path and major, increasing the time and cost associated with obtaining a degree." Furthermore, almost two-thirds of students feel "overwhelmed" by the process of selecting a major and many feel they need more help. While this study is aimed at coming up with solutions at the college level, surely giving students more opportunities for deep learning about themselves, from kindergarten through twelfth grade, could help.

Embed imperatives and conditions

So how can we shift our learning cultures to ensure that each student's brilliance can be revealed and unleashed? I was curious to view Rebecca's work through the lens of our imperatives and conditions, so I've spent the last several years capturing her story and the stories of her students, parents, and community members through videography. Here's a glimpse into that world.

Encourage wonder

Rebecca's students engage in inquiry work, but not inquiry work that's determined by the teacher. It's all guided by student voice and student choice. She establishes and opens up spaces of learning that encourage her students to delve into themselves. They're inspired to discover what really matters in the world around them; to investigate with an open mind and a collaborative spirit; and to imagine and set in place ideas that can make an extraordinary difference in their own lives and the lives of others, across their school, within the community, and sometimes across the globe.

Rebecca encourages her students to think of themselves as change makers. She pushes them to look within themselves and out into the broader community and ask, "How can I make a difference? What can I do to make the extraordinary happen—in my life and in the lives of those around me? What am I passionate about? How can I use that passion to catalyze positive change?"

This isn't always easy for the students. Pose the same questions to many adults, and they would really have to think about their answers. But at fifteen-, sixteen- and seventeen-years of age, many students have no idea! They're used to a traditional curriculum where what to learn, when to learn it, and how to learn it are pretty much decided upon by the school system. So for years, too many students plod through their learning. They take notes in class, study them, take tests, and finish assignments, knowing that they have to play the game. As for curiosity? That's for after school.

Then along comes a teacher like Rebecca Chambers, and their minds are blown. "Choose something I'm passionate about, something that matters, something that makes me curious—and go make a difference in the world? I've no idea where to begin!"

During the first few weeks of the term, Rebecca helps students over this hurdle. Not all—some know exactly what they want to do, especially those who are taking their second, third, or fourth class with Rebecca. Many kids, once exposed to having choice and control in their learning, can't get enough of it.

Invite the outside world into the classroom

Rebecca, along with students, also invites community members from all manner of organizations to come into the classroom and talk about their work. They come from all walks, from businesses, nonprofits, science, retirement homes, hospitals, plumbing companies, and more, to help spark the students' imaginations and ideas.

And sure enough, the project ideas start to emerge, along with the students' unique seeds of brilliance. Sometimes it's a student working by themselves, or with a partner. And sometimes a group of students will be sparked by a similar idea and decide to work together.

Here's a look at how a few of these projects evolve, which will give you an idea of the steps taken to conduct these learning projects.

The AND Project

For several years, with the aim of creating true inclusivity and cultures of belonging, Rebecca's students have partnered with a class of high school students with cognitive disabilities. The work and friendships that have formed through this joining together are inspiring. But recently a group of Rebecca's students took it a step further and created AND: Abilities Not Disabilities.

The thinking behind AND is that the student can say I can do this, AND I can do this, AND this, AND this. It doesn't limit an individual to disabilities; it helps them see beyond.

With AND, plumbing becomes more than a pipe dream

There are many amazing examples of the impact AND has had on the students. One student told me about a boy who, in spite of challenges, had a keen interest in plumbing. He loves fixing toilets and sinks and has now opened a YouTube channel to share his passion and teach others how to do it.

AND lessens the sting of segregation

As a society, we tend to segregate ourselves. Students with serious developmental delays or cognitive challenges such as those with Down syndrome are often set apart in segregated classrooms. "The General Learning Program (GLP) students are very segregated from the rest of the school," explains Jessica, one of the students involved in the project. "We want people to know they have strengths, talents, and gifts, just like everybody else. The girl who came up with this idea (for AND) was in the GLP class, and she wanted everyone to know they are the same as everyone else."

Socializing is another key need for GLP students. "You see how us being there with the GLP students just once a week brightens up their day; they are so excited to see us," Jessica told me.

Bringing young and old together

Two other students decided to volunteer with seniors at a local retirement home. They soon noticed that a lot of the seniors appeared isolated. They were sitting alone and not interacting with each other.

The students talked to Rebecca about it, as well as the class's two mentors, a past vice-principal and a teacher. Through discussions of project design, the girls came up with the idea for a project call Mapping Your Roots.

The map included all of the places the seniors were born, with a pin and a string attached to their name. It was hoped that the map would help the senior residents get to know each other better—a map would be a great way to help people start conversations, especially as they often came from a similar geographic area.

After creating the map with the seniors' help, the students then planned a gathering with food and music from the seniors' youth and talked to them about their life experiences.

"Just to see the transformation of them sitting alone and not looking too well to then glowing and being so happy that someone wanted to talk to them was amazing," says student Jillian. "One lady, after I said hi, said, 'Oh, are you talking to me?' And it just touched my heart because they just want a friend."

One senior gentleman involved in the project was from Italy. He said that he had previously tried to talk to people in the lunchroom, but no one really wanted to talk to him. That touched Jillian. "You have this whole community in the retirement home, and they don't talk to each other. So this gentleman became a part of the project to see if there was anyone else from the same place he was from, so that he could make some friends."

Putting it on film

The two students then decided it would be important to capture some of the seniors' stories on film. At first, it wasn't easy to convince the seniors to participate. As Jillian pointed out, "A lot were nervous because they felt they didn't have cool stories."

But as the girls heard how some seniors had moved eighteen times, or had experiences in the war, they realized the power of what they were doing and that "all of them had something special to talk about."

The girls partnered with a videography company for the project, so they also had the opportunity to learn about production. They created footage of card games and doing puzzles with the seniors, all while asking them questions about their lives.

Jillian explains, "We got to have a big event, and they could be excited about something that they did. I think in a lot of cases when you're in a retirement home, you're not really connected with the outside world. But you have so many interesting ideas and stories to tell . . . this event was an amazing opportunity for people to hear them and to hear about them."

The girls said the biggest lesson they learned was the importance of communication and about a whole new community that's often hidden from society.

As student Rachel summed up, "Both [young and old] generations are stigmatized. Our generation is seen as not good in the workplace, and they are seen as people who have already had their chance and aren't really as important. So bringing the two together can connect us in a special way."

Point your phone's camera at the Video 6.1 QR code to hear students Rachel and Jillian talk about their project.

Video 6.1

Building Bridges Between the Generations

Students Rachel and Jillian describe how their project worked to alleviate isolation and loneliness in a seniors' home.

Video 6.2

A Hilarious Moment With Marjorie

Hear what one of the senior citizens had to say about Rachel and Jillian's project.

As we see in these projects, Rebecca's student teams think and act from strength-based perspectives. They have the intent to make the extraordinary happen wherever and whenever they can. And in doing so, they naturally foster cultures of belonging, whether for students with disabilities or residents in a home for senior citizens.

Moreover, they succeed in their endeavors through storytelling and listening, by honoring the stories people tell, by personalizing their learning, by bringing a lens of sincere inclusivity, and by infusing celebration and a culture of joy through their interactions.

Assessment of a Different Kind

So if there are no tests or exams to assess the students' learning, what then? How do these extraordinary youngsters demonstrate their understanding and insights? Reveal the impact of their learning? As we touched upon in the chapter about Fiona, at the end of each term, Rebecca organizes a Celebration of Learning where individual students or teams present their work. But it's never a conventional presentation: she challenges them to present in a way that brings their stories to life, very often through the use of metaphor.

While this may sound unstructured to some, the students can always express the connections to curriculum, whether that be world affairs or human growth and development. Rebecca leads the students to make the connections between their area of passion and the specifics of curriculum.

Rebecca's engaging methods resonate among the educators and business leaders Jane and I have met. These leaders understand that if learning is to matter, it needs to connect to the heart of the individual learner—and that means starting with the concept of "know thyself." Rebecca allows her students to explore who they are and what matters to them and to gain the insight of how they can use this as a catalyst for change.

When you look at the videos of Rebecca and of the students whom I interviewed at the Celebration of Learning, you'll notice the students' candid reflections and personal stories on Rebecca's new approach to learning. The following examples provide a glimpse into the meaningful and poignant work that grows from their minds once the seed of brilliance has been provided with the right soil.

From the Students' Perspective

As with Fiona in Chapter 5, I've interviewed many students during Rebecca's Celebrations of Learning to gain their insight. Here are some of their perspectives.

Carter's story

Carter had struggled in school. He described how he wasn't a great student and has trouble following "step-by-step" instructions. He credits Rebecca with saving him "huge time by taking me on a different route and exploring different ways of learning."

Rebecca leveraged Carter's passion for hockey to help him explore certain cultural aspects of the 20th century, including encouraging him to watch a television documentary series called *Hockey: A People's History* (McKinley, 2006). This approach had a transformational impact on Carter's learning. In his words, "It changed the way I looked at school, and how I developed my ideas, because I was experiencing learning stuff in a totally different manner.

 Normally you'll look at the board or whatever and take your notes, and just flip the page, take more notes or maybe read a book and get your ideas that way. But with Ms. Chambers, I got to learn history through something I love, which is hockey. So I had a sense of, I want to learn, I want to watch the movie."

Rebecca used Carter's interest in hockey to spark his interest in history.

"The movie started off talking about the invention of hockey," says Rebecca. "But then with the invention of hockey came the market crash in 1929, which led to the Depression. And then through all that there was the First World War and the Second World War and how hockey players and people had to live when men went away, and women came in to do their jobs in the factories and service industry. So through the hockey aspect, it gave a whole sense of the first half of the 20th century. That made a huge impact."

Carter agrees this changed him as a learner. "I just feel better about myself because in other courses, when I received bad marks, that's like a really shitty thing, right? But even with receiving maybe not the greatest marks in this class, it still brings out my confidence because I know I'm learning. I might not be able to express it properly, but I know I'm learning because of my interest. So it totally changes the way I look at school, and how I enter the situation."

Carter says he also enjoys the camaraderie in class, that culture of belonging. "There's a lot of sharing for sure. We've all shared ideas and worked together and made something incredible, really, that most people, most other classes, won't ever get to experience. So it's had a huge impact."

As I listened to Carter that day, it baffled me that he has an ingrained belief that he can't express himself well, yet this is belied by the very articulate expression of his journey during the interview.

> *"But even with receiving maybe not the greatest marks in this class, it still brings out my confidence because I know I'm learning. I might not be able to express it properly, but I know I'm learning because of my interest. So it totally changes the way I look at school, and how I enter the situation."*
> *—Carter*

Video 6.3

Carter: Learning Through Hockey

Carter describes how teacher Rebecca recognized his love for hockey and showed him a different way of learning that incorporated his personal interests.

Saxon's story

As I've interviewed more students like Carter over the years, I've found they give very astute insights into this conundrum of how students' seeds of brilliance are missed all too often. When I first met Saxon at a Celebration of Learning event, he was in an unusual place. He was seated inside a cardboard jail cell with his wrists handcuffed on the outside. Some quite provocative words were written on the jail wall.

Video 6.4

Saxon: Saxon in Jail!?

Student Saxon has cuffed himself to a homemade jail cell at the Celebration of Learning. Find out what that's all about!

I told Saxon I was sorry to see him in this state and asked him what was going on.

Here's a bit of our conversation that followed:

Saxon: "I am being restricted by school."

Me: "How on Earth did that happen? School is such an open place."

Saxon: "Well, there's a lot of stuff that we're forced to do. There's a lot of stuff that we're forced to learn. We don't really have freedoms in learning those things."

Me: "Can you give me an example of that? Have you felt that all the way through school?"

Saxon: "Through most of school, yes. I've been told how to learn, I've been told what to learn, and I've been told what to present."

He mentioned that Rebecca's class was somewhat different, and I asked him how.

Saxon: "Well, you see, we have inquiries. Basically, we pick an issue, and there are freedoms and restrictions, but we have more freedoms than in any other class I've ever been in."

Me: "What's that done for your thinking?"

Saxon: "It's opened up my mind a lot and I've learned to think a different way. I've learned to think way more creatively."

I was very impressed by the way Saxon had chosen to express these thoughts and ideas. The metaphor of the jail and the handcuffs was very powerful. I asked him how he had come up with it.

Saxon: "This semester hasn't been a great one in terms of grades (in my other classes), and I've been thinking, in a lot of these projects, if I had been given the freedom to do what I really wanted and show what I really wanted and how I wanted to, I think I could have done a lot better. And I think I would have learned a lot more, too."

I asked him what advice he would give to the public school system, thinking of the young people coming behind him and his experiences.

Saxon: "You should treat everybody as an individual and not have them as cookie-cutter people. Everybody is different and everybody learns differently . . . if we could figure out a way where everybody can learn in the way they learn best, and the way they want to learn, I think everyone would be way smarter and we would advance as a race."

In another of Saxon's inquiries about social norms, he chose a similarly clever metaphor of "Don't Follow Suit," in which he wore a suit and tie. He explained to me, "With sociology, you study societies and get to learn why people do certain things for whatever reason. And I came across social norms and I found them quite preposterous, to be honest.

"Because there's a lot of social norms like guys can't cry, for example, things people think are unacceptable for really no reason. So don't follow suit or you're going get one of these around your neck." Here, he pointed to the tie dramatically and talked about how it would choke you.

"And sometimes the suit doesn't fit so you gotta find your own thing. That's what I took away from this class was finding your own thing, your own path, being your own person and not trying to let society influence you."

Seeds of brilliance can grow in more than one garden. Recently, Saxton's English teacher told him she thought he would get a better mark in English if he was less restricted regarding being told what to write and how to write it. She recommended he take a writer's craft class, because it would give him more freedom in his writing.

"She told me I'm creative and smart, it's just the restrictions within her course that is minimizing my mark and not letting me expose my full capabilities," he told me.

Anika's story

When I met up with Anika at a celebration, she talked to me about how learning was much different in Rebecca's classroom.

"We just learned so much more; we think more. In traditional classrooms, you get a piece of paper and here this is, learn it, do the test and it's done," says Anika. "But here we found topics we really liked. We would elaborate, we would research, we would find things we're passionate about. We had the choice to look at things we wanted to learn about. We would share and learn from others, and it was just a whole mix of creative thinking, and so many different points of view."

Anika believes this type of learning could happen throughout all schools.

"Of course, there has to be basic guidelines but it's so easy to implement. With traditional learning there's always boundaries; there's no room for looking at other things. Here you can explore, see everything you want to see, learn everything you want to learn, and then find passions and keep going in life with those passions. It's just so much fun and I enjoyed it so much."

Video 6.5

Anika Compares Traditional School Structures to Passion-Based Learning

Ever wonder how students feel about traditional ways of learning compared to passion-based projects? Anika explains it in no uncertain terms!

Anika found this type of learning had a deep impact on her. "I found out things I didn't know about myself . . . I found a passion for human rights and helping other people. It makes me very happy to change other people's lives as much as mine. It's about learning about myself, and there's so many people that can be impacted, not just the people learning but the people who learn from the people that are learning."

Emma's story

I shared an interesting conversation with Emma.

"My two inquiries were body shaming and homelessness," she said. "This mannequin has a really small waist, and the two oversized shirts represent the spectrum of body shaming. Then I've got this old, ripped shirt to represent homelessness and the belt kind of wraps everything together.

"Then I also have the brown shirt that's kind of boring, and that just represents my mindset towards the class at the start of the year, and then the really colorful shirt is my mindset towards the end of the year. So, the brown is kind of like my brain when we didn't get to use any of these set outcomes in our regular classes, but now the color represents my brain because we've gotten to use these outcomes and we've learned so much, not just about history but everything in the world. And I really, really enjoy this."

So if her brain was brown in her other classes, I asked her what color her brain was during her previous eight years of schooling.

"The color was definitely brown and boring because in each subject it's always one way: write notes, and memorize information to pass the next test," Emma said. "You're not learning to learn; you're learning to pass. But in this class, we're *learning*. We got to pick things we really wanted to learn about.

"That's what I learned in this class as well. You can do whatever you want to put your mind towards, as long as you have the passion, the drive, the desire."

Owen's story

Owen told me he had enrolled in five of Ms. Chambers' courses. The reason, he explained, was that everything is firsthand in her classes. "It's learning real life skills, interacting with different people, and it's stuff that I won't just learn it, cram, do the exam, and then forget it the next day. It's stuff that's transferable into anything I do."

Owen described how he's learned a variety of skills like resiliency, passion, critical thinking, and many other attributes that will contribute to his success. "I can do anything I put my mind to."

For Owen, the self-directed approach is essential. He emphasizes the importance of the guest speakers, the use of social media, and the interaction with peers; the connectedness catalyzes the learning.

"For example, I follow my classmates on Twitter and everyone's doing a different inquiry, learning something new, and they tweet out every day what they find, and I scroll through my feed, and I learn what they're learning."

In one of Owen's inquiries, which I thought was very clever, he compared his life growing up to his grandparents' generation. "I wanted to know how our childhoods differed and how it affected our values throughout the lifespan."

Another of his inquiries explored the idea of why people conform.

Owen: "I did one of my inquiries on why we conform and conformity in general. And if you relate that to the school system, looking at schools 200 years ago, and even before that you have the desk, you have the teacher at the front teaching the lesson, chalkboard, pencil, paper. You write the test, turn it in. It's the exact same as it is now. That's what I mean about conformity; no one is really willing to change the system, because they think what they have does the job. But it doesn't and times are changing now. I think there's a lot of work that's been done but it really does need to change."

Me: "When people say, 'Everything is fine and we don't need to change,' what would you say to that?"

Owen: "I'd say the people who say that lack creativity. They don't want to step outside the box. They just want to get the job done. The good old poster board, PowerPoint presentation, that doesn't work anymore. People will look at it, they might read it, then they'll forget the information and they don't care. But the stuff that's going on in this room is all creative stuff that people will remember, and it'll stick with them. Every school should have something like this."

Video 6.6

Video Playlist Featuring Rebecca's Students

Browse the playlist for more student interviews
from Rebecca's class.

CHAPTER 6

Key Takeaways

▶ Schools and communities are inextricably and symbiotically linked.
Engage the community in an ongoing way, by bringing the inside out
and the outside in. See classrooms and schools as extensions of the
community, and vice versa.

▶ Students get engaged when the learning is personalized, when the
learning deeply matters to them and when they have the opportunity
to make a difference. Such learning makes a lasting impression, unlike
memorizing material for the test and then forgetting it.

▶ Allowing students to demonstrate their learning through meaningful
ways, rather than the standard written report or PowerPoint
presentation, stimulates creativity and enables students to showcase
their work at a Celebration of Learning.

Reflective Questions

1. Who are the Carters in your school? What are you doing to ensure
that all children understand that they have brilliance within them?

2. How do you open spaces of trust, in which students can express
their true feelings and thoughts just as Saxon did?

3. The support of leaders is essential to enable teachers to be
innovative and try new things. How do you support staff who
want to try to do things differently?

Try This!

Turn Classrooms Into Innovative Learning Environments

Rebecca—and several other teachers you'll read about in this book— maintains a best practice of designing her classroom in unstructured and innovative ways. One of the most enjoyable ways for teachers and children alike to draw out their seeds of brilliance is to create spaces, both literally and figuratively, that encourage learning, creativity, and curiosity.

From an emotional standpoint, students and adults need spaces where they feel valued and where it's safe to give their contributions, where they can discuss, disagree, and collide ideas—which is the mother of innovation.

Bear in mind that supportive leadership is key to the ability to create such spaces.

From a physical standpoint, there are all kinds of things your school can do to make spaces more inviting.

- Have a meeting and invite teachers to talk about the ideas they have. Write them down and see what's feasible. Remember to consider partnerships with the community—an idea that doesn't have expertise on staff or seems too costly may come to life if an interested local business or organization comes into play.

- Start by bringing the inside out. Expand classrooms by getting the students outside. If you have the space, let the children grow flower and vegetable gardens, or plant a few fruit trees. This will provide infinite possibilities for learning while beautifying spaces.

- Then bring the outside in. Cut flowers and bowls of fruit and veggies from your school harvest always brighten up a room.

- If a teacher would like a class pet but isn't sure they can commit the time, see if other teachers would be interested in sharing a pet, where each class keeps the pet for a week or a month before passing it on to the next classroom to enjoy.

- Set up a Wonder Wall—a place where students can write down things they're wondering about! Each week, explore a few of the wonderings and invite all the classes to look for answers.

(Continued)

(Continued)

- A small cottage-style couch or comfortable chairs can make a conversational area, either in a classroom or a common area of the school. Alternatively, oversized cushions can be used on the floor (a great sewing project for students!).

- Take candid photos and place them around the room.

- Put a few board games or other interesting items around the classrooms if students have finished their work early. (Or have them design their own games to share with the school.)

- Set up a brainstorming center with a board to write ideas on (large sheets of paper, chalkboard, or dry erase), lots of colorful pens, and sticky notes.

- Ask students for feedback as well. What would they like to see in the classroom or on the school grounds? What about the gym or the library?

- Meet again at the end of the school year to see what went well and discuss new ideas for the fall!

CHAPTER 7
IGNITING THE FLAME
BLUE SKY SCHOOL

"We've created an environment in which students are inspired to find that thing that lights your flame and makes you follow through with your dreams."

—Shauna Pollock and Karen Hill

When Shauna Pollock and Karen Hill wanted to reimagine what school could be—to imagine spaces of learning that inspired and unleashed the brilliance in all students—they embarked on an audacious adventure. They went out for dinner one evening, and by the time the meal had ended, they had made plans to open their own school, one that would shine a light on the potential and brilliance within each learner.

Blue Sky became Canada's first full-time school designed as an innovation center and entrepreneurial incubator for youth. It offered a completely new kind of learning experience, welcoming youth from a wide range of backgrounds.

Shauna had been a very successful teacher in the public school system, where she received the Prime Minister's Award for Teaching Excellence. But she was ready to try something different. She felt too many youngsters weren't thriving within the traditional school structure; indeed, many were suffering not just academically, but in relation to their well-being.

Karen, with her background of working in group homes, counseling, and behavior intervention, wanted a better way to serve young people in need—especially those slipping through the cracks of our social systems.

Karen's own daughter was a very different learner, due to a lack of confidence.

"Not only did students I work with need something different, but my own daughter did. I wondered how we could look at the complexity of needs and see if there are a few solutions that can address those needs so teachers aren't overwhelmed."

Getting Started

Shauna and Karen created a presentation for the prototype model of their newly imagined learning culture. Its critical characteristics included a school that's holistic, child based, and more focused on learners becoming self-directed. Desirable outcomes would see a child become a lifelong learner, empowered to be a change maker.

"We then created our hypotheses based on 'if we have the time, the space, the people, and the resources, how can we experiment and build a new prototype for education?'" says Shauna. "And then within a year of that fateful dinner, we were opening the doors to Blue Sky School."

Cultivate Core School Values

Both wanted core values to be foundational to all aspects of the school, to guide them in decision-making as co-founders and directors of the school, and in what the learners are doing.

They started by making a long list of all of the things they valued in education. Then they sent the list to people of all ages and backgrounds: friends, family, educators, and other people they respected, and asked them which values they would like to see in a school.

This culminated in the creation of a values wheel.

Figure 7.1 Blue Sky School Values Wheel

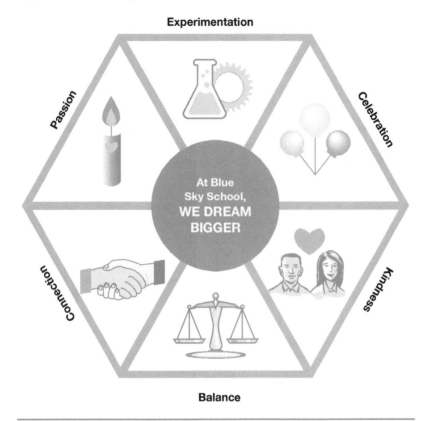

At the center, they placed their key guiding value, that at Blue Sky School they don't just dream big, they dream bigger. This supported the school's motto, "Blue Sky Dreams."

That key guiding principle is upheld by six supporting values on the wheel, as Shauna explains.

Six Supporting Values

1. **Experimentation:** "We value experimentation in everything we do, as do the learners. It's not just about a product they're creating, it's about the process of what they're doing."

2. **Celebration:** "We take every opportunity we can to celebrate and make school a really joyful place."

3. **Kindness:** "Once you've created an environment that's kind to absolutely everybody, it feels safe—and wonderful."

(Continued)

(Continued)

4. **Balance:** "Balance is a really interesting one that Karen and I are both trying to model. As a start-up, there's a tremendous amount to do. I'm running a business with Karen and am the principal and primary educator, so the changes in my life are challenging. We don't have the answers, but we're constantly exploring that with our learners."

5. **Connection:** "Then there's the meaningful relationships we make within and outside the school. We say the city is our classroom. We just had our forty-second field trip within a hundred school days. The learners have had all kinds of opportunities. They went to the Senate of Canada, met with the senator, and then spent the afternoon at Impact Hub doing a consultation with Environment and Climate Change Canada. And then in the evening they joined a discussion about student voice with one of our coaches who's a graduate student at the University of Ottawa."

The also bring the outside in. "If we don't have the content knowledge for them, we bring in people with a passion or profession to work with them, and they consult in person, via email, and social media," Shauna explains.

6. **Passion:** Shauna and Karen were determined that students would be ignited by their own passions and interests. They created an environment in which students were inspired to "find that thing that lights your flame and makes you follow through with your dreams."

Placing students at the center of their own learning was transformational and modeled throughout the learning environment. "Our curriculum will continually be built around the students, so it will never be something that's finished."

Build a Community Before the Curriculum

After determining Blue Sky's values, Shauna and Karen wanted to ensure their school was, first and foremost, a community. The idea was to get to know the students deeply, build a community where the magic could happen, and then add in the curriculum according to the individual student's unique passions, interests, and needs. With that, each student's seeds of brilliance can flourish.

"People learn when they're in communities, when they're connected to the people around them, when they feel safe and secure," says Karen.

Shauna and Karen also focused on two questions to guide their curriculum:

1. What are the outcomes we want for our learners?

2. What do we want them to know?

They wanted to avoid "retention and regurgitation of content," for their learners to develop a deep understanding of concepts and the ability to "dig into their own ideas."

They codesigned curriculum with each individual learner, their pedagogical coach (teacher), and their families. This is one of the most distinguishing features of Blue Sky and one they believe most differentiates them from the traditional school model.

Video 7.1

The Centrality of Wellbeing

Teacher Shauna explains how Blue Sky School's learning culture nurtures the wellbeing of students and teachers alike.

The Blue Sky learning culture was structured around three strategies: The Socratic Wheel; The Four Quadrant Model; and the Nurtured Heart Approach™, developed by Howard Glasser. These ensured learning was personalized in the context of an emotionally supportive and safe environment.

Structure 1: The Socratic Wheel

The Socratic wheel is used in participatory action research, so the students can self-assess throughout the year. It also allows each learner, along with their parents and their pedagogical coach, to meet three or four times a year to design the child's curriculum.

"As we were imagining what our report cards, IEPs (Independent Education Plans), and a host of other documents might look like, the Socratic wheel seemed a perfect fit," says Karen.

The beauty of the Socratic wheel is that it can be customized to personal goals and situations, as simple or as complex as you need. Despite the name, it can be shaped into a rectangle, square, or snail shape. It can document what the student wants to achieve, where they want to be, and the steps they need to take to get there.

Once the student has determined their objectives, they can map out their goals, skills, seeds of brilliance, alternative choices, and other variables in detail. The wheel can be divided into as many sections as you like, depending on the number of variables to be assessed. Typically, one section contains one goal. The wheel can then be used as a planning tool, as a means to view and assess progress over time, or to spark conversations about new goals and ideas, and to decide what steps or conditions are needed for success.

You can also design your own rating criteria for the variables on the wheel. There are a number of ways to do this. One example, typically used for measuring increments toward skills attainment, includes

0 = I've never tried this

1 = I've done it a few times

2 = I've done it often enough to feel confident

3 = I could teach this to someone else

For someone who's just beginning a skill, they would start at the point in the center of the wheel. The journey from the center to the outside of the wheel is a journey to mastery of the goal.

Figure 7.2

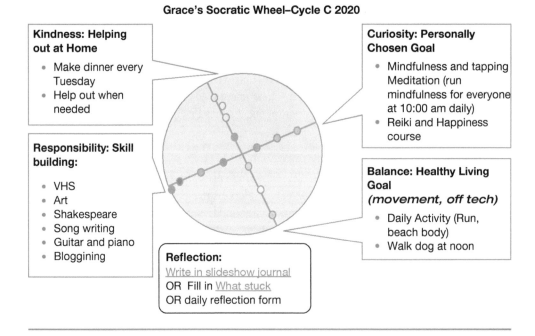

Grace's Socratic Wheel–Cycle C 2020

Kindness: Helping out at Home
- Make dinner every Tuesday
- Help out when needed

Responsibility: Skill building:
- VHS
- Art
- Shakespeare
- Song writing
- Guitar and piano
- Bloggining

Curiosity: Personally Chosen Goal
- Mindfulness and tapping Meditation (run mindfulness for everyone at 10:00 am daily)
- Reiki and Happiness course

Balance: Healthy Living Goal
(movement, off tech)
- Daily Activity (Run, beach body)
- Walk dog at noon

Reflection:
Write in slideshow journal
OR Fill in What stuck
OR daily reflection form

The more specific you are, the better. If you look at Grace's Socratic Wheel in Figure 7.2, she doesn't simply write, "Be kinder." She includes where she'll be kinder (at home), the specific activities to achieve that (make dinner, walk the dog), and when (every Tuesday, at lunch).

Curriculum starts with a question: What matters to you?

A powerful aspect of the Socratic wheel is that it facilitates a conversation between parents and learners. It opens up possibilities because parents are invited in to contribute to the learning priorities for their child. Students are asked to create projects on topics of personal interest and to be asked, what skills do you want to develop?

"Even just asking that question develops reflection," says Shauna.

Using the Socratic Wheel

At Blue Sky, the students design their own Socratic wheels. They identify their own learning goals, along with input from the parent or guardian and coach. When Shauna and Karen first introduced this tool to students, the very idea that a child was designing their own learning was quite a novel concept!

But it didn't take long before the Blue Sky learners had developed the ability to design and use their Socratic wheel to

- identify personal goals

- set concrete actions to achieve goals

- pick a starting point

- reflect on their progress

The Socratic wheel planning process

At Blue Sky, the following process is used as a starting point. The creative ideas generated serve as a catalyst for conversation. The "team" looks for patterns and themes in the ideas and, from these, develop specific learning goals to create the spokes for the Socratic Wheel.

Setting up Socratic Wheels

1. Meeting with learner, parents, and coach

2. Generate an array of learning ideas and use cue cards or sticky notes to display on a chart:
   - What are the learner's interests?
   - What gives the learner enjoyment?
   - What experiences provide the learner with the experience of engagement or "flow?"
   - What makes them curious?
   - What do you wonder about?
   - What do you want to learn about yourself? About others?

The conversations are guided by the previous experiences of the young learners. "Many of these youngsters have been filled with external judgment about their learning and abilities in the past, which provides a very important context for the conversations," says Shauna. "We're at the point where a lot of learners make a draft of their wheel and pitch it to their parents and coaches. We ask them questions and help them with a bit more depth and clarity. Then they go start the learning!"

Students discover their unique learning style

Because so much of the learning is self-directed, the learning environment itself is a joy to behold. On my first visit to Blue Sky in 2017, the difference with this approach was tangible. There was an enormous array of diverse learning happening—podcasting, Mobius strip models of the brain, dance, environmental projects, and more. And all of the learners could describe precisely what they were doing, why they were doing it, the stage they were at, and their thinking.

This self-reflection was so common among them that I asked Karen about it.

"One of our central goals is to help the kids 'learn how they learn,' so we talk a lot about neuroscience and brain development, especially teen and tween brain development.

"Then each learner digs into their own learning style; they're not limited to auditory and kinesthetic, for example, and they think about how their own mind works. We split the school year into three segments, and after each one, we have a learning showcase where we invite members of the community to see our space and the learners tell their stories.

"Several of them focus on how they learn and actually build physical models of their brains. One of them wrote an entire book describing seven different types of brains and created an online quiz where you can figure out your learning style."

Structure 2: The Four-Quadrant Model

Karen and Shauna were aware, from personal experience, that there's a huge diversity in the individuals of any classroom. They wanted to capture that as a foundational aspect of Blue Sky, so they tried to define what a learner is. As they began creating their new learning culture, they included a four-quadrant model to help individuals see themselves in a learning system. The tool is structured around two concepts: the learners' perception of their success and their perception of their motivation.

They designed the instrument as a self-reflective process, for the child or adult to think about where they saw themselves. This self-reflection immediately creates an entry point and catalyst for future learning.

"It's not as important for an adult to say this child is capable. This is all about self-reporting, and there are no external metrics used."

The upper left quadrant is someone who identifies as a capable learner, willing to take risks, curious, open to exploration and experimentation, and to failure.

Figure 7.3 Where Students Land on the Four Quadrants

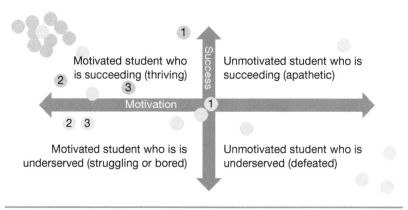

The upper right quadrant is someone who self-identifies as an unsuccessful learner, of not being capable. Shauna reports it's not uncommon for some to tell you they believe themselves to be stupid.

"The vertical line is the perception of a fit within a system. Beneath the horizontal line are learners who are underserved for a number of reasons. They can be our middle-of-the-road learners. They can also be learners with extreme learning difficulties or giftedness, or behavioral difficulties, all kinds of things. We ideally wanted learners from all four quadrants. This balance demonstrates this learning culture can work in larger systems."

One of the most powerful aspects of this tool was the way it resonated with all manner of different people, including partners, parents, and community members. People almost invariably place themselves where they fit through their own experience.

Structure 3: The Nurtured Heart Approach™

Karen spent much of her career working with students with behavioral challenges, children who found it very difficult to find success in their learning. One approach she found helpful is the Nurtured Heart Approach™ (1999) designed by Howard Glasser (see Glasser, 2016).

"It's great for kids who are super intense and need something different, but the more the approach becomes embedded in my soul, I realize they're magic for the kids that do well, too. People thrive on clarity and clear expectations, especially when we're noticed for doing the right thing."

While the methodology is more complex than what's described here, Karen says that generally the child's actions are responded to in the following ways:

▶ Stand One: Absolutely No!

I refuse to energize negative behavior.

▶ Stand Two: Absolutely Yes!

I will relentlessly energize the positive.

▶ Stand Three: Absolutely Clear!

I will maintain total clarity about rules that demonstrate fair and consistent boundaries.

"We often talk to kids about what they've done wrong as a teachable moment. This approach flips that on its head and uses moments of greatness as teachable moments. It's a beautiful approach. Like the second imperative you have to constantly think and act from a strength-based perspective."

Three Differentiators: Lifelong Learning, Change Makers, and Release of Responsibility

With these three structures helping to guide the learning, Shauna and Karen have established three core differentiators in their learning approach: a goal for students to become lifelong learners; to become change makers; and to adopt a gradual release of responsibility from other-directed learning to self-directed learning.

"We're always experimenting with how much the child can do on their own. That's why we have coaches, instead of the teacher judging how to make experiences challenging but at the right level for each child. We're constantly assessing and having learners self-assess their readiness for self-direction. Some questions we ask include the following."

Assessing Leaners' Readiness for Self-Direction

- Do you want coaching now?
- Do you want time to work now?
- What is it you want from someone right now?
- Do you want me to model for you how I did my Socratic wheel before you do yours?

It's that ongoing collaborative experimentation with each learner that really individualizes each part of the program, from the design and use of each tool to their day-to-day scheduling and learning.

Grace's Story

To show you how Blue Sky's approach affects students, I spoke to Grace, one of the first students to attend Blue Sky, in 2017. I very quickly came to understand that what Shauna and Karen had made real was a learning environment that was very special.

My first conversation with Grace was illuminating in several ways. First, the project on which she was working gave me real insight into the open-ended, project-based approach that's core to the learning culture.

Grace had found life in her previous school quite challenging. "I get very distracted. I'm in class listening to someone speak, then I not only notice the person speaking, but all the other things that are going on in the class. And that just kind of piles blankets on top of my brain and it's really hard for me to learn that way."

But at Blue Sky, with the strategies she's worked on with her coaches and the culture of belonging, things have changed.

"Blue Sky has been very beneficial for me because I've come up with strategies, like breathing and focusing. And somehow the blankets have come off. I think it's more like a comfortability thing. I just feel so comfortable in this environment. So it's been amazing for me—transformative."

Peter: "Based on your experiences, what one or two things would you include in a learning environment?"

Grace: "The family feeling has been an amazing experience for me, having that really close connection with your peers and your coach. I feel like this is a family, my second family at Blue Sky School. To do that in your classroom, just take the first two or three weeks to really get to know your class. Just really one on one, because if you're an educator or a teacher, you need to cater to the students' individual needs. That connection lets your student know you believe in it, and they can achieve great things and it will be really amazing to watch."

Video 7.2

Grace: Blankets on Top of Her Brain

Grace gives an eye-opening account about what she's learned in her first hundred days at Blue Sky School.

Grace continues, "It's actually taken a while for me to figure it all out. In the traditional education system, the academic stuff could be easy for me, the social stuff could be easy for me, but it just wasn't. I think it's because of several reasons.

"First, I could feel all of the energies about competing against my fellow learners, my fellow peers. We're all separated based on our skill level, and that can make people feel lessened. Also, it's hard for me to learn in a classroom where there's a lot going on, so sometimes the information wouldn't come in.

"For those reasons, the traditional system didn't really work for me, and I felt stupid and alone. I wanted something different, so being at Blue Sky has been amazing."

Grace describes the learning in her first year at Blue Sky as a "creative mess. That's my favorite type of mess, and we were doing projects with our hands and with our hearts and with the world. And I not only felt like I was a brilliant student, but I also felt like I could possibly change the world. And I had this almost superpower ignited in me that I could do pretty much anything I set my mind to."

> I not only felt like I was a brilliant student, but I also felt like I could possibly change the world. And I had this almost superpower ignited in me that I could do pretty much anything I set my mind to.
> —Grace

This awakening experience wasn't just about academic work but also for the deep connection she felt with her community.

"I was hanging out with all different types of people, all different groups, in all different races and orientations. We had a whole range of everything at Blue Sky, and the diversity of the learners brought us together as a community, and for that I am eternally grateful because now I have 20 to 40 new friends that I feel like I can really be myself with."

I asked Grace what aspects of Blue Sky's learning culture enabled that transformation.

Learning for Different Days and Different Ways

Grace: "We say at Blue Sky that people learn on different days in different ways and I don't think that could be truer. We nurture every type of learner for a few reasons:"

Self-directed learning

"First, we're a self-directed environment, which means learners can choose their own projects, choose their own skills, and within that the coaches give them support on how to make these projects, these dreams, these skills a reality."

Undercover learning

"Second, we're often asked how we feed in the academic stuff that doesn't hold as much interest. We usually do a lot of undercover learning, which means we learn, and we don't even know we're learning. We do that with field trips and with projects. For example, if someone's building a robot, and we want to feed in some literacy skills for them, we say now write a letter to this person and they'll do it right away, no matter how much their preconceived notions are with literacy skills."

Personal projects lead to sense of purpose

"Third, we've seen that as soon as learners are engaged with these projects and moving forward, they have this sense of purpose and direction in their learning. Then they'll do anything to get there. They'll do the numeracy or literacy skills because they're inspired. And that's been a magical, beautiful thing for me. I've never really been a math person. I don't think I've ever been a literacy person. But at Blue Sky, I feel like I've been a genius in both of those areas and that's definitely been an epiphany for me."

Intentionalize a community of kindness

"In this community, everyone is connected, everyone is our friend. We don't do exclusivity, we do inclusion. We do that every day by teaching not only academic skills, but those permanent skills you need in everyday life like kindness, like responsibility. We do this through organized games and practice every day. We have posters all over our board as a reminder. The environment is unlike anything you've seen before. We lift each other up. We empower each other and that's how we all feel like we're brilliant at the end of the day."

Heartbreak to heartache

"Another thing the coaches encourage learners to do is to become the next generation of change makers. Each and every one of us wants to make an impact in our community, or on a more global scale, whether that be from the little thing—I remember this one student had this idea to make eating popsicles easier—all the way to building homeless shelters. We have a specific process on how to become change makers and we do lots of design sprints, lots of activities. But one of our most critical is this idea of finding your heartbreak in the world, learning from heartbreak to heartache. Something that touches you in a way that nothing else does. For example, for the past four years I've been working on helping and supporting people in South Sudan because we went on a field trip to a conference called The Future of Good. A speaker from South Sudan talked about the inequality of women there and it really kindled something in me. Heartbreak also gives you a sense of purpose, like I'm meant to do this."

I asked Grace, "What characteristics in a learning environment bring out the best in people and makes them all feel healthy and brilliant?"

"I think at Blue Sky it's the people: the coaches, the mentors, the learners. That's what makes the culture. These people are dedicated and passionate about what they're doing and about teaching.

"It's also that we take the time to build those relationships, whether that be learner to learner, learner to coach, or learner to mentor. We build those connections and the best way to nurture a creative and sustainable environment is to nurture those relationships. It's absolutely essential that everyone feels safe and accepted. Because when we feel safe and accepted, we're able to flourish, we're able to fly.

"Reflecting on this whole beautiful process of Blue Sky School, I realize the core of all the success I've had here is the people around me and the people I've met. That's definitely the magical thing."

Brad and Chris's Story:
Building a space through partnerships

Another interesting aspect of Blue Sky is that a community partnership helped the school facility come to be. Brad McAninch and Chris Hill are senior executives of Modern Niagara, a company that installs building requirements such as plumbing and electrical for facilities. They were so taken with the Blue Sky vision that they offered to transform a space in one of their buildings for the cutting-edge school.

Brad says, "When we met with Shauna and Karen, we realized this was something special. We're in the construction and services business, so we didn't pretend to understand the education system. But we understood these individuals were extremely passionate, and we realized, hey, we can bring our skills and play a part in this. We know how to make things happen; we can put a space together where they can get started."

"Blue Sky presented a unique value proposition where we could invest in creating the next generation of great humans," says Chris. "We're a company based on the work of our tradespeople, and our jobs exist because of the good work our plumbers and pipefitters and electricians and service techs do in the community. If you look at the journey of some of those trades people within their school experiences, it's been less than optimal and unnecessarily so.

"Shauna and Karen talked about authentic learning, following your passion, and reframing trades work as a noble and worthwhile profession and career of choice. They wanted to introduce the trades' curriculum at the primary level. It became doubly compelling for us and, quite frankly, a no-brainer in terms of investment for the modern era."

Brad adds, "We wanted to be a part of creating something that could make an impact, starting with one life and then multiple lives. Who knew where it was going to go? We were believers in Shauna and Karen and the potential of Blue Sky."

To me, Brad and Chris demonstrated a beautiful example of strength-based thinking, asking the questions, "What could be? How can we use what we have to bring out the extraordinary in our children and our workers? How can we join forces with others and build partnerships to make that happen? How can we bring joy and hope into this situation?"

The way Brad and Chris described this story to me was so matter of fact, I got the impression they had no idea what they'd done. They live with these wonderful core values, and their commitment to community just shines through. I think of them as a model for other corporate-school partnerships.

> *"How can we use what we have to bring out the extraordinary in our children and our workers? How can we join forces with others and build partnerships to make that happen? How can we bring joy and hope into this situation?"*
> *–Brad McAninch and Chris Hill*

Video 7.3

Brad and Chris: Building a Partnership, Part 1

Hear the story of why two businessmen decided to provide a space for Blue Sky School, and why they saw it as a worthy investment.

Video 7.4

Brad and Chris: Building a Partnership, Part 2

Brad and Chris describe how they recognized Blue Sky School as something that would positively impact individuals and the greater community.

Video 7.5

Blue Sky School 2020

Students describe what it's like to be a Blue Sky student in this promotional video.

CHAPTER 7

Key Takeaways

▶ Early on, the leaders of Blue Sky created six foundational core school values. Having core values not only supported the vision they had for the school but also helped guide their decision-making and building the learning culture.

▶ There is value in teaching students how they learn, to be cognizant of their own learning styles and how the learning brain works. This helps them to take ownership of their learning.

▶ A community of caring and kindness rarely happens by accident; it must be intentionalized. Encouraging children to think of themselves as change makers empowers them to make a difference in the world.

Reflective Questions

1. The Blue Sky leaders and students recognize that people learn on different days in different ways. How is this visible in your school? Or is it a one-size-fits-all teaching strategy?

2. The power of community is demonstrated in the inspiring story of Chris and Brad. What are you doing to engage the community in an authentic way to enrich your learning culture?

3. What characteristics in a learning environment bring out the best in people and makes them all feel healthy and brilliant? What are you doing to incorporate these characteristics into your learning culture?

Try This!

Use Your School or District Values as a Powerful Decision-Making Tool

This chapter described how teachers Shauna and Karen identified school values early on in co-founding Blue Sky School. As illustrated, identifying your school or district-wide values isn't just about warm and fuzzy feelings. The journey toward determining just what your values are can lay the foundation for behavioral and academic expectations; bring together individuals and groups for a common purpose; foster a sense of community and belonging; and play a powerful role in short-and long-term goals, planning, and decision-making.

Already have school values? There's never any harm in reviewing or updating them from time to time or even starting with a fresh slate!

Once you've defined your values, they should never simply sit on a plaque near the school's front door. They should be used to guide everything you do, from vision and mission statements to everyday operations and guiding leadership characteristics.

With so much riding on your values, it's worth taking the time to develop them with participation from all levels, to think deeply about what they mean for your school or district, and to celebrate them with joy.

Here's a guide to help you get started:

- Don't go it alone. Invite everyone in your community into the conversation. That includes not only your formal leadership but also teachers, faculty, students, parents, volunteers, local business owners, shopkeepers, baseball coaches, the municipal government, volunteers at the food bank, and more. Inviting others into the conversation will help you ensure that you get more ideas and will be better able to build consensus on a strong set of values.

- Take stock of your school or district. Every school is different, so you need to create values that are uniquely your own, that recognize the distinct challenges, opportunities, and the culture and vibrancy of the surrounding community.

(Continued)

(Continued)

- Take a strength-based approach and think about what you would like your school or district to be. I've found a good way to begin is by asking my signature question: "If you were given a blank slate, and a magic wand, and the opportunity to reimagine and redesign a culture of learning—what would be some of your unshakable, foundational characteristics?"

- You'll likely end up with dozens of suggested values but limit yourself to no more than six. The more you have, the harder they will be to remember and the more diluted each one will become.

- To narrow down the suggestions, see which ones are most often mentioned, but don't discount ones that might only be mentioned once or twice yet are deeply meaningful.

- Distribute the narrowed-down options to your participants and take a vote.

- Once you've selected your values, start putting them to good use. You should be able to create a mission statement (the tangible objectives your school or district will focus on today) and then a vision statement (the optimal state your school or district is working on for the future).

- When it comes to decision-making, whether it's to allocate budgets and resources, set curriculum, or to dream up the next charitable project for the school or district, your values can make the decision clear. For example, if two of your values are *sharing* and *sustainability*, you could perhaps implement a board-wide project to grow vegetables and donate them to a food bank or shelter; or sell them and donate the proceeds, with all the math, science, reading, writing, and business skills that involves.

CHAPTER 8
SEEDS TAKE FLIGHT
ROAD TRIP

"Ms. Windham made a complete change within my life. She made me realize learning can be outside of school, that learning is more than just books, that there's more out in this world that's a pleasure to learn. She made me love to learn."

—Cam Traylor

Every community has a lot riding on their teachers. People who aren't in education might think I'm being a bit biased, but just do the math. A teacher interacts with around three thousand students (Tornio, 2019) over the course of their career. If we assume each student will attain the average American wage of $52,000 (Kopestinsky, 2021) per year and will spend forty years working before retirement; that means each teacher is overseeing the future potential of more than $6 billion in earnings—which will be realized only if the teachers are effective. Multiply that by the average 187 teachers in a U.S. school district (National Center for Educational Statistics, 2012), and we're talking about trillions.

It doesn't stop there. School rankings on standardized tests, whether an accurate indicator of a school's overall quality or not, have a direct impact on home values in the area by as much as 23 percent, or nearly $80,000 on the average $340,000 U.S. home (Fitzgerald, 2020). This makes school rankings a vested interest even for those who don't have school-aged children. While this is an indirect and probably unavoidable side effect of standardized tests, the consequence will still be public pressure to maintain focus on increasing test scores above all. Imagine any other job where your place of employment is publicly ranked every year, with the results so heavily impacting on not only your students but also on every member of your community.

Jane and I aren't pointing out these amplified numbers because we believe standardized tests deserve the almost-exclusive focus they receive (we don't), but because we know there are so many decision-makers who do. And we get it—we understand the appeal of the stats, of the simplicity of working with crisp, clean numbers that aren't cluttered by extenuating circumstances, footnotes, or asterisks. And we're not suggesting doing away with testing: they have their place and can provide valuable information when taken in context.

But if our number-crunching friends are serious about wanting to increase student achievement and all the community benefits and potential future wealth that comes with it, then we'd like to invite them to collaborate with us on something that's too often considered a "nice-to-have": teacher well-being. Growing research shows teacher well-being has a far-reaching impact on student success. We'd like to give equal credence to those numbers in this chapter, along with three inspiring examples of supportive teacher environments.

Cultivate the Brilliance in Teachers

So far we've been talking about bringing out the seeds of brilliance in our students, but the first imperative Jane and I put forth for innovative, healthy learning environments is to recognize there's a seed of brilliance in *everyone*, children and adults alike. It seems only logical that having engaged, supported, thriving teachers will in turn help their students and their broader communities to flourish.

Even before we get to the numbers, brain science and common sense support this. Studies continue to show it's not really possible for learning or optimal performance to happen if you're feeling anxious, stressed, scared, or overwhelmed. That's because in the presence of these emotions, the brain goes into "fight or flight" mode and shuts down anything that's nonessential to those two actions—like learning and memorizing. Stress, in particular, also causes the release of cortisol, which can impair brain structures over the long term, involving memory and executive functioning.

> *There's a seed of brilliance in everyone, children and adults alike. It seems only logical that having engaged, supported, thriving teachers will in turn help their students and their broader communities to flourish.*

The bad news, according to a Gallup poll described in *Teacher Stress and Health: Effects on Teachers, Students and Schools* (Greenberg, 2016), is that 46 percent of teachers report high levels of *daily* stress during the school year, which impacts their health, quality of life, and teaching performance, with the cost to U.S. schools estimated to be in the billions of dollars. (That 46 percent, by the way, is from before the pandemic; the percentage is very likely higher today.) Stressed-out teachers are also less likely to form close relationships with students (Sparks, 2017), which, as we've seen in the previous chapters' examples, is essential to student growth and learning.

So how does that affect test scores? The same research report includes a survey of 78,000 students from grades 5 to 12 in 160 schools, which showed that "higher teacher engagement in their jobs predicted higher student engagement, which in turn predicted high student achievement outcomes." And if the goal is to get test scores up, another described study found that students who began the school year with weaker math skills and had a teacher with more depressive symptoms had the lowest rate of achievement.

Teacher Well-Being

Given the immense benefits of teacher well-being and the impact on student achievement and success, the need to see teachers thrive and bring out their own seeds of brilliance becomes all the more critical. To see what can be done and the results, I'd like to explore three examples of supportive teaching environments I've had the good fortune to work with. I'll start at the end, with the culmination of a Canadian-U.S. road tripping adventure.

The Roadies: Teacher Leader Fellowship Program and Duke TeachHouse

I was asked by Dr. Betty Sternberg, the founder of the Teacher Leader Fellowship Program (TLFP) at Central Connecticut State University, if

I knew of a school district that was placing teacher voice and creative pedagogy at the center of their learning culture. I had worked with Betty on a number of interesting initiatives over the course of a few years and readily followed the program's impact on teachers and administrators alike. So it was only natural that I invited her on a field trip up to Canada.

Betty accepted, and she didn't come to Canada alone. She was joined by a group of educators and administrators from her own TLFP, as well as four young teachers from Duke University TeachHouse in North Carolina, and their leader, Dr. Jan Riggsbee. Both Betty and Jan have founded inspiring hubs for bringing out the seeds of brilliance in teachers, so let's take a side road while I tell you a bit about them here, as it will allow you to see why this field trip was so special.

Teacher Leader Fellowship Program, Central Connecticut State University– Connecticut

The Teacher Leader Fellowship Program (TLFP) at Central Connecticut State University was founded by Dr. Betty J. Sternberg, commissioner emerita, who currently directs the teacher development program. It draws from fifteen districts around the state and has connected with hundreds of teachers and administrators. It equips teacher leaders to enable students to be creative, collaborative, and innovators in their classroom and beyond. A critical question addressed through the program is, "How can the teachers themselves exercise leadership to allow their students and their colleagues to flourish?"

Duke TeachHouse, Duke University, Durham, North Carolina

Launched in 2015, the Duke TeachHouse is the brainchild of Dr. Jan Riggsbee, director and professor of the practice of the program at Duke University. The TeachHouse provides an intensive living and learning community experience for teachers enrolled in the faculty of education at Duke University. The program focuses on equipping early career educators with knowledge and networks to support teacher health and well-being and to cultivate leadership, creative problem-solving, and innovation skills.

Fellows are awarded two-year fellowships and work full-time as teachers in the local schools. The first year of the program focuses on transitioning to the professional workplace, building relationships, and navigating the school community. In the second year, fellows work collaboratively with faculty and administrators at the school sites to identify a critical school priority and design an innovation project to help address it. In the year following, the fellows launch the innovation project at their home school.

The magic of this program is that it fosters an environment that makes brilliance proliferate. It brings together a group of highly motivated educators with enormous potential and provides support for both intellectual growth and well-being, so they can succeed.

Destination: Renfrew County District School Board

Now as it happened, I had just been engaged by my friend and former colleague, Dr. Pino Buffone, the director of the Renfrew County District School Board in Ontario, Canada, to assist him and his district on precisely that journey.

Pino wanted to create a very open and welcoming learning environment where people felt they could thrive. He and Wendy Hewitt, the chair of the school district at that time, had outlined three goals for their vision:

▶ To build and learn from the amazing creative and innovative practices already taking place in our organization, both in schools and in central departments.

▶ To create an informal action inquiry around what conditions enable us to be creative, curious, imaginative, and innovative as a learning culture; and

▶ To showcase and celebrate the magic already happening, and build on it.

These goals were a natural extension of the wonderful vision statement already created by Renfrew County District School Board:

"We will be a community of learners where curiosity, creativity, imagination, and innovation are celebrated and where students are engaged to explore and discover their own pathways to success."

Listen to the conversation between Pino and Wendy here.

Video 8.1

Pino and Wendy: Putting Creativity Into the School Culture

Pino and Wendy describe their quest to define what creativity means to them, as they embed it into the Renfrew District school culture.

Like me, Pino was absolutely delighted at the prospect of touring some American guests around Renfrew County schools and departments. We saw this as an opportunity to explore the healthy learning cultures going on in this district, using the visitors to glean perspectives through fresh eyes—as they in turn learned from us. We believed this external lens would bring a powerful clarity and deepened understanding of what was happening in the schools and that this would make a wonderful starting point to unleashing creativity.

The Spark: The Action Inquiry Begins

Pino and I traveled for five days with these teachers and heard their fascinating stories and perspectives on reimagining learning for the future and how they planned to incorporate their learnings from the tour into their own teaching.

On the first evening, we gathered with people from Renfrew and some other like-minded souls from the Ottawa community for dinner and a very open-spaced, informal "Spark" brainstorming activity.

The purpose of the evening was threefold. First, it was to give the group a chance to get to know each other in an informal setting.

Second, it was to engage in genuine conversation about themes essential to setting a culture of optimal learning, cultures in which everyone feels comfortable to explore their own seeds of brilliance, with a profound impact on their emotional well-being.

Finally, the evening was to set the context for the four-day tour on which we were about to embark. By identifying factors, conditions, and cultural imperatives that are so pivotal to healthy and dynamic cultures, it helped us understand what to look for in the schools and classrooms that exemplify this learning. Pino and I also believed that the experience of the "inquiry" would enrich the learning of the visitors and their feedback and observations would be rewarding, inspiring, and motivating for the staff and students.

We had decided to frame the tour as a strength-based appreciative action inquiry, founded on observations of the extraordinary. The Spark activity allowed us to discuss critical themes about fostering optimal learning environments—cultures where people could explore their learning in novel and personal ways. We asked everyone to reflect on the topics of learning, leadership, creativity, and the intersections of these concepts with individual and organizational health and learning.

The animated conversations that emerged that evening were thought provoking, sometimes provocative, and most importantly, conducted in a culture of nonjudgment, trust, and complete openness.

What I found interesting was how the trust within the group was established so quickly. It's been my experience that if you can set conditions where people are given a voice and feel comfortable to speak honestly, then innovation quickly ignites and takes hold. Such environments unleash imagination and brilliance, and the connection between people becomes almost tangible.

We gathered ideas on charts placed around the room, which led to some rich discussions. Many different themes emerged, and we asked people to keep these in mind throughout the next four days as we toured the Renfrew school district. The entire trip would be an opportunity, individually and collectively, to engage in an informal inquiry framed around our questions and wonderings. Some questions that emerged from that evening's dialogue included these themes:

How is leadership enacted?

Who are seen as leaders?

What aspects of the learning culture foster teacher and student well-being?

In what ways are learning environments personalized to students' needs?

What does inclusivity look like?

How is creativity defined? Enacted in practice?

Pino and I created artifacts from that first evening. We asked people to put their thoughts and ideas and "wonderings" onto sticky notes and charts exploring each of the critical themes we had identified.

The next day we began our tour. Our original plan was to hire a bus to take the visitors from site to site, with us joining them whenever possible. But the more we thought about this plan, the less we liked it.

We wanted this trip to matter. We wanted to model cultures that supported teacher well-being and the types of learning we sought to foster throughout the school community. It was learning that was curious and inspired, fuelled by conversations that challenged assumptions (and the assumptions on which the assumptions were based), and that collided ideas.

We realized we could only accomplish this by being physically present with the group for the entire four days, so we could get to know each other, enjoy each other's company, laugh together, and of course, engage in vigorous discussion about what we were learning, observing, experiencing, and feeling. The best way to do that, we figured, was to be the tour guides using our own cars. And so, the bus tour was swiftly transformed into a road trip. It turned out to be a great decision.

See Through the Lens of a Newcomer

Pino's primary goal was to ensure that what our guests saw and experienced was authentic, rather than trying to impress them. He asked the schools to simply allow the teachers, students, and staff to go about the day as they normally would.

Pino and I were excited to learn from the insights of our American friends on what they had witnessed over the four-day road trip. Throughout the journey and culminating on the final day, we had countless discussions among pairs, larger groups, and the whole team.

What was especially interesting was that these participants had the benefit of a different lens, leadership and learning provided to them through TeachHouse and the TLFP, and this gave all of us a higher quality of insight into environments that invite teachers' seeds of brilliance to emerge. Indeed, the conversation often jumped back and forth among experiences between Renfrew, TeachHouse, and the TLFP.

Here's a quick view as to who everyone is and where they're from.

Who's Who
Renfrew County District School Board, Canada
Pino Buffone, Director
Wendy Hewitt, Chair
Tim Demmons, Teacher
Jamie Owen-Martin, Teacher
TeachHouse, Duke University, North Carolina
Jan Riggsbee, Founder
Corey Bray, Fellow
Savannah Lee Windham, Fellow
Brianna Tuscani, Fellow
Emma Paradiso, Fellow
Teacher Leader Fellowship Program, Connecticut
Betty Sternberg, Founder
Tawana Graham-Douglas, Principal
Janie Perez, Principal
Lynn Logoyke, Principal

We've listed here some of the major themes and takeaways that inspired our visitors. It was very clear that if we are to bring out the seeds of brilliance in our students, we must first ensure we're bringing out the seeds of brilliance in our teachers.

Lessons Learned

1. **Leadership support is critical**

   Leadership arose as perhaps the most essential component of creating environments that give space for teacher voice and choice. Without the cooperation and support of leaders, virtually nothing can move forward. As Janie said, "Leaders set the conditions for that to happen."

   Corey said, "When we were talking about how leadership converges with learning and creativity, I was thinking how the leader has to make that foundational, and make changes and decisions based on that undergirding to get the learning culture right. Organizational culture is the lifeblood, it's the heartbeat of what the organization believes and how it governs the decisions that are made."

2. **Empower teachers to personalize learning**

   While the value of personalized learning was universally accepted among this group, being provided with the time and support to achieve it is difficult.

   "What's the groundwork to ensure every child is thriving in the room, that every child has that little spark?" was a wondering of Emma. "I can see (the Renfrew schools) trying to build on student interest, and the resources they have, and the different paths students can take allows them to do so."

   Tim, a teacher from Renfrew, had told me earlier, "If you give students an opportunity to do something a bit different and use practical skills when they're learning, they just thrive. We saw a real need for kids to learn some things our normal curricular courses don't provide. We started bundling credits and having them work all day in the outdoors and inside. It's worked better than we could have imagined."

3. **Give teachers the power of choice**

   Closely related to personalized learning was having the power of choice—not only for students but also for teachers. I would say, in fact, that we must think about the need for personalized teaching for teachers in addition to personalized learning for students.

   Savannah said that during the first evening's Spark discussion, she was lucky enough to sit with both a superintendent and a math teacher. "We had a variety of perspectives and what was really inspiring was one of the intersections of those three characteristics of leadership (curiosity, the challenging of assumptions, and collision) comes from student voice and prioritizing student leadership and choice in the classroom. While that might look different across subject areas and levels, we talked about ways you can allow students to express themselves in both formal and informal academic ways to spark that creativity."

   (Continued)

(Continued)

4. **Give teachers an atmosphere of celebration and positivity—especially in building relationships**

Savannah said, "You're always going to have people who aren't on board or are negative. But overwhelmingly, everywhere we've been this week I've seen how positive, how happy everyone is to be here, the students as well."

Corey noticed how this attitude had the power to build stronger relationships. "There's been an intentionality about relationship-building at all levels, between students, teachers and students, teachers and teachers, teachers and administration, administration and students, all the way up to director and superintendent. They care for each other as people as well as professionally. Everything at any level of the hierarchy, any level of organization, has been based on relationships."

5. **Give teachers the ability to create spaces that enable innovation to happen**

Brianna brought up how people need a space where they feel safe and valued to give their contributions, but she also spoke of spaces that enabled and allowed people to disagree, to discuss, and to collide ideas—which is the mother of innovation. "We talked about creating space for disagreement and if someone feels safe expressing their views, it's okay to express that disagreement and have that productive collision of ideas so you can go in a new direction."

Several Renfrew tour participants were especially impressed with the welcoming, physical space that Jamie Owen-Martin, one of the Renfrew teachers, had created in her classroom. The place looked magical, with a feeling of calm and creativity within.

Jamie explains, "The students come in and feel very comfortable. Everybody's calm and that gives me the starting point I need to teach. Once they want to be in the classroom, then you can do the educational work with them."

Jamie also personalizes her classrooms to include student interests. When she had students who were very artistic, she put paint-by-numbers around the room. When some were interested in the circus, she added juggling balls.

Jamie says, "Having a welcoming space is really important to me. A lot of my students come from backgrounds of low socioeconomic status. They might be very transitory in where they live and having a space that feels like home is very welcoming."

Once again, leadership is key to creating such spaces. "The kids have to be warm, fed and rested to prosper, but it can't stop there," Jamie says. "The relationship aspect has to be coupled with strong leadership, and the leadership needs to set up the conditions to build on that."

Several tour participants discussed the need to create spaces for belonging. Snippets of conversation emphasized that if there isn't a reciprocity, with respect, nurturing, and caring, there's not a whole lot of learning that's going to happen.

Video 8.2

Jamie and Savannah: Watch This Space

Jamie and Savannah discuss the importance of creating beautiful spaces of learning.

6. **Give teachers a voice**

As the fellows from TeachHouse and TLFP attested throughout our road trip journey, the ability to own your teacher voice, to be able to use it and to have it be respected, is essential to teacher well-being. This is something that both institutions strongly believe in and foster within their fellows. Seeing how teacher voice is encouraged and supported in the Renfrew schools was therefore of keen interest to them.

Jan explained, "The intentionality of the individual and collective voice of all stakeholders really resonated with me in terms of the importance and power of teacher voice. I think teachers feel their voice is heard and valued."

"It's not just giving students and teachers a voice in order to check off a box; there's an openness to that feedback," said Janie. "They're interested in feedback from everyone, even from a group of visitors. They believe they're going to learn something valuable from them."

A Lasting Legacy

I talked earlier about sympathetic resonance, how what we do as teachers and educators and business leaders can have powerful, rippling effects that spread outward into our community and far beyond. Quite some time after our road trip ended, I had the pleasure of reconnecting with Savanna. She said she wanted to let me in on an inspiring and far-reaching project that had come about from that trip.

On returning to her school, Savannah really wanted to share the experiences of her trip to Canada with her students. What had particularly impressed her was the openness with which the schools allowed access to staff and students. She wanted to have the same kind of conversation with her students, about how to unleash creativity and innovation. She created a PowerPoint virtual tour of her Renfrew experiences, including how the conversations shaped the action

> *What we do as teachers and educators and business leaders can have powerful, rippling effects that spread outward into our community and far beyond.*

inquiry throughout the tour. Then she posed the same questions from the Spark evening to her students.

Video 8.3

Savannah: Bringing Home
the Lessons From Canada

View the presentation slides Savannah created to share her Canadian adventure and lessons learned with her students, kick-starting them onto their own personalized learning project.

"They recorded their answers on the iPad, and then, I let them design their own curriculum for the last days of school," Savannah told me.

As a result of these conversations, one class focused on an initiative of a fellow student, Cameron Traylor, called Cam's Closet. This charity supplied students in need with basic clothing and hygiene products, without anyone else knowing.

The students used their collective power to lift Cam's Closet to a different level, and Savannah gave Cam time to lead the class in the project.

What struck Savannah most powerfully was the degree to which her students engaged in self-directed conversation throughout the process. They organized themselves into teams and honed all the details for a community fundraiser, gaining support from businesses and other community agencies, to raise $4,000 in short order. Just as importantly, the students developed a bond as they grew together through this social-enterprise project.

"None of that would have happened if we weren't inspired by all the stuff we did in Canada," Savannah said. "It really made a big difference."

I spoke to Cam personally, to find out how Savannah's "seed of brilliance" and new learning culture had impacted him.

"Ms. Windham had a major impact on not only me, but my family and my organization," Cam told me. "She made a complete change within my life. She made me realize learning can be outside of school, that learning is more than just books, that there's more out in this world that's a pleasure to learn. She made me love to learn."

Cam identified qualities in Savannah's leadership and personal style that helped him. One was taking the time to form a relationship. "She took the time to understand who I am. Even though we spent one semester together, she knows me better than probably any other teacher I've had. Ms. Windham actually takes the time to learn about her students, to learn their learning styles, and their pet peeves, so she can teach them the best way she can."

The genesis for Cam's Closet began at the kitchen table. Cam's mom had always encouraged him to be aware of peers who might need shoes, hygiene products, food, or clothing.

"She always said don't ask them but recognize it and let her know and figure out what we can do to help them," Cam told me. "We both started Cam's Closet, I'm the CEO, my mother is COO. Nothing gives my family more joy than giving back to people."

Cam pitched his idea for Cam's Closet in a competition for young entrepreneurs and won first place in the social-enterprise category. This gave him the seed funding to start making the dream a reality.

Cam says Ms. Windham's assignment was the first time he had had free rein to do a project on something he truly cared about and was inspired by.

"A lot of teachers, I can see they follow a system and they're not really happy about being there for their job. With Ms. Windham, she allowed students to learn how they wanted to learn."

Cam says his classmates were also inspired by this approach. "She was such an inspiration to us."

Video 8.4

Cam: How Teachers Can Inspire Students

Cam talks about the experience of getting free rein to do a project he truly cared about, and how he envisions what a reimagined school would look like.

Hearing From the Students

As mentioned earlier, the well-being of teachers has a direct impact on student engagement and success. One of the highlights of the road trip was the chance to hear from students themselves about their learning experiences and their insights on their teachers' influence. If we want students to succeed, then the well-being of teachers is paramount. Here's a sample of how students thrive when teacher well-being, teacher voice, and teacher choice are fostered by leadership.

Culinary arts

I asked Cole and Tim, in the hospitality program. "What's your experience of being in the kitchen, and why does it matter?"

Cole said, "I personally cook for my family and everybody because that's what I want to do as a career. We have a great chef and he's super good to us and honestly, it's awesome."

Tim said the classroom is like his second home. "I love coming to this class . . . it warms my heart. I can trust everybody in this class, we're like a family."

Video 8.5

Cole and Tim: Teacher Makes School Engagement Sizzle

Hear how one chef's teaching style makes students want to go to school.

Automotive

Nick, in the automotive course, said, "I want to be a mechanic by the time I'm 25. I have dyslexia and dysgraphia and don't like to work in a classroom, but this class actually pushes me to come to school. It's given me an experience of a lifetime and just helps me out as a person."

Video 8.6

Nick: Steering Toward a Career With the Automotive Program

Nick shares how the Special High Skills Major program sparked a renewed interest in school, and how it's driving him to reach his goals.

Music and the Riverside Boys

The Riverside Boys band, Hunter, Jayden, and Kiefer, got a great reception from our visitors. Hunter told me he'd been interested in music for a long time, but only really started chasing his dream and playing guitar recently. All three boys agreed it was great to practice as a band on school time.

Asked if it had shifted his attitude toward school, Hunter said, "I used to really not like school. But now I have two music classes this semester, and it really brings me to school. It makes the day fun."

Video 8.7

The Riverside Boys: School Hits a High Note

Three students talk about the impact of music on their lives and how pursuing music has shifted their attitudes toward school.

The OSPREY Program

Another highlight was seeing the OSPREY program, a locally developed wildlife and research course, at Opeongo High School.

I asked Jordan, a student in the paddle-making class, "If you could design a learning environment, what one or two characteristics you would want?"

He described the power of strength-based, personalized learning. "There has to be some sort of structured curriculum, but it also needs to pinpoint people's strengths and weaknesses and personalize learning to a degree."

Alexa, another student in the paddle-making program, said hands-on projects teach and reinforce deep subject-matter learning and meaning in a way that chalk and rote memorization simply can't. "I'm really glad to be part of this program. I wake up every morning wanting to come to school. I don't want to miss out on anything we're doing."

Video 8.8

The OSPREY Program: Learning to Paddle Our Own Canoe

Students in the paddle-making class talk about the many things they've learned, from chainsaw certification to bird identification, and how these fit into their future career plans—even though this doesn't feel like school at all!

This doesn't happen by accident

The reason I'm sharing these students' insights is because this kind of deep learning and positive attitude—of being engaged and *wanting* to be in school, no less—doesn't happen by accident. Nor does it come about by teaching to standardized tests. It takes real leadership, both formal and informal, to set the stage and an environment where it's okay for teachers to be innovative, to take risks, and to make mistakes and learn from them.

Teachers make it all possible

As with most schools, many of the opportunities for students to explore areas of personal interest and passion come from teachers and community members generously volunteering their time. Teacher Jeff Scott is one of these amazing people, and he directs the Opeongo drama club, or Odyssey Theatre. Their playbook describes how the goal "is always to select plays with a journey in mind. Ideally, each play is a voyage of discovery, an odyssey for our casts and crews to embark upon."

When I asked Jeff about the importance of providing the opportunity for these young people, he responded, "I think the most beautiful thing, with Shakespeare, is when you see young people breathing it out again and picking these characters off the page again and making them real. That's the most incredible thing."

Video 8.9

Video Playlist of Renfrew Road Trip

Browse the Video Playlist for more student and road trip participant interviews during the Renfrew School District road trip.

CHAPTER 8

Key Takeaways and Reflective Questions

For this chapter, we've included key takeaways and reflective questions from a few of our road trip participants.

Brianna

I'm going to carry with me a lot of what I saw this week.

▶ Creation of physical space

   ○ Creating a physically conducive space to learning in my classroom

- Incorporating frameworks with things I really value such as student voice, choice and collaborative inquiry, and synthesizing them on many levels:
  - What are we doing? And why?
  - What are our main skills that we're working on here?
  - What are our community values?

As I start to build my foundation, I'm also a dreamer so I like to think forward.

- I like to think about what might be future roles that I take up. Seeing the student leadership organizations here have been encouraging.

- If nothing else, I know I can come alongside the work that's already being done in our school spaces to help magnify them while we wait for more systemic change.

Emma

Purpose, intentionality, and space—making learning flourish—ask students their ideas on space—allow them to dream.

Being a second-grade teacher, it was important for me to see people talking about purpose and how intentional everything is.

- The space was very intentional. It was created so that students can explore and learn by having hands-on opportunities in the room.

- Making outdoor learning, physically taking students outside for project work, has become a big idea for me. Seeing in the classrooms how they brought outdoor learning inside, where they had plants in the classroom and were even planting inside, is a great idea because it takes a long time to get little people outside and back inside safely. It's seeing those bigger ideas being possible in more compact ways.
  - How can we spark that innovation in kids?
  - How can we make a space that's creative for them?
  - How do we learn to actually ask that question of our students?

While I have an idea that I think would be the best learning environment for my kids, they might have a completely different idea. And just because they're young doesn't mean they can't dream, and they can't create these spaces for themselves. We talk a lot about voice, and I think that would be an important way to have their ideas heard.

Janie

I'd like to go back and use some of the structures for our meetings that we experienced here, in my school with my teachers.

(Continued)

(Continued)

▶ The intersections around leadership, creativity, and learning. I'd like to foster and facilitate those discussions because I think we've had powerful discussions around those concepts, and that's where I'd like to start.

▶ I think it's a good time in my organization to reflect on and look at a lot of what we've learned here, so that's the first step. There are many other things I want to share with them, but I first want to set it up as we did the first night here with the Spark and see where that takes us.

Try This!

Five Steps to Empowering Teacher Voice

The *Teacher Voice Report 2010–2014* (Quaglia, 2014) found that barely half (53 percent) of teachers agreed with the statement, "I have a voice in decision-making at school," and only 59 percent felt confident "voicing my honest opinions and concerns." Further, a mere 48 percent felt that people communicated effectively at their school. This is critically important because, as the same report points out, feeling they have a teacher voice can have significant impacts on teacher well-being, motivation, and confidence. For example, believing that they have a voice in decision-making correlates to being

● three times more likely to work hard to reach goals;

● four times more likely to believe they can make a difference in the world;

● four times more likely to be excited about their future career in education;

● twice as likely to support and foster student voice.

Of course, there are also benefits for the school, such as increased teacher retention and the opportunity to learn from teachers' ideas and opinions once they are shared.

Here are five steps to help build and support teacher voice at your school.

1. **Ask**. Start by getting a baseline of what your teachers and staff are thinking and feeling right now. Due to the number of people who may feel

uneasy disclosing honest answers, the best way to do this is through an anonymous survey. Be brave enough to ask the hard questions of how people feel about leadership, the school culture, and teacher empowerment.

2. **Listen**. Once your survey is complete, pay careful attention to the results. Then share them with teachers and staff, but don't tell them, "Here's what your leaders are going to do about it"—tell them you want their input on what needs to be done.

3. **Collaborate.** Hold celebratory brainstorming sessions on a set schedule, perhaps every three months, to gather ideas on how to address specific issues in the survey. Remember to also brainstorm "what could be," taking a strength-based approach.

4. **Earn trust.** You must take the survey feedback seriously and start putting ideas into action if you are to maintain credibility. Earn trust by fostering an ongoing, cultural transformation, welcoming and expecting a continuous flow of teacher and staff input, recommendations, insights, and questions.

5. **Empower.** Teachers need time and the freedom to try new things on the way to developing their teacher voice. Be generous with both. Establish parameters that set them up to succeed and support them rather than hem them in.

CHAPTER 9
SEEDS TAKE ROOT
GOLDEN HILLS

"The mind involves learning strategies, critical thinking skills, collaboration, and the like, but also it involves the bigger piece that captures kids' hearts and engages them to release those seeds of brilliance in the most innovative and imaginative ways possible."

—Kandace Jordan

Have you ever watched one of those TV shows where a team is building a house or undertaking a huge renovation, and the camera speeds up and there is rapid-pace hammering and sawing and dry walling, and at the end of the show, everything has been transformed and is all ready for the big reveal?

Unfortunately, that's not how the transformation of your learning culture is going to happen.

Transforming your school, your district or your organization isn't an overnight process. It can also be messy, chaotic, and unpredictable, and trust me, mistakes will happen, and you'll encounter push back and nay-sayers. And at the end of it, while you should indeed have a big reveal and a celebration, you'll also recognize there's no final destination for innovation. This is a never-ending odyssey where you'll always be finding new ideas to try, new possibilities, new partnership opportunities, and new variables to engage with.

But I promise you, it will also be one of the most rewarding endeavors of your life. Soon after taking the first steps, you'll feel stretched, challenged, and invigorated. As you go on, your mind will be bursting with new ideas and possibilities, and you'll feel, along with your colleagues, that you've become a part of something greater, something that will brighten and better the futures of those within your sphere of influence and beyond. You'll feel a sense of purpose and a great sense of achievement in your day-to-day interactions. And best of all, you'll see the transformation in your students. You'll see their seeds of brilliance, and you'll watch them blossom and grow and take their brilliance out into the community. You won't be building nice, neat houses in a thirty-minute episode, but you'll be building young lives with an inspiring future ahead.

Golden Hills: In It for the Long Term

I got to experience this powerful metamorphosis from a school district's perspective with the Golden Hills School Division 75 in Strathmore, Alberta. In November 2017, I received an email from Cathy McCauley, then the executive director of the Calgary Regional Consortium in Alberta. Cathy had read *The Wonder Wall* and wanted to explore the opportunity of us working together with school-leader teams in Alberta. We agreed to meet, along with Kandace Jordan, at that time deputy superintendent of Alberta's Golden Hills School Division. When they walked into the room in Ottawa, they dropped a copy of *The Wonder Wall* on the table. It was jam-packed with all manner of sticky notes—clearly, they had done their homework!

Kandace told me how, under the umbrella of an initiative they called Powerful Learning (powerfullearning.com), they'd focused on numerous strategies to unleash potential in staff, students, and colleagues. Their goal was to make Golden Hills a world-class learning culture. They wanted me to build on their extensive work by bringing the ideas, imperatives, and conditions for innovative environments, as described in *The Wonder Wall,* to the Golden Hills district, schools, departments, and classrooms.

They understood the long-term nature of their mission. Kandace explained, "We came up with the framing concept of Powerful Learning, and we've grown a shared ownership for it across our systems. You'll hear the superintendent talking about it, you'll hear the teachers and support staff too, so it's become something continuous. It requires a vision sustained over time."

Powerful Learning in Golden Hills achieves deep understanding through strategic instruction, authentic engagement, and connecting and contributing. It uses proven research-based strategies to bring the best learning experiences for our students. Visit the Powerful Learning Facebook page—facebook.com/powerfullearning—to see further examples.

I was excited to see *The Wonder Wall's* imperatives and conditions play out, and gladly agreed to work with them over a sixteen-month period. The structure would include four full-day sessions, spaced four months apart, with all of the school-district leaders, managers, coaches, and teacher teams. I would also spend time at each of the district's schools and departments to work with the teams on their personal quests.

Sleep chose this time to ghost me

It would be easy to lay out now, in retrospect, how I and the Golden Hills team bravely surged forth through the messiness and uncertainty, with no road map, no rubric, no charts, or linearity, other than the three imperatives and four conditions to guide us. But I have to confess that after agreeing to the project, I went into a bit of a panic. I didn't get a lot of sleep.

While I was excited to embrace this opportunity with Golden Hills, I was a bit overwhelmed by the complexity of it all. It's one thing to put into action the ideas you've crafted for many years, but it's quite another to do it in a school district that's more than 1,800 miles away, over the course of nearly a year and a half. In the cold light of day, I kept wondering: How do you make the extraordinary happen within the complexity of distance and time? . . . And with four months elapsing between each visit, with the realities of day-to-day school life in between? I went through a period of significant self-doubt and questioning.

I know I'm not alone. I've talked to people from all walks of life and this theme emerges nearly every time people step into uncertainty. By expressing my own anxiety here, I hope it gives you the strength and courage to try new things. The fear of facing new challenges is often what impedes progress and innovation. We share a deeply human urge to avoid challenging the status quo and to keep our heads down. But if you look

up, you'll see there are others who think you have good ideas, who want
to work with you and support you, who are cheering you on. Sometimes
we already have cultures of belonging without even realizing it.

And I realized it wasn't just the teaching teams who would be
learning. I would learn from this experience as well, witnessing how the
three imperatives would evolve in a real-life school district's environment
to seed and cultivate innovation.

A new idea sets the stage

After a couple of nights of tossing and turning, I had an idea around
3 a.m. When Jane and I had written a report about the leadership journey
to innovation and creativity at the Ottawa Carleton District School Board
(2012), we called it *Unleashing Potential, Harnessing Possibilities: An
Odyssey of Creativity, Innovation and Critical Thinking*. We chose the
word *odyssey*, defined as a long series of wanderings or adventures, filled
with notable experiences and hardship, for a good reason.

First, the initiative had been a journey of close to ten years and was
designed to continue evolving infinitely. Second, it involved a long series
of wanderings, adventures, and definitely some hardships. In many ways,
it was like the enactment of a play, with a beginning, several acts, many
scenes, and multiple entrances and exits. It also had a multitude of crowd
scenes, several soliloquys, conflict, subplots, and climaxes and, trust me,
a fair bit of drama!

Thus, I began to think of the next sixteen months with Golden Hills
as an emergent, living, four-act play rather than the project in its entirety.
The play had a beginning: the Golden Hills Powerful Learning initiative they'd already been working on. My task was to build on Powerful
Learning by fostering and unleashing creativity, grounding the belief that
within everyone lies seeds of brilliance. Breaking it down this way made
the process a lot easier to envision:

> ▶ **ACT I** would catalyze the imperatives and conditions to foster
> a learning culture that inspires and encourages individual and
> organizational creativity and innovation.

> ▶ **ACT II** would build on those themes and engage teams in
> identifying initiatives within their own worlds; initiatives
> grounded in the imperatives, conditions, and realities to cultivate
> the unique potential of their staff, students, and the broader
> community.

> ▶ **ACT III** would bring some remarkable people to join us through
> Zoom and Skype, to share their remarkable journeys and help
> catalyze thinking.

▶ **ACT IV** would be a celebration of the extraordinary, where we came together to share the stories and initiatives that exemplified the sixteen-month odyssey.

Starting at the end: A Celebration of the Extraordinary

I'll lay out how this long-term project was structured, so you can replicate it if you wish.

On my first day with Golden Hills, casting all spoiler alerts aside, I started at the end instead of the beginning. I described how, sixteen months into the future, there would be a *Celebration of the Extraordinary*. Each school and department would present an artifact on that future day, essentially a story, to demonstrate how they'd used the imperatives and supporting conditions to bring about an innovative shift in some area of their organization.

It didn't matter if it was a small project, perhaps working with a group of children who were struggling or felt no sense of belonging, or if it was an intensive, school-wide initiative impacting the entire community. What was important was that it germinated a cultural shift through one or more of the three imperatives: a movement that fostered the brilliance in all; that turned a deficit focus to strength-based thinking; or built cultures of belonging, opening up space for story, personalized learning, genuine inclusivity, and celebration.

With that end goal in mind, we went on to the opening scene, to lay the groundwork for our district odyssey, and the individual odysseys of each school and department. On the walls of the venue, I placed four charts:

Four charts to gather teacher insight

1. Why Creativity and Why Now?
   - Why in this age of complexity do we need, more than ever, to unleash the seeds of brilliance that lie in everyone?

2. Your Story; Our Journey
   - An opportunity for the participants to reflect openly on some of the learning they've had through personal experience.

3. Fostering Cultures of Creativity: The Imperatives
   - What will be the underpinning beliefs upon which your creative learning culture will be founded?

4. Conditions
   - What learning conditions will be critical to maximize the opportunity for learners to find their potential and creative possibilities?

These themes and questions were among those that Jane and I had posed to ourselves to guide our thinking while writing *The Wonder Wall*. Throughout the book, we emphasized that while the three imperatives and four conditions had been the most impactful in the experiences we had witnessed, these could change depending on a school's specific situation. The important thing, then, is for people to think deeply about their unique situation, especially in this complex age, to figure out what cultural imperatives and conditions are critical to manifest.

Thus, the team was encouraged to ask,

▶ *Why is it important to foster the potential, creative seeds of brilliance in students and colleagues?*

▶ *What aspects of our own stories, or those around us, might inform our pathway—or spark questions?*

▶ *What fundamental beliefs about learning and culture are foundational in defining learning?*

▶ *What are our unique imperatives and conditions to bring learning to life, so students and adults are inspired to be curious, to challenge assumptions, and to collide with ideas?*

Much of the first day was engaged in thinking and sharing around these topics. To start, I shared some of my fundamental characteristics of healthy learning:

Critical characteristics of a healthy, creative learning culture

1. A culture of curiosity

2. The challenging of assumptions (and the assumptions upon which the assumptions are based)

3. Colliding ideas are welcomed and encouraged

I asked the participants to reflect on this throughout the process, hopefully jotting down their ideas, key insights, thoughts, and feelings on card stock anyway they liked. If something piqued their curiosity, they could make a note of it or write a poem, draw a picture, or sketch a cartoon. Many did so in a very creative way! See Figures 9.1 through 9.3. At the same time, if something was said and they wanted to challenge the assumption or collide with an idea, they could jot it down to address later or pose the question in the moment.

Figure 9.1 Participants Could Capture Their Thoughts Anyway They Chose. Some Decided to Sketch Instead of Take Notes. Artist: Scott Sackett

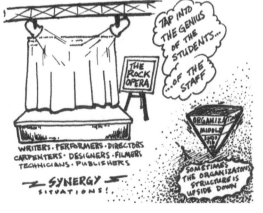

Figure 9.2 Lightbulbs, Rocket Ships, Spilled Liquids, Surfing, and Mountains Are Just Some of the Images Used to Illustrate Key Insights. Artist: Carley Blaseg

Golden Hills Context: Powerful Learning

Kandace described how Powerful Learning had shaped their learning culture with two interconnected elements, mind and heart. "The mind involves learning strategies, critical thinking skills, collaboration, and the like, but also it involves the bigger piece that captures kids' hearts and engages them to release those seeds of brilliance in the most innovative and imaginative ways possible."

Feeling from the heart

She further emphasizes the importance of merging "the feeling from the heart stuff" with tangible structures. "You must have both of these married to achieve a culture of powerful learning. The heart piece is the way you work with people, the way you actually notice when somebody has an idea and you support them in running with it. In (our sessions) that was the magic. We learned what made a difference to people; what they got

Figure 9.3 Such Creative Note-Taking Could Easily Be Transformed Into a Poster. Artist: Carley Blaseg

excited about; what was meeting a need in their work or with their group of kids; and then how to allow it to blossom, like a seed."

Kandace further noted that Golden Hills has a highly skilled superintendent, Bevan Daverne, who provides exceptional leadership for the school division. He articulates the district's vision and actively supports professional learning and innovation toward that vision. He recognizes and nourishes the seeds of brilliance in Golden Hills staff, which further energizes Powerful Learning and innovation.

During the four all-day sessions I facilitated, I noticed the senior staffs were all present and taking part in the collaborative learning with everyone else.

Jeff Grimsdale, Golden Hills' associate superintendent for Learning Services and First Nations, Metis, and Inuit Coordinator, says Powerful Learning is also positive thinking. "Our motto is about powering hope and possibilities for students and developing positive relationships. Building trust and belonging, is one of *The Wonder Wall's* three imperatives."

Jeff believes it's the positivity that enables people to take risks, supported by three pillars woven through discussion and practice: a culture of support, of achievement, and of collaboration. Most importantly, there needs to be trust.

"Change happens at the speed of trust," Jeff told me, quoting author Stephen Covey, who noted that change takes time and can happen only if we've developed trusting relationships and value others' contributions.

"I believe the power of trust is easy for an organization to say but is rarely achieved," he added. "It's one of the greatest stumbling blocks to learning. Once you lose trust, there's no openness, there's no comfort.

"When we start our collaborative days, our new teachers are challenged to learn our Powerful Learning initiatives. We need our other teachers to take them under their wing and help them feel a connection."

When I asked Jeff his most essential characteristic for a learning culture, the answer was a sense of belonging. "If people feel they belong to something that gives them purpose and trust, it creates that openness for dialogue. As someone said, 'If both of us always think the same, one of us is irrelevant.' It's about hearing what someone has to say and what you can add on to that. That's how innovation starts; it's that collision of ideas and adding pieces onto it from different perspectives."

For Jeff, the goal for students shouldn't simply be to pass the test or check off an achievement. "The point of education should be to inspire students to reach their potential and to encourage people of all ages to continue to learn regardless of what they've already achieved."

The importance of structure

The second critical focus for Golden Hills is the structure upon which the Powerful Learning culture is built, with five core competencies: creativity, critical thinking, communication, connecting, and collaborating. These competencies prepare students for their future but are equally crucial for educators.

Jeff explains, "Within our structure of Powerful Learning, we have strategic instruction, which gets to those high-impact strategies; authentic engagement, to build the culture of learning; and connecting and contributing to go beyond school, so we can transfer the learning and apply it to new situations. This collaborative foundation creates a relentless commitment to improving student learning. It's a place where we support each other, but we also push each other. It's a strength-based approach, which is another of the three imperatives."

Kandace elaborated: "Golden Hills had, over a significant period of time, very purposely envisioned and invested in the ongoing professional development [PD] and learning of staff. Much of this PD emerged from the collaborative efforts and ideas of people in their own learning. This results in extraordinary and, yes, powerful learning."

Administration Days—
Focus on Learning

The administrator meeting days first focused on sustained inquiry for critical thinking. Then the focus expanded to building capacity, celebrating what was happening in the schools, and learning from one another. System leadership days invite external experts to infuse their expertise into the Powerful Learning model. This started with vision building and nurturing a collaborative and thinking culture and later, using *The Wonder Wall* as a tool to spark initiatives, knowing everyone has a seed of brilliance.

This commitment to professional development, built on the competencies and structure of the Powerful Learning model, has deeply impacted Golden Hills. "Teachers can develop this relationship where they can be vulnerable and experiment with new things, and then take it back to their schools," says Kandace. "It's an environment of trust, and ideas that collide. So these fantastic ideas happen here and we create opportunities that engage students with purpose, as well as provide this emotional attachment, so it has meaning to them. It's about mastery, urging them to get better at something that's purposeful."

Powerful Proposals—Making
the Extraordinary Happen

A best practice at Golden Hills is to intentionalize vision into action, making their imagination of Powerful Learning synonymous with practice. Not many organizations I've worked with practice this. Imagination, as with creativity, is too often diminished to a "nice to have." But Golden Hills has created structures that support imagination and creativity. They focus on proven instructional strategies to improve performance and teach these to teachers.

Leadership support is, of course, essential for anything to unfold. Says Kandace, "You need to provide that support, that nurturance, so the idea comes to fruition, because a lot of time and energy is spent on the teacher's part. Celebrate it and appreciate those pieces from the heart, the ways you interact on a daily basis with folks. You need to have eyes that see what you have, and not what you don't have."

At Golden Hills, the process for new ideas is formalized. Jeff says, "We have Powerful Learning proposals schools and teacher groups can submit if they have ideas for which they'd like support, such as bringing in external experts, for example. As long as the proposals meet our criteria of Powerful Learning and building capacity, we provide funding."

> *Golden Hills has created structures that support imagination and creativity. They focus on proven instructional strategies to improve performance and teach these to teachers.*

Over Acts II and III, the teams sowed the seeds of their own journeys, and they shared them during each session. I encouraged them to be open, to challenge assumptions, and to collide with ideas in the pursuit of making each other think more deeply about what they're doing.

The Celebration of the Extraordinary

When the day for the Celebration of the Extraordinary finally arrived, the culmination of sixteen months of hard work, there were stories of children, schools, classrooms, communities, families, and departments— and all the noisiness and messiness and beauty that came with it. People spoke of personal discovery, of models of inclusion, and of the joy and pain of learning when stepping into uncertainty. It was indeed extraordinary. As the stories unfolded and ideas collided, assumptions were challenged and curiosity came alive.

The following videos I captured will show you the engagement and genuine interest that is sparked when the right conditions are in play. Listening to these stories will provide you with rich information that will spark ideas for your own journey.

Video 9.1

Claire: Celebration of Learning and Nature Connections

Claire introduces students at the Celebration of Learning, who have been running their own company.

Video 9.2

Shelley: Inspiring Learning Through Passion-Based Projects

From Genius Hour to a life-sized Bigfoot, Shelley describes the fun and learning being demonstrated at her school's Celebration of Learning.

Video 9.3

Sue: The "Shift" Across the District

Sue went around the Celebration of Learning and asked the question, "How did your sessions with Peter shift what you did over the last year, and how does that drive what happened here?" Here's what people said.

A critical part of the process was the creation of the artifacts that had tracked the learning journey. This was demonstrated in many ways: charting, journaling, photography, video, podcast, social media, and a host of others. (You'll notice I didn't mention "testing" or "grading," which I believe would have been contradictory to this learning process.) The artifacts needed to show

- the unleashing of curiosity;
- a culture where it was okay to challenge assumptions, and the assumptions on which the assumptions are based;
- a learning environment that ultimately thrived on the collision of ideas;
- any other cultural elements they found crucial, through our sessions.

The stories and the documenting artifacts were all so different, reflecting on the unique journeys people had taken to cultivate seeds of brilliance and grow innovation in their own circumstances. Story 1 and Story 2 are two examples . . .

Story 1: The NetZero Project

NetZero made a big impact on both the students involved and the community. In February 2020, I went back to Golden Hills for some follow-up work and met with Mark and Leslie, two teacher leads for NetZero.

NetZero (later named Students for Sustainability) began when a group of teachers wanted to bring together some of the key learnings we'd discussed on my earlier trip—addressing imperatives and themes and allowing for creative exploration. They were curious about how they could enhance deep learning with a project-based approach. Mark and Leslie had a shared interest in the environment, sustainability, and solar energy, and through this emerged the seeds of a plan.

Leslie's courses involved applied science and biology. She wanted hands-on activities to pique her students' curiosity, and she thought sustainability initiatives would engage her learners in a practical and fun way.

When Mark came across a grant opportunity through Energy Efficiency Alberta, Leslie was immediately interested, even though she hadn't worked with grants before. Not to be deterred, they put the proposal together and submitted it thirty minutes before the New Year's Eve deadline. It was well worth it, as the NetZero project was awarded a grant of $113,000. They quickly honed their vision to make Strathmore High School the first NetZero energy school in Canada.

One of the students involved in the project, Rodrigo, had a vision to make Strathmore High "stable" by making its carbon footprint net zero. The school would need to generate the energy it consumed, benefiting the school and community, and contributing to sustainability efforts around the world.

Partnerships were key, as Rodrigo worked with EnMax, an Alberta company exploring the possibility of car ports with solar roof panels. Rodrigo had been using software to design the carports and had connected with another Alberta based company, Carbon Busters, who helped with the software's learning curve.

Another student, Liam, described how his role involved coordination. "There were a lot of people joining this project and it's grown. I've been helping people decide what they're doing as well as resolving energy issues. I'm currently looking at getting an electrical company in here to install an intelligent meter that measures the electricity the school uses, so we can have in-depth, up-to-date tracking of the energy our school is using. Then we can observe and log any changes as a result of the changes we make to lighting or systems we're running."

Liam's plan required a two-step process. The first was to reduce and prevent energy use by cutting down on everything from water to heating. The second was to produce their own energy, which was a cost-savings measure as well. "If we can cut usage down first, then that's less that we have to install in terms of solar, heat exchange systems or whatever."

Video 9.4

The NetZero Project: Students for Sustainability

Meet four of the amazing "students for sustainability" here, as they provide a glimpse into their journey.

The reduction and prevention aspect became a focus for Leslie's biology students. After discussing microplastics in class, they began to see if recycling and composting could be incorporated throughout the school.

Meanwhile, another group of students in the applied science class phoned companies about recycling bins. They ended up getting a substantial grant, so all of the recycling bins in the school were cost free.

The students have a longer-term plan to develop a school composting project and a greenhouse, and they're already working with the local town council waste management department for support and insight and have attended town council meetings. "It was really nice to have recognition from the town about what we're doing and collaborating with them," says Liam.

The business plan: Funding applications and quarterly reports

The NetZero project was carried out as a real-life business transaction, and I must say I was deeply impressed. It was extremely well thought out and sophisticated and outlined in a detailed business plan.

As one student, Florence, explained, "With the grants, the students needed to write quarterly reports and even apply for more grants so we can get the funding we need. It meant a lot of sitting down and trying to figure out what the questions were asking us, and then Mr. Schweitzer helped out as a guiding hand."

In the end, the project saved money by changing the lighting structure and determining where the school was losing heat. Everyone, teachers included, were "learning as they went."

The students created a website to highlight NetZero, and it was clear this project was deeply personal to them. Leon spoke about the economic and financial benefits of the sustainability project and how the money saved could be put to use in other areas. He also described how the group planned to present to children in younger grades and at other schools. Florence said the project allowed people to come together for the "greater good of the community." It was an opportunity to work as a team and to learn in depth about issues pertaining to solar power and heat exchange.

For Rodrigo, the project taught him about teamwork, along with an enriched language experience by working with people who didn't speak his native Spanish. He further learned, "how to join your skills with others to make yourself a better person in terms of the message you're sending by engaging in this project—not only the students but the staff and broader community."

The students emphasized that it is important to be personally invested in their work. Liam said, "You want actions to bring a better future for humankind. I think that sums up what a lot of people are doing with sustainability and all-around technological, ecological, and even social advancements. We're trying to share a message to get people to pursue a better future because there's always something you can improve."

Learning reimagined

I asked the students, "If you could reimagine and reshape learning cultures, what would be your priorities to make them alive, meaningful, and creative?"

More hands-on, real-life learning projects was a popular answer, and Liam built on that with unique analogy featuring Aldous Huxley's *Island* (1962). "It's meant to highlight an ideal society, based not only on material learning but also on spiritual, mental development and ultimately the attainment of oneness. I guess with oneself, being content with who we are could theoretically work. Money is a limiting factor in lots of societies; it's also an amazing enabler for lots of amazing stuff to happen in development and communication. Being content with less material I think could realistically produce a society of people that are more content. And so this is where NetZero is going, trying to find more sustainable, self-procured solutions to problems."

Video 9.5

Liam: Imagining Learning for a Better Future

Hear Liam describe what a better future looks like to him.

A surprise ending

You might think all of this learning was folded into an environmental science course. I thought the learning was so rich that it encompassed business, social studies, English, mathematics, biology, and more. But there was no course involved. The students received no credit for this project. All was done on their own time, with the exception of thirty-minute blocks for personal study during school hours. It was passion-based learning at its best, undertaken not for a grade or mark on a standardized test, but for the sheer love of learning and doing something that mattered deeply to them. If you'd like to learn more about this project and find out how to make it happen in your organization, take a look at the website that Leon and his classmates created—sustainablesolutionsforschools.com.

It was passion-based learning at its best, undertaken not for a grade or mark on a standardized test, but for the sheer love of learning and doing something that mattered deeply to them.

Video 9.6

Playlist for NetZero Project

Browse the playlist for more interviews surrounding the NetZero Project.

Story 2: A Celebration of Inclusivity, or How to Put on a Play with 410 Students

Another initiative was the production of a school-wide play at Westmount School. I was curious to know why the school chose this avenue and how it had shifted and built the learning culture to exemplify the imperatives and conditions.

Teacher Amanda Ball and Karen Oliphant, a teacher in the Strive program for students with a variety of physical and learning challenges, explained that the fifth and sixth-grade students had always put on an annual drama production. But this year, as a result of our conversations pertaining to creativity, inclusivity, the power of personalized learning, and the importance of celebration, the team decided to involve the entire school. As Amanda said, "Rather than reinventing the wheel, we decided let's take something we already do, but involve everybody."

After a considerable amount of brainstorming, they created twenty-five mini departments, each of which would have responsibility for one aspect of the play's production. This was a challenging idea given that the school had 410 students. How do you structure inclusivity on that scale and ensure it's personal for each child? The level of organization was complex, because to make their choices, everyone, students and adults alike, had to understand what the twenty-five different mini departments were about.

Amanda described the process. "We put kids from multiple grades in each department. So you had kids from kindergarten to sixth grade in the makeup department, for example, working with a teacher creating makeup for all the characters in the play."

Because certain departments were more popular than others, giving every child their choice was a bit tricky. The driving idea was to give each student a chance to celebrate what makes them special, perhaps to show off a passion or discover one they didn't know they had. Teachers also got

Video 9.7

Amanda: A Play for 410 Kids!

Listen to Amanda describe the process for putting on an all-school production, showcased at the Celebration of the Extraordinary.

to choose their departments. "For example, teachers who love art chose the advertising department where they created the posters, and so the students got to show their seeds of brilliance in a different way."

Each department had seven meetings throughout the course of the project. Karen added. "We had the seniors' tea department making cakes and creating menus, the props department, the costume department. We also involved some experts. Rosebud Theatre helped us with production; we drew in expertise from the local newspapers and radio stations, and documented the whole process. So once it's finished, we can have the families and community back into the school to share our documentary."

Karen reflected on how the school-wide play fostered inclusivity. "Some of us were outside our comfort zone in our departments. But I thoroughly enjoyed learning along with the kids, too. When we watched the play, each kid could say, I painted that chair, or that's my costume idea. They have ownership in the play. They've all learned and loved being part of a department."

The Strive classroom

As a special education teacher, Karen wanted to ensure her students felt involved and included. She carefully worked with each student to ensure a balance of choice and guidance, according to their needs.

"I had to collaborate with our educational assistants to make sure all of our inclusive education students got to their departments. Some of them could go independently, but some had to pair up with EAs."

Karen had thirteen students from first grade to sixth, and all worked in a department. "We have some very eloquent and vocal students who love to talk and tell a good story, so those guys were certainly very apt for our advertising department. One student was in the photography department and every time the group popped by to take pictures, you could see that big smile of pride on his face."

The project seemed massive at the beginning. "But as a team, we pulled together and it didn't become as daunting. And our school is very welcoming. We've had the Strive program for many years, so our classroom is a huge part of our school. The other students see my students as 'our students.' I think it creates empathy and understanding of everyone's differences. So whether it's a kindergartner, a Strive student, a sixth grader, they all supported each other. It was just part of their culture, their nature, and their empathy.

"My students felt proud to be part of a department. They shared their stories and built friendships. I saw them all catching up with each other in the hallway and on the playground, and they'd introduce me to their new friends."

Teacher Corrine described how her department had lots of kindergarten children, as well as several fifth-and sixth-grade students, some of whom were struggling in different ways. She noted how the older children rose to the occasion of circulating around the classroom to help the younger children in their work. "This had such a positive impact on them. I don't know if they had ever had that role before."

Karen advises other teachers, "Just give it a go. As teachers, I think we're all very stuck in our boxes and afraid to let go. But I found when throwing a group of students of mixed age and mixed ability together, they kind of figure it out for themselves. Just give them the chance and they run with it."

The power of collaboration

It struck me how much the success of the play was dependent on the cooperation of the entire staff. I've worked in many schools and departments and have spoken to endless numbers of educators and business leaders around the world. One of the recurring conversations is how to foster a learning culture that inspires trust, understanding, and collective action. It's a difficult thing to do. Leadership needs to create space where the natural, informal leadership of those throughout the organization can flourish. As I explored some of the stories surrounding the production, I became even more curious about this school culture.

The play's script was written by teacher Dana Graff, who takes the time to write the script every year for the Grade 5/6 production. "We write scripts because we don't turn down any kids who try out. We can't find scripts with 40 or 50 characters, so I write a play with enough parts," Dana explained. "For this year's school-wide production, I wrote a play with a green theme about conservation. So everything we do at school for the year is based on that green theme."

Behind any successful venture lies structure. Dana told me, "This project was developed from our sessions with you. That team of teachers came back and decided since we always do the Grade 5/6 production, we want it to be bigger than it is. So we carved out some time, and we all sat together and created a format. We looked at a million different schedules, planned six meetings around our hockey program, around swimming lessons, around preps, around gym. Then we created authentic departments and presented it to our staff."

And there was pushback, but not as much as might be expected. "There was definitely some reluctance, and lots of questions, but everybody was willing to give it a try."

A structure of support

It's one thing to create a structure, but Dana and his team also wanted it to be supportive. "We wanted to take the logistics off the teachers' hands so all they had to worry about was their department, not about planning around other school events."

At each regular staff meeting, a priority agenda item was to ask what needed to be changed or tweaked for the play. Department meetings were held separately from staff meetings, and the planning team was provided half a day to work on the logistics. Feedback from previous productions was used to hone the plans.

For example, teacher Corrine noted in previous years, one teacher was responsible for each department. "I personally work better collaborating with others, so I felt very isolated. I need to have all this information percolating and to bounce it off somebody, so that was a welcome change we made."

It doesn't matter who you are—you belong

Principal Cori Hanson thought the play's inclusivity captured who they are as a school. "Strive students are very much a part of our school, but we're always trying to make them even more so. A parent mentioned the inclusivity to me and how her daughter feels like she belongs at her school. That's what we're all about. Everyone belongs."

Video 9.8

Cori: Exploring the Celebration
of the Extraordinary

Hear principal Cori describe what she's seeing at her school's learning celebration.

A celebration department!

It truly delighted me to see the school created a celebration department. One of the four conditions to foster an innovative environment is to understand that celebration isn't an event, but an attitude that should be infused in all aspects of school and life. Jane and I were touched that the team had taken this to heart, weaving the critical importance of celebration of learning into the structure of the production from the start. It was the job of the celebration department to trace the journey of creating the play across the school and document it through photography. The work was captured in a final video that celebrated the diverse range of activities and learning that occurred across the many different groups.

Path flexes with ideas emerging from students and teachers

Corrine co-led the celebration department with Cori. For her, what stood out most was the dynamic and fluid nature of the process. "It changes depending on what the kids are saying. What I thought was going to happen evolved and turned into something much greater than I had foreseen."

Chloe and Kennedy: The power of choice

Curious to learn what some of the students thought about the play, I spoke with two girls in fifth and sixth grades. Chloe worked with the photography department and Kennedy with the makeup department.

Chloe described how they had learned the importance of taking photos from different angles "to get better shots for all of the scenes of the play" and created the effect of "movement." Chloe chose photography because it sounded like fun, and it was something different.

The photos were on display throughout the school as a celebration and reminder of the school's accomplishment and how hard they had worked. They were also used by the video department to create a celebration video.

Kennedy chose the makeup department because she loves art and thought it would be a great opportunity to learn how to use art skills in painting faces. She learned "how to use the brushes and to practice painting with all of them."

It was very compelling to hear the children talk about how the entire process involved people from inside the school, but it also drew on outside talents, providing a wonderfully enriched opportunity to learn from experts. This deepened the commitment to "community" in the learning process.

I asked the girls why they thought it was so important for everyone to be involved.

Chloe said, "We can all learn to get along a lot better with lots of people, and like different opinions sometimes, too."

If you create the right space, the learning will emerge.

Video 9.9

Video Playlist for Celebration
of the Extraordinary

Browse the playlist for more interviews with
students and staff.

CHAPTER 9

Key Takeaways

1. School district cultures can be transformed by embedding the three imperatives and four conditions into the learning environment.

2. Asking students to view themselves as change makers, to work on projects that have strong personal meaning for them, enables deep learning to take place.

3. You need a collaborative foundation to create a relentless commitment to improving student learning. To create a "place where we support each other but we also push each other" requires a strength-based approach.

Reflective Questions

1. Why is it important to foster the potential creative seeds of brilliance in students and colleagues?

2. What aspects of your own stories, or those around you, might inform your pathway to nurturing seeds of brilliance—or spark questions?

3. Superintendent Jeff Grimsdale says he believes things happen at the speed of trust. Do you have a trusting organization? What are the hallmarks of an organization where deep trust exists?

4. What are your unique imperatives and conditions to bring learning to life, so students and adults are inspired to be curious, to challenge assumptions, and to collide with ideas?

Try This!

Foster an Ecosystem of Celebration

This chapter describes how one school created a "celebration department" for its school-wide play, demonstrating the critical importance of the celebration of learning, one of the four conditions supporting healthy and innovative environments. The department's goal was to "create a tribute and celebration of the diverse range of activities and learning that occurred across the many different groups as they contribute to the final production."

Such celebratory events and attitudes aren't simply about showcasing the work. For every student and every adult in your organization, you need to create an ecosystem in which each individual is known, valued, and cherished for exactly who they are. Seeing their unique contributions celebrated helps to build that ecosystem and that culture of belonging.

Plan to hold a Passion Project Day, where everyone, students, staff, parents, and even community businesses and organizations, are invited to create a project or pursue learning regarding something they are passionate about—on their own or in a team.

Ask everyone to present their project in a unique way at a later Celebration of Learning. You can brainstorm ways to celebrate your learning, allowing students to have their moment in the sun. During the celebration, document the learning that has taken place in a video and play it at the next school assembly.

CHAPTER 10

WHERE LEARNING COMES NATURALLY

REGINA STREET ALTERNATIVE AND CARSELAND SCHOOL

"(At Mud Lake) . . . the student drops down those walls, and shares not just what's going on, but how they're feeling. And when you're here with five or six students, you naturally end up walking beside one and having those conversations. That would never happen in the classroom."

—John Cameron

There's certainly no shortage of research showing that outdoor physical activity and play, as well as simply being exposed to nature, helps our physical well-being to flourish. Outdoor play allows children to exercise, improve motor skills, get more vitamin D, and burn calories, which lowers the risk for obesity and related chronic diseases.

Nevertheless, some school districts are shortening recess or eliminating it altogether, while others are putting physical education on the sidelines or calling for year-round school. In an increasingly competitive global marketplace, the driving motivation is that we must devote as much time as possible to the top-hierarchy subjects of language and math. The thinking is that physical activity and the arts are considered just "nice-to-haves" and do little to increase scores on standardized tests, so out they go.

What the advocates for less playtime don't realize, however, is that research over the last decade shows being exposed to nature is *significantly* correlated with an increase in student scores on standardized tests (Lloyd-Strovas, 2018). The higher the exposure is to greenery and outdoor play, the higher the test scores and general student achievement. And those increases hold fast even after researchers adjust for sociodemographic variables such as student-teacher ratio, school attendance, family income level, race, gender, and English as a second language.

I should also add here that Finland, a country much admired and celebrated for its academic outcomes, devotes one and a half hours, or a quarter of the school day, to recess and unstructured play for first graders (Stainburn, 2014).

So how does nature and outdoor play improve test scores (Kuo et al., 2019)? Teachers and parents have known about a few of the reasons for generations. A good runaround outdoors helps kids "get the ants out of their pants," relieves stress, helps them focus, and just makes children feel physically better. The ability to use their outdoor voices and move more freely than inside the classroom can also lessen anxiety and even reduce symptoms of ADHD (Dunckley, 2013).

Most kids also just like being outdoors. Depending on the quality of the outdoor environment, it's more novel: There are always changes going on and something new to see. And as a bonus, kids are more engaged in learning not only when they're outside but also after they come back in (Kuo et al., 2018).

Intriguingly, our brains are biologically designed to learn better after interacting with nature. This is explained through attention restoration theory (Berman et al., 2009), which says there are two types of attention. (There are days we wish our students could pay *any* kind of attention, so this is good news!)

[The theory was initially explored by Rachel and Stephen Kaplan in their book, *The Experience of Nature: A Psychological Perspective* (Kaplan et al., 1989)]

"Directed" attention involves our prefrontal cortex, which is used in a wide range of higher executive functions for learning, such as memorizing, planning, paying attention, impulse control, reasoning, and problem-solving, to name a few. You can imagine the vigorous workout the prefrontal cortex gets during an intense classroom lesson, where it's continuously trying to figure things out, make decisions and choices, and take appropriate next steps.

But during "involuntary" attention, which involves the brain's sensory processing systems, we simply take notice of pleasant things around us without feeling we must pay strict attention or take action. You've experienced this yourself when you've sat on a park bench, admiring a butterfly flit around some lovely flowers, or when you've taken a walk on a nature trail during an autumn day, listening to the birds sing. While this involuntary attention is going on, the prefrontal cortex takes a backseat to recharge and is then rested and refreshed to start learning again. In other words, taking breaks and letting our minds wander actually makes us smarter! How great is that?

In a moment, we'll explore two inspiring examples of schools immersed in nature-based learning, but first, you may be wondering: even if it helps us learn, what does the great outdoors have to do with being innovative?

I'm glad you asked.

Walk on the Wild Side

First off, nature is an untapped and often overlooked gold mine of learning resources. You can literally never run out of ideas and possibilities to make nature an imaginative and engaging foundation for your healthy learning environment. It solidly supports all three imperatives and four conditions for well-being and innovation:

Three Imperatives for Innovative Learning Environments

1. **Recognize there's a seed of brilliance in everyone**. This is an easy one. Every aspect of nature contains seeds of brilliance. Helping students to recognize the process through which the hidden seed, even as a metaphor, emerges into something extraordinary, can help them recognize and value the seeds of brilliance within themselves. At the same time, exploring the interconnectedness in nature and the unique roles and essential contributions every player makes can help them recognize and appreciate the seeds of brilliance in others, the power of diversity and inclusivity, and empathy. This ability to look—not just at the big picture but also at the whole picture and all of its possibilities—supports learning and ultimately innovation.

2. **Think and act from a strength-based perspective**. There are countless demonstrations and metaphors of strength-based perspectives in nature, from the survival mechanisms and behaviors that animals have developed

(Continued)

(Continued)

to the fragile flower that bursts through the concrete in the middle of a city sidewalk. Invariably, every animal and every plant appears to ask the same questions we do: "What are the amazing possibilities that we want to achieve today? How will we make that happen? Who can we partner with?" Thinking about how we can help repair the damage done to nature, like Boyan Slat did with his ocean-cleaning invention, The Interceptor (see Chapter 3), is also ripe with possibilities for strength-based thinking.

3. **Foster a culture of belonging**. Nature teaches us that biodiversity is essential; if one part is diminished, taken away, or excluded, then entire ecosystems are put at risk. Learning about this firsthand is an insightful way for students to recognize and appreciate the need to value every person and the contributions they make.

Four Conditions That Support Innovative Learning Environments

1. Storytelling and listening—There is magic in teaching children to close their eyes and actively listen to what they hear: the honking of geese, the wind rustling in the leaves, the sound of falling rain. Each sound tells an important story that students can expand on, learning why some sounds are only heard during the changing of the seasons, for example.

2. Moving beyond diversity to true inclusivity—Again, we must recognize that every person, of all levels and backgrounds, has important ideas, experiences, and talents to share. Encouraging that kind of inclusivity is what drives real, innovative change. Exploring biodiversity, inclusivity, and partnerships in nature can give students the founding for inclusivity among their peers. It helps them to not only see the forest for the trees but also the trees for the forest.

3. Making it personal—We need to make learning deeply personal to allow learning to be embraced, to connect the subject being taught to something that is deeply personal for the learner. Nature is deeply personal to every individual, particularly our desire to understand our place within it. In fact, science shows our brains are hardwired to be drawn to nature (Worrall, 2017).

4. Recognizing that celebration is not an event, but an attitude—There is no more convenient and affordable means than nature to foster a sense of joy and novelty, with the sheer wonder of learning and stretching the imagination.

And as for living in an Age of Complexity, there's nothing more complex than nature. Learning about its awe-inspiring interconnectedness helps students appreciate the complexity of our own world and all of its moving parts.

Even if your school is in the inner city or is on a tight budget, you'll find several ideas at the end of this chapter for how you can incorporate nature into your classroom. Research has shown that merely looking out of the window at a garden or having more daylight in the classroom can have positive effects on student well-being and test scores (Uncapher, 2016). The following two examples illustrate how some schools are incorporating nature to create healthy and creative school environments.

Regina Street Alternative School: Bringing the Outside In

From the outside, Regina Street Alternative School doesn't look much different from countless other elementary schools dotting the Canadian landscape: a plain one-story, red-brick building, constructed during the pragmatic, baby-booming era of the 1960s, albeit a bit on the small side.

The wide, flat school yard consists of packed-hard earth, driven down by the hundreds of sneaker-clad shoes that pound through the schoolyard each day. Patches of barren soil are interspersed with brown grass that won't green up until the school year ends in June. There are a few play structures, and bordering the back of the lot, a solid line of trees forms a curtain, blocking the eye's view.

The surrounding neighborhood is high density. A jumble of high-rises, low-rises, and townhouses, mingled with a few single homes, hugs the school tightly. Two social housing communities flank the area. A large number of the students who attend Regina Street Alternative are new Canadians; more than half speak a language at home that isn't English. With many still struggling to put down roots in their adopted homeland, these families have chosen this established neighborhood to call home.

If beauty was judged only on the outside, one might be forgiven for not thinking such an ordinary little school would be a place where the extraordinary happens. But as I've learned over the years, appearances are often deceiving, and every person and every place contains a seed of brilliance. It just takes brave and inspiring leadership to set the imperatives and conditions in place for it to emerge.

You see, behind that curtain of trees I mentioned, that canopy of green lace at the back of the school, there's a rather magical place called Mud Lake. Now I admit the name Mud Lake doesn't conjure up visions of environmental beauty. But step behind the curtain and you'll suddenly find yourself in a natural oasis in the middle of an urban area. The Mud Lake conservation area spans some 400 acres and nurtures a complex ecosystem bursting with plants and trees, tadpoles and turtles, and mammals from rabbits and raccoons to coyotes and foxes. The rumble of the city traffic, even though it exists just a block or two away, quiets here, the noise drowned out by the individual songs and melodies of some 200 different bird species, croaking frogs, and buzzing bees, all rising to a crescendo with the breeze that rustles through the leaves.

Turtles sun themselves on a log at Mud Lake.

Photo credit: Janet Wilson

Bringing the inside out

With such a treasure in their own backyard, it's only natural Regina's teachers would look to this city wilderness for educational purposes. But they've done much more than make Mud Lake a once- or twice-a-year field trip. Several years ago, they decided to bring the inside out. And the outside in. They made Mud Lake an extension of their classrooms, not just for science and environmental studies but also for every subject in the curriculum—writing, math, music, gym, and so much more. And the results have been refreshing.

Changing the environment can not only bring out seeds of brilliance, it can even turn perceived weaknesses into strengths. For example, I know of one student who had great difficulty sitting still and focusing on a task. That made being in a classroom setting very challenging for him. He was constantly drawn to things beyond his task at hand. A sudden movement would cause him to focus his attention elsewhere, pointing out to everyone what he saw. He regularly distracted other students, and in addition to making it harder for him academically, it didn't make him popular with his peers.

Out in the middle of the conservation area, this student's "weaknesses" suddenly became strengths. He was the one who could home in on the tiny movements of an insect. Students wanted to see what he was seeing. They wanted to partner with him. His seed of brilliance was suddenly shining through.

The former principal of the school, Rob James, told me, "I think removing them from the classroom environment just changes things.

Conversations change, relationships change for the better when we come here. It's almost like the school walls are walls between us and they come down. While looking in front of us, where we think we should be looking, a distractible child is looking all over the place and spotting the squirrel, the frog, the turtle, the heron."

The key point about this "transformation" is that the student hadn't changed at all. He was still the same child he was in the classroom. But by changing the environment, the "problem" student was now confidently learning new things and being a leader among his peers. By allowing his unique abilities to shine through, the student himself was perceived differently. And that helped him to flourish.

Teacher John Cameron (now retired) explains very poignantly what happened at Mud Lake: "You're able to have those much deeper discussions, you're able to really understand, because the student drops down those walls, and shares not just what's going on, but how they're feeling. And when you're here with a group of five or six students, you naturally end up walking beside one and having those conversations with them. This helps you so much as an educator, getting to know them better and I think it does a lot for them too, knowing you care and they're comfortable enough to share that information with you. That would never happen in the classroom."

Out in the middle of the conservation area, this student's "weaknesses" suddenly became strengths. He was the one who could home in on the tiny movements of an insect. Students wanted to see what he was seeing. They wanted to partner with him. His seed of brilliance was suddenly shining through.

The key point about this "transformation" is that the student hadn't changed at all. He was still the same child he was in the classroom. But by changing the environment, the "problem" student was now confidently learning new things and being a leader among his peers.

Video 10.1 and 10.2

Carter: The Impact of Mud Lake on Learning

Listen to Carter as he talks to me about the impact Mud Lake had on him and how nature helps him learn across all subjects in the curriculum.

Part I   Part II

Bringing Mud Lake into the curriculum

Rob and John told me the story of how the magical marriage of Mud Lake and Regina School began.

"Mud Lake is like a Disney World for nature," says Rob. "There are about 250 species that have been identified, and we can walk down and see turtles, beaver, frogs, snakes, raccoons, skunk and all manner of birds. There are pathways winding through the area, there's water, there's forest—it's a pretty diverse natural area, and there's always something to see."

Several years ago, John had the idea to use Mud Lake as a natural learning opportunity. "Before that, the school used the area sporadically, such as for a science unit, or a writing or art activity.

"We had always taken our Grade 5 and 6 students on an annual three-day camping trip. They learned so much there and talked about how we created that connection with nature for them. So I thought we could try going to Mud Lake once a week, connecting it to the curriculum not just in science and social studies, but also by basing our writing, reading, and art activities around it."

Reaching out to the broader community

Once the idea had laid down roots, the school wondered if the Mud Lake programming could become more formally entrenched.

"We discovered the Teacher Leadership and Learning Program, a joint program between the Province of Ontario Ministry of Education and the Ontario Teachers' Federation," says John. "We applied for and got some funding, which allowed us to do a self-directed professional development approach. We also become more informed, because it allowed us go see what other schools were doing.

"We didn't see anything in the education curricula resources, so we thought we could bridge that gap by showing other teachers what we do here at Mud Lake."

Depending on leaders to blaze new trails

No matter how many good ideas an individual or group comes up with, they won't get very far without leadership support. In the case of Mud Lake, the school and community were fortunate to have Rob James as their principal.

"No matter how many good ideas an individual or group comes up with, they won't get very far without leadership support." –Rob James, former principal, Regina Street Alternative School

"I got familiar with what John was doing with Mud Lake," says Rob. "Thinking about the opportunities, I wondered why we weren't all doing this. I just gave people permission and helped facilitate it."

Once a leader signals that it's okay to take risks and try something new, a project takes off. "You can just imagine people coming at the initiative with all different kinds of expertise and ideas. I encouraged them not to be afraid and said it was okay if we didn't have all the answers."

Being allowed to revel in ambiguity was another attitude that helped spur the project on. One teacher asked, "What if I go down there and a student asks what kind of bird that is and I don't know?"

Rob responded with, "That's great, you figure out the answer with the student together. That's the joy in the learning. We had just started inquiry-based learning, and nature is the ultimate place for inquiries. But without the teachers wanting to take that chance, that risk, none of this would've happened. Our students now treat this as a classroom, an extension of the school we share with the community."

Rippling out into the community: The Mud Lake Symphony

One day, Regina's school librarian contacted a man named Jesse Stewart after hearing him talk on CBC Radio about his music related to nature. She told him what the school was doing with Mud Lake, and he wanted to learn more.

"He met with us, walked around Mud Lake, and said he wanted to do an internship," says Rob. "He worked with our students for a full year on a weekly basis. It's such a gift to have someone like Jesse be so giving of their time."

During the walk at Mud Lake, Rob says, Jesse listened to the birds and was knocking on the trees, a big hollow tree in particular. "He's a percussionist. And at that time he said, 'We'll create the Mud Lake Symphony, and we'll perform it onstage with the National Arts Centre Orchestra.' That happened five years later, and it was an amazing experience for our kids. That's the power of making connections outside the community, someone who brings something to the students that we often can't as teachers."

Jesse brought a variety of instruments into the school such as shakers and rattles, and he showed the students how they could repurpose items as musical instruments, such as plastic buckets for drums. He also provided sonorous stones, which can be rubbed or tapped together. He made it clear that everyone can make music, even without access to traditional musical instruments or instruction. Every other week for eight months, Jesse led the students in making improvisatory music together.

Taking Mud Lake as a source of inspiration, Jesse also initiated the collaborative musical performance that would eventually play out at the National Arts Centre. For the basis of the creative piece, he used R. Murray Schafer's concept of the soundscape (Schafer, 1993), the immersive sonic environment within a space. He led the students on a fascinating discovery of all of the sounds they heard at Mud Lake, including the geophony, the Earth sounds such as rain drops on the water; the biophony, which are animal sounds such as frogs and birds; and the anthrophony, the human sounds of fellow hikers and traffic noises.

Together, Jesse and the students also researched the history of the area and imagined how the Mud Lake soundscape has changed over time. What did it sound like a century ago before there were cars? Or a thousand years ago when the only human inhabitants were the Algonquin First Nation? Or 13,000 years ago when the area was covered by the Champlain Sea?

Implicit in Jesse's process of sonic investigation and imagination was one of the central tenets of critical pedagogy—namely, that students and teachers should be co-investigators of knowledge through critically engaged dialogue that leads to collaborative problem-solving toward a common learning objective.

Through this collaborative learning process, musical parts were developed for all 160 students: junior and senior kindergarten used stones to create the sound of rain; first and second grades used ridged wooden frogs to create frog sounds; third and fourth grades created bird sounds; and fifth and sixth grades played drums. Two narrators provided context for the sounds, one in English and one in French.

The *Mud Lake Symphony* premiered in the school's gymnasium and was enthusiastically received by parents and school officials. Word of the project soon got around, and they were invited to present in a variety of settings, providing a broader range of learning experiences.

The flexible and adaptive nature of the project means it can be used as a model for community-based collaborations in other contexts. Educators, students, and community members can adapt the piece itself, or the collaborative process, to their own unique sonic, cultural, and educational environment.

When the day of the performance at the National Arts Centre finally arrived, Rob says most of the students had never been to the location before. "I'll tell you, someone walked us down to the stage and when the students turned around, they were just in awe, looking out at all the seats. I thought our students would be a little intimidated, but it was like they were meant to be there. They were so confident about the whole thing."

Jesse later created a presentation of the entire project and the process titled *Music and Social Justice: Bridging Public Education and Higher Learning Through Community Engagement*, which he shared at the Teaching Roundtable: Community Engagement in Teaching in January of 2016.

The Mud Lake Math Trail

Another project that Rob and John mentioned was the Mud Lake Math Trail. "Math Trails are established in a lot of museums and public places, and we thought we could create one," says John. "We had students go through a series of math problems that they could solve going through Mud Lake or bring the information back to the classroom to solve the math problems.

"The students were really engaged in the process when the teachers created the math trail for them, but we soon realized our older students would be able to create a math trail for students in kindergarten or Grade 1. Looking at the curriculum from a student's point of view took student voice to a whole new level."

Video 10.3

Mud Lake: A Natural Place to Learn

Take a peek at Mud Lake and hear school leaders describe the impact this natural environment had on their students.

Carseland School's Passion for Nature-Based Learning

Carseland is part of the Golden Hills School District in Alberta, Canada, where (as described in Chapter 9) I was invited to do a sixteen-month project. I wanted to mention Carseland School here in Chapter 10 because they, like Regina Alternative, have immersed themselves in nature-based learning.

Teacher Claire Wade catalyzed the nature-based learning initiative, which she believes has many implications for health, wellness, and meaningful learning. She discovered her passion for it when she stayed home with her two young boys on an extended maternity leave.

"Watching them grow and explore and learn, I noticed how the wonders of nature and the outdoors, that experiential learning, just brought everything alive. They pick things up so easily in this space. So when I returned to school, I wanted to create one of those climates where learning was experiential and hands-on and nature-based, because I could see the value."

Microcosms of awesomeness

Claire refers to these powerful learning climates as *microcosms of awesomeness.*

"They're little zones where everything grows and people are like, how does it grow so well here? And I'm like, it's a little microcosm of awesomeness! I was at a professional development opportunity and we spent six hours outdoors with a bunch of passionate, nature-based, place-based, like-minded people, and I felt that excitement and climate for learning."

The initial seeds—outdoor garden

Claire's first adventure to create microcosms of awesomeness started with an outdoor garden, where the students designed and co-constructed garden boxes. The goal was to create a connection with nature, "so the children could be outdoors and learn in a natural environment."

She soon co-created a school-wide program called Nature Connection and proposed an outdoor program in collaboration between Carseland School and Alberta Parks. The school is located very close to Wyndham Carseland Provincial Park.

"The Siksika Nation is a close neighbor and the school works very closely with an elder. We meet regularly at the Provincial Park and take part in a variety of place-based learning activities."

The program is called *Ik Ka Nutsi,* which is a Blackfoot phrase meaning to shine brightly or to be bright. In a climate of authentic engagement that deepens the impact of the learning, the students connect and collaborate with elders and community members.

Claire's emphasis is on community-based, not community-placed, learning initiatives. While definitions vary, place-based education uses the local environment as a basis to teach school subjects such as math, language, or science, while community-based learning immerses students in, for example, local cultures, heritage, experiences, and issues or opportunities as the starting point for learning other subjects.

community-based learning: immerses students in, for example, local cultures, heritage, experiences and issues or opportunities as the starting point for learning other subjects.

place-based education: uses the local environment as a basis to teach school subjects such as math, language, or science.

"Community-based gives you the direction, knowledge, wisdom, and support from the community," says Claire. In this context, she sees her role as a facilitator of learning.

Listen to student Caleb Eagle Speaker (Video 10.4) and his dad Simon (Video 10.5) reflect on the importance of community and land-based learning.

Video 10.4

Caleb: Learning From Nature

Student Caleb talks about what he's learned about nature and why he thinks other schools should be doing this.

Video 10.5

A Parent's Perspective: Caleb's Dad

Caleb's dad, Simon, explains why he thinks nature-based learning is important, particularly from a Blackfoot perspective. He also talks about the effect it's had on his son.

Personalize land acknowledgment

For Claire, land acknowledgment is an important aspect of the children's learning. Although the students heard the acknowledgement on the morning announcements, she wanted to ensure they had a deeper understanding. Together, they explored why the land is so important in this space, and then, the students co-created their own land acknowledgment for the park area in which they were working.

The students also got to take part in a very creative, real-life project, thanks to the collaboration with Alberta Parks. The class was invited to review the campsite map for visitors to make sure everything was in the right place and provide feedback. To conduct their research, the children went on a snowshoeing expedition around the campsite. They found a typo on the map and made some corrections, as well as provided several suggestions, such as a section describing the park's chickadees.

Learn from the land: Levels of the forest

Levels of the forest is a sixth-grade science objective in the Trees and Forest learning unit. Claire had previously used Google slides and photographs to show her students the forest floor and upper canopy to guide the learning. But being in the forest took the learning to an extraordinary level. One student told me how learning the levels of the forest, while actually being in the forest, was pretty cool.

"Outdoor learning makes the walls of the classroom disappear," says Claire. "When you're actually in the forest and feeling the forest floor, and you're looking up at the canopy and the birds up there, that experiential opportunity when all of your senses are firing; the kids just get it. And so often I hear, 'well, how do you have time to do that, to do outdoor learning or nature-based learning?' But I find you can embed many curriculum objectives quite simply and effortlessly."

Claire underscores the need to first have a full grasp of the curriculum. "Once you have that, you can figure out how to bring it to life anywhere."

Learning that sticks like burrs to your pants

One of the most beneficial aspects of learning in the park is to see the interconnectedness of life so authentically, so up close and personally, and develop an understanding of these connections.

"As we're learning about the forest floor, we're also observing flight, and the chickadees are landing on us so we're learning about aerodynamics and Bernoulli's Principle. We're seeing how lift happens, we're learning about adaptations. The learning objectives weave so naturally into this outdoor classroom," Claire says.

Claire distinguishes between the "compartmentalized" learning that often occurs within the regular school curriculum, which is broken down by subject- and time-allocations throughout the day. "You know it's science time, or language arts time. But place-based learning just flows naturally and easily. When you're looking at the deciduous and coniferous trees and they're right in front of you and you can see the differences, it's learning that sticks. I always say it sticks like the burrs on our pants!"

Learning starts out as play

"I love it when kids start to play and explore because that's when the real learning starts. They're constructing their own understanding. This space is dynamic and provides a multifaceted learning lab or playground for all learners."

This nature-based experience impacts not only children's learning but also their well-being. As Claire explains, "Students just feel confident and comfortable in nature because this welcoming space allows all students to experience wonder and success. Everyone has curiosity, everyone has an interest in exploring, and I see this confidence building in the students and it's really beautiful."

Claire describes how one student's parents expressed how much they were learning from their son. "He was going home and telling them stories about deciduous and coniferous trees and discussing moss and lichen. This student didn't say much in class, so it was awesome, that confidence and engagement when they're intrigued."

The power of story:
From the elder to the students

Claire agrees the human brain is "hard-wired" for story, and she sees how engaged her students become when listening and learning through the stories of the elders, weaving through metaphor the core values of the Blackfoot values and culture. "The children are very connected to the stories, and they draw on them to make sense of their own realities."

The students create nature journals in which they reflect upon the stories. "We're creating park signage for the park that contains those stories. Our dream is to create a trail with interactive narrative, so the students can share that knowledge with park visitors and do some virtual reality pieces as well."

Jeff, associate superintendent, is working on bringing augmented and virtual reality to the park. "There'll be QR codes on the signs to access a story from an Elder. You'll see what's happening, hear the story, and it will come to life. We're hoping it will bring people to the park, but if not, this is a virtual field trip to gain that experience."

Advice from Claire: Be the river

If you're ready to try nature or community-based learning, Claire's number-one piece of advice is, "Don't fear failure. Embrace it. I was so worried about making a mistake; I've had to really step out of my comfort zone. I set a lot of parameters. But then you have to just do it, and sometimes you learn on the spot."

Claire adds you need to be confident in the uncertainty and messiness of learning. "You're in a fluid environment and sometimes you have to 'be the river.' Just go with the flow. Every minute, everything's changing. You never know what you're going to experience so be open for it."

Video 10.6

The Carseland School Video Playlist (Various)

Learn from other student and teacher interviews on the playlist.

Key Takeaways

CHAPTER

10

▶ Nature-based learning and incorporating nature into the school setting may increase the health and well-being of the people in your schools as well as improve student test scores.

▶ Learning cultures need to be microcosms of awesomeness.

▶ Students, teachers, and the community need to be co-investors of knowledge, as highlighted in the partnership that resulted in the Mud Lake Symphony.

Reflective Questions

1. How do you incorporate nature into your learning?

2. What are you doing to bring the inside out and the outside in, to enrich the learning experiences and make them authentic?

3. How can you create projects with partnerships, like the Mud Lake Symphony?

4. Who are the elders in your community? How does your organization draw upon their knowledge?

Try This!

Nature-Based Lesson Plans to Try in the Classroom

Nature can be the basis for every subject imaginable, including history, geography, art, literature, math, social studies, civics, problem-solving, outdoor education, and science, as well as for integrating subjects. It's possible to design your entire curriculum around and within the natural world.

Outdoors, students experience an imaginative, colorful, ever-changing milieu that stimulates all of their senses. It's a joy that doesn't come with instructions, enabling kids to make sense of the natural world on their own terms and engage in more creative and innovative thinking and play.

As a school leader or teacher, you'll also never run out of fascinating material. The natural world is estimated to contain 8.7 million species of living things, of which scientists have documented only about 1.3 million, or 15 percent (California Academy of Sciences, 2011). From the peacock and the platypus to the praying mantis and the pygmy python, nature beckons to curious minds.

Helping students develop a love for nature is also the first step in creating a lifelong respect for our environment. "Take only pictures and memories and leave nothing behind" is a great first lesson to learn.

Here are three lesson plans that can be adapted for various age groups, followed by a bounty of activity and project ideas.

Grade 1 Math

Curriculum outcome: *Apply developing reasoning skills (e.g., pattern recognition, classification) to make and investigate conjectures (e.g., through discussion with others).*

What's in a Leaf?

Create a template with eight to ten different kinds of leaves. Invite students to examine the different shapes, sizes, and patterns of the leaves, and in a group discussion, list how they're similar and different. Students will learn a lot more from collecting leaves and studying patterns than from filling out a worksheet!

Then head to a forest or treed area where students can participate in the Annual Autumn Leaf Hunt, where they can search to find at least one example of each leaf on their template. The students can measure and count the leaves and make any number of charts or graphs comparing which leaves are bigger, smaller, or more numerous. Add in a school district-wide competition for the biggest and smallest leaf of each type, and young students will enjoy seeing how these records track leaf sizes over the years.

To encourage cultures of belonging, a discussion can explore how leaves are a lot like people: some things are different; some things are the same; some things are common, and some things are rare; and all have an important role to play. But avoid the poison ivy and poison oak!

Grade 5 History

Curriculum outcome: *Understand and relate major historical events over the last century and their impact on today.*

The Tree's Story

Students can count the rings on tree stumps to see how old a tree was before it was cut down. They can then explore a tree's "biography" by researching the major events that occurred during its life span. The following provides an illustrative example.

A 151-year-old tree

When this tree first began to grow . . .

- The population of our city was less than 500 people.

- No planes flew overhead, no cars drove by, no light bulbs shone, no telephones rang, no tractors farmed the land. None of these had been invented.

(Continued)

(Continued)

- Albert Einstein has not been born yet.

- Louis Pasteur had not figured out how antibiotics worked.

- No one wore zippers on their clothes.

- This tree celebrated its 40th birthday during the Chicago World Fair, its 60th just before the 1918 World Flu Pandemic, its 70th during the Roaring 20s, and its 80th during the Great Depression. It lived through World War II, the coming of TV, and the first man on the moon.

- When this tree celebrated its 120th birthday, the average income per year was $12,900.

- This tree saw the end of disco and the rise of computers and the internet, and the fall of the Berlin Wall.

Plant a tree for the future. Your class can also plant a tree and make predictions for what will happen in the world as the tree grows older and older. Put the predictions in a time capsule to be opened in twenty-five years by future students.

Grade 10 Civics

Curriculum outcome: *Students must analyze a current public issue that involves conflicting beliefs and values, describing and evaluating conflicting positions.*

Learn About Forest Conservation. Discuss the various stakeholders surrounding the development of a forest. In a class discussion, students list what they believe the values and motivating factors are for each of the various groups. Students are then broken into small teams and, drawing from a hat, are assigned to "become" one of the various stakeholders. They must research and develop a solution that tries to satisfy not just their requirements but the requirements of each stakeholder. This collaborative approach will encourage students to work toward innovative, empathetic solutions, taking a strength-based approach to problem-solving.

The Possibilities Are Endless . . . .

Take a Nature Hike or Walk. Whether in the country or the city, there's always nature to be found. Encourage students to intentionally observe the nature they see, hear, and smell and document it. Get up close and personal and notice all the little characteristics of the plants, bugs, worms, birds, rocks, wood, whatever you find! From art to math, this easy and affordable first step can evolve into infinite learning activities. Don't rush into a lesson though—let your kids relax and destress in the natural surroundings first. Find a "sit-spot" and encourage them to quietly breathe it all in.

Make a Nature Documentary. While on your hike(s), why not make a nature documentary of all that you discover and learn?

Annual Bioblitz. During a bioblitz, you measure the biodiversity of an area by documenting and counting every species you find in a given time period. A great place to start is by identifying the trees, plants, animals, and insects in your own schoolyard. See how many you can find and keep track year over year.

Urban Forests. Invite the manager of your city's urban forest to speak to your class. They may even be able to take your class on a walking tour to see the trees.

Feathered Friends. Birds are everywhere! Discover why birding is the fastest growing, most addictive outdoor hobby in the world. Before going, learn about the food sources, migration, and nesting habits of your local birds. See how many you can spot and identify.

City Mouse/Country Mouse. Many mammals have adapted to life in the city, including raccoons, skunks, rabbits and even coyotes. Contact your local government to see if they have any materials on the animals in your town and how these animals and humans can co-exist.

Orienteering and Survival Training. Students can learn self-confidence and resilience by knowing how to use a map and compass to navigate through any terrain, and what to do if they ever got lost in the wilderness.

Spiritual Celebrations. Find out if there are First Nations-led ceremonies honoring nature that you can participate in or guest speakers in your region.

Weird and Wonderful Wombats, Etcetera. Wombats have cube-shaped poop. An octopus has nine brains. Emus can't walk backward. Explore the many strange animals of the world and their cool factors. Even though they're very different, they all play a role in the ecosystem.

Animals in the Classroom. Contact your local wildlife rescue center to see if they do classroom visits.

Rock On. Ask each student to bring in a rock or two or find rocks in your school yard. Identify each one and find out its approximate age. How many different kinds did you find? What are rocks used for?

Bug and Slugs. Once you've done Rock On, what are the creepy-crawlies you find *under* a rock? Get up close and personal with some downright amazing bugs and slugs.

Frogs and Bogs. Get an up close look at just what goes on beneath the surface of the swamp and learn how your everyday actions can make—or break—a better life for our gilled and web-footed friends.

(Continued)

(Continued)

The Global Seed Vault. Talk to your students about the Global Seed Vault, located deep inside a mountain on a remote island halfway between Norway and the North Pole. It contains one million samples of different seeds from all over the world. Start your own classroom seed collection. Ask students to bring in seeds from the vegetables and fruits they eat at home or from flowers, and learn how to store them for later planting.

Grow Veggies, Herbs, and Flowers. Use your saved seeds from the Global Seed Vault activity to plant a school garden, or recycle empty cans, water bottles, or milk jugs to use as plant pots in a sunny window. Once you have a harvest (herbs grow quickly, even inside), find some recipes to use them or create your own!

Go Geocaching. Geocaching is called the world's largest treasure hunt. Look online for sites around your community. You can also create your own geocaches on school grounds for other classes to find. See geocaching.com/play.

Picture This. Invite a local photography store to come in and provide tips on how to get the best shots of animals, plants, and birds. Practice taking your own photos, research and write captions about what's in the photo, and create a gallery in the hallway for other students to enjoy.

Other Ideas:

- Create a teachers' database of online lesson plans for all subjects, specific to your local environment and habitats.

- Team up with other teachers and schools to create a resource document of online lesson plans and more, to bring environmental education to each discipline.

- Regular exposure to nature can actually help increase students' test scores. Try pairing older students with younger ones for some in-forest tutoring sessions.

- Consider working in partnership with school boards, private schools, homeschoolers, and other educational groups and outdoor education centers to enhance their online and on-site programs, including field trips and guest speakers.

CHAPTER 11

HOW TO BUILD A STRONG COMMUNITY

ODYSSEY'S NORTH STAR

"Ultimately, each individual has different gifts within them and if we can create the right atmosphere, if we can nourish them in the right way, then we can see them really grow into their full potential."

—Scott Martin

This chapter explores a story of three people who will move you, inspire you, and show you how strength-based thinking and cultures of belonging can enable people, working together, to achieve the extraordinary.

The first person is **Scott Martin**. After teaching for twenty years in inner-city, suburban, private, and tuition-driven institutions, he saw too many great kids "chewed up" by the overarching structure of the traditional-education system. So in 2015, Scott took a risk and opened the doors to the Odyssey Leadership Academy (OLA), in downtown Oklahoma City.

The second person is sixteen-year-old **James Golston**. At the age of nine, James's aspiration, like many boys in his neighborhood at the time, was to become a gang member. It wasn't because he was naïve about what that would entail. Even at that young age, he knew that if he joined a gang, he would likely be dead by the age of eighteen—and he was okay with that.

And the third person is **Tonya Golston**, James's mom, who was determined not to lose her son to a gang. "As a Mama, you pray. [His father and I] had divorced, and James was striving for attention, good or bad. It's hard to see your child going down a path that you know is not going to bring them any good and just trying to figure out how can you stop something before it gets worse." As a single parent of two, Tonya found there were important things James needed to help him turn around and bring out his seeds of brilliance.

Scott's Story: The Formation of Healthy Human Beings

In creating the vision for the Odyssey Leadership Academy, Scott Martin made "human flourishing" the primary goal, rather than the more traditional objective of getting the highest grades possible as a means to college admission and job preparedness.

In fact, Scott threw out grades altogether, which meant no grade transcripts for college applications. The website for the Odyssey Leadership Academy quotes Scott affirming his goals:

> *"I am convinced that what we offer colleges and universities are students who are well-versed in thinking deeply, engaging critically, working collaboratively, expressing creatively, exploring curiously, and leading from a place of service; but we are just as proud of the fact that we offer communities leaders who are walking out the virtues of humility, openmindedness, gratitude, civic responsibility, attentiveness, compassion, and wisdom"* (Odyssey Learning Academy, 2021).

This was the school that James Golson and his mother Tonya would eventually choose for him.

In the higher echelons of educational institutions around the world, I can almost hear the blood pressure cuffs being pulled out of the desk drawers, the Velcro sleeves wrapping the arms snuggly, as the idea of such uncertainty pushes hypertension to new heights. And they have my sympathy. In our Age of Complexity, where tests and grade-point averages are the gold standard control for college-admission decision-making, how can we possibly rank and measure such seemingly intangible characteristics as creativity, curiosity, and deep thinking?

I'd like to assure them that they can put the blood-pressure cuffs away. The student outcomes at Odyssey fly in the face of conventional thinking:

- 100 percent of Odyssey graduates who apply to college are accepted to their top college of choice.

- Odyssey graduates have received President's, Dean's, Regent's, Trustee's, Chancellor's, Honor's College, and Academic Excellence scholarships from their universities of choice, averaging $80,000 per college-bound graduate.

- Odyssey graduates go on to major in mechanical engineering, psychiatry, cognitive science, business, marketing, architectural engineering, history, creative writing, videography, philosophy, and more.

"We made a commitment that we'll never brand a student with a number or letter grade," Scott says, "because as research shows, striving for numbers and letters creates stress and anxiety that leads to depression, angst, and self-harm. We're committed to reimagining the very fabric of what education can and should be."

Stop building the schools that are failing our students

The main reason Scott embedded human flourishing as the school's vision was the growing amount of empirical data related to teenage stress, anxiety, depression, sadness, loneliness, and self-harm—and his belief that the traditional model of schooling plays a role in these alarming statistics:

- Cigna U.S. Loneliness Index shows that young adults are now the loneliest generation of Americans, more disconnected and isolated than elderly people.

- A National Health Service (NHS) study shows "a shocking rise" over the last ten years for children and young people for self-harm, including poisoning, cutting, or hanging themselves.

- Admissions of patients aged five to seventeen for suicidal thoughts and actions more than doubled from 2008 to 2015.

The group at highest risk for suicide are white males between fourteen and twenty-one.

This increasingly dire situation made the formation of healthy human beings Scott's top priority. He wanted to create an environment—an ecosystem—where each and every student is known, valued, and cherished for exactly who they are. His ideal is not just to prepare them for the real world but to help them shape a better world for everyone, and to inform not only the mind but the heart. The school has vowed to promote joy, creativity, discovery, and voice while celebrating students' learning, not ranking it.

"By getting to know each student individually, we're able to monitor their progress relationally rather than numerically," he says.

Prioritize teacher-student relationships

Scott is a strong believer in the power of mentorship.

"If the goal is human and communal flourishing, then we need to ask ourselves, what does it take to help raise a flourishing child, who in turn wants to help shape flourishing communities? What has to be in the soil for that?

"For us, mentoring is a big part of that soil. Everything we do revolves around mentoring. It's offering a curriculum that's engaging and explores deep questions. It's offering opportunity for passion and purpose and play and creativity. There's a deep sense of community."

Odyssey even uses a different vocabulary, in which teachers are called mentors and the surrounding district is called the community. The goal is to foster deep, covenantal, mentoring relationships between teacher and students and between students and students in a safe, caring environment.

"Ultimately, each individual child has different gifts within them, and if we can create the right atmosphere, if we can nourish them in the right

> *"The pressing issues of our times demand individuals possessing the skills, desire, and courage to bring light to dark places."*
> *—Scott Martin*

way, then we can see them really grow into their full potential. The pressing issues of our times demand individuals possessing the skills, desire, and courage to bring light to dark places."

I asked Scott why he had founded Odyssey.

"I've been in education for about 25 years, and I've worked at all kinds of schools: inner city schools, large public schools; private schools; and major research universities. Early on I saw a lot of poverty, a lot of gang influence, a lot of drug and alcohol abuse. Fatherlessness. Acting out. At the time I attributed it to socioeconomics and thought if we could just pump more money into these schools, these neighborhoods, these families, we would be able to solve that.

"Fast forward a decade or so and I ended up at a private day school and the tuition is about $25,000 a year. These students want for nothing.

The classrooms have all the bells and whistles, we've got smart boards, we've got laptops, everything brand new. The parking lot looked like a scene out of *Casino Royale* (2006); it was just incredible, the money that was there.

"So the money problem was solved, but what I saw in the lives of students was still high stress, high anxiety, depression, cutting, eating disorders, fatherlessness. I saw the same woe, a lot of brokenness. I realized this isn't just a money problem. To borrow from the seeds of brilliance analogy, there was something deeper going on in the soil. An acorn has within it the potential to become an oak tree, but only if you have the right nutrients, water, and sunlight, and I just didn't believe traditional schooling had that."

By traditional schooling, Scott is clear he isn't speaking about public versus private, faith-based, or homeschooling. "If they teach in certain ways, not cultivating the soil necessary to foster human flourishing, then it's a traditional model," he says.

Make human flourishing your North Star

Scott believes the aim of the traditional model is college and career readiness. "I'm not asking students to be homeless and unemployed, but I don't think that's a full-enough vision of education. If schooling means desks in rows and tests and grades and a lot of rote memorization and regurgitation, then we're going to lose a lot of people and a lot of innovation. This in turn breeds stress, anxiety, depression, and more.

"I believe human flourishing is essential at any level, but especially during those formative years of childhood through adolescence. If we make human flourishing our North Star, we must back all the way out and reorient our North Star."

Change the story

"To me, the story we tell students goes something like this:"

Student: "Why does this matter?"

Teacher: "Well, it matters because it's going to be on the test."

Student: "Why does the test matter?"

Teacher: "It matters because you want to get a good grade."

Student: "Why does the grade matter?"

Teacher: "Well, because you want to go to college and get a degree."

Student: "But why do I want to go to college and get a degree?"

Teacher: "Well, so you can get a job to make money to buy stuff."

"And so, the moral of the story is that the highest goal for humans is consumption. Not creativity, not wonder, certainly not flourishing.

"I thought that was a self-defeating story, so I began a new story, one where the North Star is human flourishing. What needs to be taken out of the soil and what needs to be put in for that? And I realized that what needs to be deeply embedded, nonnegotiable, is our deep-rooted relationships [in] a highly accountable community.

"The way schooling is set up now, with 45-minute classes, kids are running all over the building and it's a frenetic pace. They go home with hours of homework, most of which doesn't connect to anything of any meaning or value to them.

"What really gets missed in these fast-paced days is the idea of the Elder in a student's life. If you go back historically, whether we call them elders or rabbis or whatever, we've always had this culture of elders who get the youth to flourish. It takes a long time, a lot of exposure to the exemplars in the community, the grandmothers and the grandfathers. But traditional schooling followed the Industrial Revolution model instead."

Cultivate scholars

"I wanted to reimagine curriculum, reimagine the ways in which we engage, and reimagine the role of teacher. So I quit my teaching position in 2013 and spent two years dreaming up this education system whose North Star is human flourishing.

"We do things differently here. We sit in circles so everyone can see eye to eye. When you're sitting in a circle, it's that old campfire feeling; something magical happens. There's an alchemy there.

"Instead of grades, we do a narrative transcript that allows us to talk about the student as a human being, talk about their intellectual development as well as their moral development. Our narratives are a full page or so for each of the student's classes.

"We'll talk about the books they've read, the projects they've done, the ways they've collaborated, the growth they've experienced and things like intellectual humility and creativity. Let's say a student does a spoken word for the first time. We'll talk about the moral courage it took to go outside of their comfort zone. And we've found colleges eat that up: they love the narratives as it gives them so much more.

"We've created a model where students can do really beautiful, deep scholarly work. I believe a student just consumes information and regurgitates it back, but a scholar creates learning—they contribute something new to the field. It is creativity, collaboration and new research being done."

Require students to be active citizens in community life

"We try to blur the lines between school and city, as school should be an integral and vital part of the rhythm of the city. That's why we're located downtown, so we can interact with some really phenomenal people. We've taken our design lab students over to Sonic's world headquarters, our STEM students to Devon Energy, we've used university science labs, and gone to the aquarium. And we've had our mayor come in to talk to us, as well as our district attorney, politicians from both sides, psychologists and psychiatrists, authors, university professors, local business owners, platinum-winning musicians. In a given class, 30 to 40 percent of the time is spent engaging with the community in some way.

"We also have dedicated time every Monday afternoon for service leadership. The students serve in the community such as [at] an animal rescue farm, helping to plant a food garden for the local elementary school, infant crisis care center, day shelter, or homeless alliance. We really try to be a school without walls, communal internally and externally.

"But so much is dependent on leadership. If a leader doesn't want to leave the status quo because their school has good grades and kids getting into college, it becomes really difficult at the individual class-room level to see systemic change. I would love to establish an Odyssey leaders' academy to help school leaders create culture and move towards this."

Offer a curriculum that's compelling, rigorous, and relevant

"We teach courses that matter," says Scott. "We don't do boxed curriculum, we create every course from the ground up, so we have classes like marine biology, Harry Potter, and ancient world philosophy."

For those who get a little nervous about such transformation in this Age of Complexity and worry that this focus on joy and celebrating and human flourishing might detract from a strong and rigorous curriculum, fear not. The Odyssey leadership are strong supporters of neuro-cognitive research showing the impact that more engaged, robust curriculum has on the formation of healthy brains. The curriculum doesn't just teach students *about* math, it invites them to *become* mathematicians, or artists, authors, scientists, astronomers, chemists, historians, linguists, and scholars in their own right, through a course of inquiry.

If you read the Odyssey Leadership Academy website, you'll see that over the course of an academic career at Odyssey, a student might

- investigate the idea of dark matter and the physics of quantum mechanics in *Math: Quest for Wonder* (Mathematics),

- present on the work United Nations Children's Fund (UNICEF) is doing around the world to defend and empower children in *Peacebuilding and Holistic Communities* (Social Studies),

(Continued)

(Continued)

- explore the environmental impact of oil and gas pipelines on natural ecosystems in *Perspectives on Energy* (Science),

- teach others about Carol Dweck's concept of growth mindset in *Neuroscience and the Mind* (Science),

- use geometry skills to help build a tiny house in *Math Class as Soul Craft* (Geometry),

- give a speech as Malcolm X while studying his response to the Jim Crow South in *Leaders of the Past and Present* (Social Studies),

- research thermodynamics and ecosystem population density in *Nature's Folklore* (Science/English),

- investigate the impact fatherlessness plays in incarceration in *Justice by Math* (Statistics),

- compose an original piece of music in a recording studio with a platinum record singer/songwriter (Music),

- create an original model of a Tesla coil designed to power an electric light bulb (Science),

- interview the local district attorney for a speech on Adverse Childhood Experiences (Debate).

Why colleges and universities want Odyssey kids

Scott says that without grades, students can work without pressure, undertaking serious academic work and ambitious projects that are driven by passion and curiosity rather than by fear and stress.

But what do you send with college applications, then, if not a transcript of grades? OLA creates full narrative assessments, a practice that other public and private schools within the Mastery Transcript Consortium are using to better reflect the unique strengths, interests, and abilities of each student.

"When colleges see the courses we're offering, when they see the conversations students are engaged in, when they see the work, what our students are reading, our narrative transcripts tell that story. So it's not a girl got a grade of 84, it's the girl who explored neurological impacts on the brain and how that influenced the cognitive thinking of Hitler's death squad in Nazi Germany. It's students who are doing really beautiful research on marine ecosystems; it's students who are looking at literary alchemy and Harry Potter.

"Odyssey itself is a university in the best and deepest ways. Kids in sixth through twelfth grade are already doing deep scholarship and original work," says Scott. "When our kids apply to colleges we send out the narrative transcript, but we also send out examples of their work. So they see this student who wrote about incarcerated juveniles and she interviewed the District Attorney and the head of a female correction facility and she has 15 original sources of work. Plus, they're good human beings, with service leadership in the community working at a senior citizen's home or an animal rescue or our local shelter. We weave all of that into the rhythm of Odyssey so they have a beautiful story to tell."

James's Story: A Community of Belonging

Now I'd like to share the story of James Golston Jr., a student at Odyssey Leadership Academy. I was introduced to James when Scott sent me a tweet with a YouTube link, inviting me to watch James perform his spoken-word artwork.

Jane and I were so captivated by the creativity of this young man that we immediately decided we had to speak with James. I called Scott and he helped arrange an introduction for us.

At the start of our Zoom session, I told James how Jane and I both, at our core, believe the current structure and manifestation of the traditional education system is upside down and damages a lot of young people because it doesn't recognize the brilliance they have within. We told him how we believe that rather than try to teach people to be creative, we need to change our environments so their seeds of brilliance will shine through. And that we were really interested in the student voice, which is why we wanted his insight.

James began, "I grew up in Oklahoma City in an area with a lot of poverty and gang violence. When I was nine, I was going to a charter school in the neighborhood, with kids whose relatives were gang members or they themselves were. And so, surrounded by that environment, getting into that gang life was my highest ideal. I saw a lot of benefits to it, so as a child I wouldn't have minded risking my life for it. Dying at 18 was something that was just so common and so in my mindset, that I thought I could become a gang member, be great at it, and if I die at 18, then I die at 18.

"Following a mindset like that does come with a heavy weight of depression. As a young male, I don't know how it is now because I'm not that age anymore, but there is this thing against any type of emotion, so you have repressed emotions. You do have depression even if you don't realize it, or some deep sense of lack of belonging, I guess."

"My value of life shifted my paradigm. My mom had been struggling, trying to get me out of this life, because she didn't want to lose me to a gang. And it's very hard to get a child out of that mindset once they're engrossed in the environment."

Scared Straight

"She got to the point where she brought me to a juvenile detention center, like in the TV show, *Scared Straight*. I don't know the guard's name who talked to me and I wish I did because I would love to tell him thank you. He just scared the life out of me. He brought fear into my heart that I didn't know was possible. And I hadn't even stepped into the facility! But he was straight up with me and very direct—blunt—about what would happen to me.

"I didn't immediately switch my behavior necessarily, but it did set me on a path to get out of that mindset. I also ended up switching to online school, to walk away from some of the bad influences that were around me at the charter school. We also moved to Midwest City, in Oklahoma, and during that period I got involved with sports. I kind of started to build a confidence into who I was through that.

"Eventually, though, I switched from sports to academics, once I was introduced to the idea that you could read books and it didn't cost money! It was this huge expansion into what I could do that I didn't know was possible."

James's advice for young boys tempted by gang life

"One, let them know they can do anything. Two, put them in front of a lot of different things, whether it's arts, athletics, give them access to the things they don't have access to. I got access to football and academics just out of opportunity. You don't know those resources exist even if you're able to technically access them, so give them the opportunity to see the possibilities."

Build a culture of belonging

James attended the online school for seven years. Eventually, he began to explore other schools. James says a school that had tried to recruit him for his athletic ability positioned their academic offering as, "You will be able to get into college with us, and get out of the situation you're in." That didn't appeal to James. But when he came across Odyssey in an online ad, he was attracted to its culture of belonging.

"Odyssey's marketing point wasn't necessarily academics, though they thrive heavily on that and it's really challenging," James explains. "The thing they focused on is community. My first day was the most welcomed I had ever felt in a school setting. So what pushed me to attend was that they valued something different from any other school in the city, and that was community."

James made arrangements to go on a "shadow" at Odyssey. "It takes you through the experience. It puts you in the classes. You talk with the students and teachers, and you just have fun. Towards the end you talk about how you felt and what are your concerns; and they talk about what they're looking for, what they see in you, things of that nature."

Notice and build on students' unique strengths

The culture of belonging, along with recognizing and encouraging his seeds of brilliance and taking a strength-based approach, continued to cultivate a love of learning in James.

"I would have never gotten into any type of public speaking if it wasn't for my teacher, Sean Beckett. It was in his brain sciences class that he pushed me to do a spoken word. And the next semester he said, 'James, you have to do spoken word, get into it.' He showed me all these different artists and I just fell in love with it. And as he saw that I began to get more interested he kept pushing. It just made it a fun experience to where I wanted to pursue it."

James gives a glimpse of what it's like to be a high school student inside Odyssey. "This is my third year, which is crazy to think of looking back. Every year at Odyssey, there's a trip to the Colorado Mountains to bond. You can't have any technology on the trips, so the new students can incorporate themselves into the community."

Having come from online school, James wasn't as used to interacting with other kids. "One thing that helped was my first mentor, Mr. Curro. He was very, very adamant about getting me into the community and just making me feel welcomed in general. He was someone I could always talk to. That was my first class, called *Science of Learning and Memory*, or SLAM. It helped tremendously in me wanting to stay at Odyssey and not being drowned by the fear of being vulnerable."

I was touched by James's words, and as an aside, I would like to say to all teachers and employers to forever be aware of who in your class or organization is feeling drowned by the fear of being vulnerable. Ensuring focus on the three imperatives and four conditions to create healthy environments will help significantly in shaping your culture so this is less likely to happen.

James continued: "Mr. Curro was that pusher to put me into situations where I had to interact with people and build relationships; and then my first trip with Odyssey was Virginia (I missed the first Colorado trip), where we stayed in this little camp far away from civilization. We had about 12 people in my cabin, and so that experience alone, having to room with 12 people I didn't know very well, made it inevitable I would build some sort of relationship.

"On one of the last days there, there were four tornadoes in the area. We're from Oklahoma, which is 'Nado Alley, so we weren't freaking out, but the administration was going crazy because our safety is paramount. We were just having fun; it was one of the best bonding experiences I've ever had because we're making jokes in the fear of danger . . . which may or may not be a good thing . . . but I did build a brotherhood with the people that were in that cabin. After that trip I not only had a foundation with the mentors I was close to, but I could also begin to interact with students and build a foundation with them. And that kind of continued throughout the entirety of my sophomore year."

> *I'd like to point out here just how important this story is, because James was somewhat of an introvert at that time and didn't have a lot of experience interacting with peers. For his mentors to get to know James, to become aware of this characteristic, and to set up situations in which he could succeed, is something very rare and wonderful indeed.*

"My first year at Odyssey was the first time I had ever really interacted or engaged with friends outside of school, because I was very reclusive and had been in online school for seven years. I just didn't have people that I could hang out with. So the trip to Virginia was definitely a fun experience to learn more about people."

Provide opportunities for deep conversations

"I was able to have a lot of deep conversations and I learned to interweave between deep conversations and fun conversations, and learning that balance within the same breath, which I think is a really important thing for me. During that time there were five major deaths in my family, people who were close to me, and three passed within the span of one month. One thing I always looked forward to was Odyssey because it was kind of my safe place.

"One thing I'm happy about with Odyssey is that while there are going to be cliques wherever you go, they're not as exclusive as other schools might be. During the trips and really that first year in general, I was able to learn how to maneuver through different groups and just to build a relationship overall with people and not get stuck in that clique mindset.

"By the second trip, I was able to be friends with a wide variety of people, I had a larger network of close friends I could rely on and my relationships with the mentors had begun to get deeper and deeper."

Create a comfortable place
where kids can be vulnerable

"In my first class, they were talking about concepts I didn't understand. There was this big pressure on my chest; how can I write a 10-page essay? I've never written a paper before!

"But it was the welcoming environment. I never really spoke up in class. The teacher always came to me to begin with, and we would just have a one-on-one conversation with no judgment. Eyes weren't staring at me; I wasn't stopping the flow of class."

Demonstrate caring

"So long story short, if a teacher cares about you and makes you more comfortable, you'll be able to express yourself.

"I've found at every level there's this push that if you don't understand something to speak up in class and that's something I'm still not comfortable doing. I'm more of an observer. If I really want to speak about something in class I will, but nine times out of ten I'll just come to you directly. Because even if they say, 'There are no stupid questions,' it's still a pressure on you so it's a lot easier to have a one-on-one conversation."

James's ideal learning culture

I asked James my standard question, of what he'd change about our education system, to bring out the brilliance in everybody. His very thoughtful answer moved us.

"That's a hard question. I've had those conversations with my grandparents to bridge off of their experiences and try to understand, because I also understand I'm very ignorant about the world; there's a lot of things I don't know or simply don't have enough experience to be at the level to explain.

"One of the conversations I had, and it was specifically a question, was why are a lot of the views people have, whether you view it as right or wrong, so streamlined, so straightforward to them or seemingly narrow-minded in a way. And so, I don't know if you can necessarily place rules around (a new education system) and I'm not sure if I can answer that question per se because it's a very hard topic."

James did offer Jane and I a few very thought-provoking ideas, however.

"The first would be to change the dynamic between student and teacher, the idea that the teacher is the one source of all knowledge, and the person who absorbs all that knowledge is the student. There's an inherent structure and distinction between student and teacher.

"At Odyssey, I've gone out for coffee with one of my teachers and just talked about the things I wanted to go into, whether it was research about pedagogy within the Bible or an independent study. That change in dynamic is very important to me, especially with me doing spoken word. I would not have taken that suggestion as seriously if my mentor hadn't already built a relationship with me during that class.

"The second thing would be creative freedom, and recognizing people learn differently. While I was able to learn and explore different things in my online school, it wasn't until I got to Odyssey and had the ability to learn visually and really connect with what I was doing that I was able to absorb the information I was getting. I would make freedom of learning styles more accessible in that structure.

"But the thing that helped me the most is just being able to reach out and talk to the mentors. Usually after we had gone over what I originally set up the meeting for, which is 'rabbit hole into life,' it felt like I was still at school (during the quarantine) because they were also struggling from a teacher's perspective."

The ability to reach out to others is a recurring theme for James, as it is with so many of the people we talk to, students and teachers alike. If we really want to engage our youngsters and team members, it seems a simple way to do so.

Still, recognizing that this could be a controversial topic, James continued. "One of the simplest ways to start this—and this would have to be further explored or explained—would just be having a conversation.

"At the beginning of the [Black Lives Matter] BLM situation in the United States, with kind of the extremist views on both sides and just the inherent arguments that happened, I reached out to a couple of people.

"One was a person who went to my old school, in response to her social media post of a Bible quote, regarding a riot that had happened, and we ended up having a conversation. I asked her thoughts, and she brought up compassion, things of that nature, and I understood those as well. I'm Baptist, I do believe in God and Jesus. And so one thing I learned was because of her world view, we didn't have the same footing as far as what our inherent opinions of the situation were.

"I do think her worldview was quite progressive. Her mom was a pastor and her church sought to prepare children for the world, how to encounter the world, how to live in the world, how to bring compassion and joy to the world. However, the world view that their specific congregation never really focused on was the one that impacts me. And so her opinion on the situation, what she saw as primarily riots, she viewed it as bad, as something that shouldn't have been happening or this overreaction. And if I would have let my initial response to what she said come out, that conversation would have ended there, and it would have been a misunderstanding.

"So we each eventually reached a somewhat agree to disagree, but also an understanding at the very least, so that's kind of how that situation stands out."

As we described in *The Uncomfortable Chapter*, as people try to grapple with today's complexity, the easiest path to control when someone disagrees with us is to stop talking to them, unfriend them and block them, rather than have the tough conversations. So Jane and I were immensely inspired by how James and his friend gave us adults such a good example to follow.

If we want children to be able to deal with difficult times, to be resilient, to collaborate so we can solve our world problems and differences, it has to start with the teachers and the parents and other adults to set a good example of how to do that. We're going to have more and more conflicts in the world, and we need to learn how to see another person's point of view, how to work together to come up with better solutions. If we can do that, we'll be giving them the gift of the innovation necessary to move forward.

> *If we want children to be able to deal with difficult times, to be resilient, to collaborate so we can solve our world problems and differences, it has to start with the teachers and the parents and other adults to set a good example of how to do that.*

Video 11.1

James: Life Experiences and Odyssey

Hear James tell his fascinating story in his own words. You'll be moved and amazed by the insights of this articulate young man.

Tonya's Story: We Really Do Need a Village

While talking with James, it became clear that his mother has been a foundational influence on his life, and that he is incredibly proud of her—he made sure to mention that she will also soon graduate with a diploma in business!

We wanted to learn the insight of this incredible woman who has raised such an articulate, bright, and thoughtful son (and daughter!), so we made arrangements to speak with her and hear her story and her ideas.

Tonya began her story with the day she took James to the juvenile detention center. "When I went up to the door, one of the officers was just coming into work and I said, 'my child is acting up, I don't want to see him dead or in jail. Can you help me?'"

"He said, 'Bring him on up here.' So I went back to my car, I got James and I said, 'You listen to this.' And the officer told James, 'Hey, if you guys come back here, it's going to be a problem,' and he scared the mess out of him."

One of the insights Tonya shared with us is that we really do need cultures of belonging, not only in schools but everywhere. For Tonya, part of this "village" involved her extended family.

"I don't know how to raise a man, so it's hard. I'm blessed to have a stepfather who stepped up and it has literally taken a village to make sure that James has everything he needs to prepare him for life.

"My stepdad has been amazing. He's been in our life since I was pregnant with my daughter, so almost 22 years. When James was acting out, he stepped in. He went to the school, he got onto him when he needed it. I also have three amazing cousins who have stepped in if he needs somebody to talk to, somebody to hang with. And I have pastors of a church we went to. I was blessed to get James into Big Brothers Big Sisters, and he had an excellent Big Brother who introduced him to college, who gave him what he needed to even be interested in college, because that wasn't something that was on James's mind at that point.

"It has literally taken a village and everybody who God has placed in our lives has played a specific role."

Believing in Myself—The Essential Role of Mentors

James also talked about the importance of relationships in giving him a more optimistic perspective for his future. "The influences that I had was a reset, and it played a very important role in influencing how I further developed.

"When we moved to Midwest City, I got a lot of mentors, including a detective who I had a really good relationship with. I also went to a church that my great grandfather used to preach at and got a lot of mentors that influenced me. I had always been into church—my grandmother was a great influence into that and my great-grandfather was still alive up until 2016 and a pastor for 30 years, so he played a big role in that as well.

"(People at the church) definitely built my idea of what my value was, even until this day. They never doubted anything I could do. They believed in me more than I believed in myself."

Seeing a different kind of school in Odyssey

"When James first told me about Odyssey, I didn't even know if it was the kind of school I wanted him to go to. But it was a blessing. Everything has been lined up in such a way that it's been for his good. Dr. Martin has really been amazing for James and for our whole family."

Tonya talked about what she was seeing in James at the age of nine, and what compelled her to put him into online school. "It had a lot to do with other students and him getting into fights. He was being bullied at one point and he wasn't comfortable within his own skin. I just didn't see him being happy. And living where there's a lot of gang activity, I didn't want to see my child in a gang. I didn't want to see him either dead or in prison by the time he turned 18. So I put him into online school and from there we eventually discovered Odyssey."

Teachers really get to know each student

Another insight Tonya shared with us, through a parent's perspective, is the power that comes about from a teacher really getting to know a student and cultivating that sense of belonging.

"The thing Dr. Martin did that was different was he learned who James was. James's self-confidence is amazing now. Spoken-word poetry is something he never even thought about—I never even thought about him doing that. His whole persona is just out of this world."

Jane and I fully agreed, noting how we actually thought he was a few years older due to his depth of self-reflection and his maturity.

It's not a school, it's a family

Tonya further explained, "It's a sense of belonging; it's not a school, it's a family, and that makes a huge difference. I recently had surgery, and Dr. Martin was praying for me because he's not just my son's teacher, it's family.

"That (connection between school and home) is something that has been lost in our schools. I remember my mom and my granddad talking about school and saying to me, 'You know you can't act up in school because the teacher knows your Mama and you're going to get in trouble at school and then you're going to get into trouble at home.' Nowadays that connection isn't what it used to be, but at Odyssey, you have that connection."

Can this happen in a public school?

I'm often asked, "Why include private schools as examples? Public schools don't have the budgets or resources to emulate what they can do!"

My answer is threefold. First, Jane and I agree we need to seek out the best practices wherever we can find them. They lie everywhere in our society—in our communities, in our businesses, in our school districts, in our services and more.

Second, the private schools we talk about here often have their birthplace in the public school system. They're often founded by educators who spent years in the public system before reimagining what learning could be and making those dreams a reality. By studying these examples, we see what could be changed in our own classrooms and schools.

And finally, you'll notice the most impactful initiatives in these examples cost nothing at all—things like respect, mentoring, and fostering students' curiosity. Odyssey, for example, focuses on the values of identity formation, virtue development, compassion, and the pursuit of wisdom through constructive mentoring relationships, transformative curriculum, and real-world experiences.

From these examples, we can take a strength-based approach and learn how to weave many of these best practices in our own school environments, helping our own students to thrive.

A Note to Parents Who Cultivate Brilliance

Before we close this chapter, I'd like to reach out to all of the parents who have recognized the seeds of brilliance in their children and felt disheartened when traditional school structure appeared blind to their child's value and magic. I hope this chapter has given you optimism and long-overdue validation.

We agree with Scott that this was not likely due to the teachers or the administrators at your child's school. It's the traditional school structure that encourages education systems to see kids as "a problem to be solved." It's a deficit-based approach in which we focus on the areas where a student is struggling rather than looking at the whole child and what brilliance and passion might lie within them. So if Joe is doing poorly in math, then we focus on trying to "fix" that by giving him more math to do. Because of that narrow parameter, we may never see the bigger picture that Joe is also a gifted diplomat, who's able to get his classmates to collaborate and achieve greater goals through synergy.

But a growing number of districts and schools, like Odyssey, are changing that. They're dedicating themselves and their schools to a strength-based approach, actively looking for those seeds of brilliance in each child and setting up the right environment to help them grow. That's not to say we shouldn't provide extra help for students who need it, of course, but their weaknesses can't be our sole focus. We need balance, and for students to understand that their worth and their intelligence encompass far more than what they *aren't* good at.

CHAPTER 11 — Key Takeaways

▶ Schools need to figure out their "North Star," the guiding belief on which the very purpose of the school is built. Note: "Getting grades to enter college" is a poor North Star to follow.

▶ To find and cultivate a student's seed of brilliance, you must take the time to get to know them deeply. As a school leader, you must ensure teachers are encouraged to take this time.

▶ Students thrive in a learning environment where they are comfortable enough to allow themselves to be vulnerable.

Reflective Questions

1. What's your North Star?

2. Does your school foster a deep sense of community? How do you recognize when students or teachers are "drowning from the fear of being vulnerable," as James once was?

3. At Odyssey, students engage in volunteer work every Monday afternoon. How do your students get the opportunity to experience service leadership?

4. Extend learning out into the community, and not just within the four walls of the school building.

Try This!

Reimagine Your School

Scott shared his guiding principles for reimagining school. Use these as a guide to start reimagining what your school could be.

1. **Place a high emphasis on community**

   - Create a place where everybody knows they belong, that they're valued and valuable. That includes students, faculty, and the families.

   - Build a culture that values and celebrates each person, where the primary goal is not to get a grade, but to build deep rootedness, an emphasis on community, an ecosystem in which every person knows they're valued and cared for.

   - Provide a curriculum that fights the "silent epidemic." A longitudinal study on why students give up on school found it was because they didn't believe the curriculum mattered or that people cared about them (Bridgeland et al., 2006). Create that caring community and make time for it. Reimagine the structure of the day so students get longer time allotments with caring adults.

(Continued)

(Continued)

2. **Mentor students**

- With a caring community, see your role not as content deliverers, but as mentors. Give students hope; provide opportunity for flourishing.

- Start the day with mentoring for forty-five minutes, in small groups. Celebrate good stuff and walk-through hard stuff, so when things come up in life and parents get a divorce or mom loses her job or a friend ghosts them, they're not dealing with that on their own, they've got a caring community. Make that your top priority.

- Schools need to have a mandate to mentor kids, to care for kids in deeply abiding ways over long periods of time. Say, "We're here to tell you that you matter and to walk through life with you." You'll still have to make tough calls sometimes and students may feel you broke trust with them, but always fight for their highest good. Sometimes it will be painful.

- Create courses with students in mind and allow student input. Make the playground, then follow their interests and let them run with them.

3. **Set your North Star to human flourishing**

- This concept will shape how you communicate with each other, how to make administrative decisions, and how to chart out courses and engage families.

- Be sure to bring out your teachers' seed of brilliance too. The concept can be tangibly felt: it's a spirit that's real, and it's not just pep assemblies on Friday before the football game. It's a deep kindness and gentleness.

CHAPTER 12

THE BUT, BUT, BUT, BUT CHAPTER
EVALUATION AND ASSESSMENT

"While we're focusing so heavily on standardized testing, how many seeds of brilliance never had a chance to take root?"

—Peter Gamwell

Things Need to Change

People have claimed that the definition of insanity is to keep doing the same thing over and over again, while expecting a different result. Jane and I beg to differ. We believe insanity is doing the same thing over and over and expecting the *same* result—especially in this chaotic and unpredictable Age of Complexity.

That's because even if we keep doing something the same way, a way that perhaps has worked successfully in the past and some may believe is still working today, everyone and everything else, all around us, is changing and moving in unimaginable directions.

Technology is continuously changing. New modes of transportation are being designed. The meaning of communication has changed: before the pandemic, teens said they preferred communicating with friends by text rather than face-to-face, but during the pandemic, young adults were the hardest hit by loneliness (Walsh, 2021). Cures and treatments for age-old diseases are planting new hope where there once was none, while at the same time viruses mutate into global pandemics that turn our world upside down. Consumer tastes are changing. Even how we shop, buy, and sell changed dramatically due to COVID-19. Supply chains were broken and twisted like a tossed plate of spaghetti. Due to rising incomes and urbanization, global diets are changing, impacting the food supply. The Earth itself is changing. New species are discovered every year while others go extinct.

Dare we say that even history is changing, or at least our understanding of it.

And instances of people who report seeing UFOs have increased significantly—we won't even speculate on what that means!

Most significantly, people change. Individuals are constantly learning, growing, and changing over the course of their lifetimes—or at least they should be.

And so to keep doing the same thing over and over, while everything else is changing, is not only insanity but futile—and a sure way to become obsolete. Organizations and societies that fail to adapt to change or to innovate will eventually get left behind, fail to thrive, or even cease to exist.

So why is it, then, that our methods to assess intelligence, brilliance, creativity, and innovation, have changed so little in the last century? We still use IQ tests to pigeonhole and label students; we still focus narrowly on the two subjects of language and math, with a hierarchy of time allotments to match; we still teach to standardized tests based on those same two subjects. When it comes to evaluating learning through tests, we too often tell students what to think, how to think, and when to think, asking them to memorize facts and then spew them back at us.

I have to say that whenever I discuss these thoughts and ideas with others, I'm surprised how many people actually agree with me. But for some—and I don't blame them—they feel a distinct sense of unease. Out come the buts!

▶ *But* standardized tests give us objective results, marked by a machine without any teacher bias!

▶ *But* we need standardized tests to compare different schools and districts. Policymakers need this information to make decisions!

▶ *But* standardized tests hold districts and schools accountable for their students' academic performance!

▶ *But* we've been doing it this way for decades!

Testing Has Its Place— But We Need to Put It *in* Its Place

To be perfectly clear, we're not against assessing students on whether they can read and write and do math at a proficient level. We need an early warning system if any student is struggling or is well above the norm. The value of testing, including standardized tests, is to see which children may need more resources or help.

My problem—and I know I'm not alone with this, not by far—is the extreme focus we put on testing and grades, to the point of teaching to standardized tests and putting language and maths above all else.

If your urge upon hearing this is to hug standardized tests all the closer to your chest, here are a few things I'd like you to think about:

▶ Was Helen Keller's seed of brilliance her ability to learn despite being blind and deaf? Or was it how she was able to inspire millions of people to persevere despite all odds, to have joy and purpose in life wherever we can find it or craft it? I'll tell you one thing: When Helen was spelling out words onto the hand of her teacher, Anne Sullivan, nobody cared what her test results were, where Helen would have ranked on standardized tests, or whether Anne even tested Helen at all. Nevertheless, inspired by her learning, Helen went on to earn a Bachelor of Arts degree from Radcliffe (the first deafblind person to do so), write fourteen books, present hundreds of speeches on a wide variety of topics, travel to thirty-nine countries, and campaign for several causes, including world peace (Perkins School for the Blind, 2021).

▶ Jon Snow, one of the most successful TV journalists in the United Kingdom, got a C in English (Dodgson, 2017).

▶ Steven Spielberg was rejected from film school (Dodgson, 2017).

▶ Michael Jordan was cut from his high school basketball team (Dodgson, 2017).

▶ Stephen McCormick, who uses math to better understand the universe, almost failed the subject in high school (Bezzina, 2016).

And then, there are the stories of so many of the young people we've had the pleasure and honor of introducing in this book—students whose seeds of brilliance were nurtured and who have spread light and good things within their spheres of influence and beyond.

These individuals, famous or not, were able to find their seeds of brilliance despite the low expectations some had for them. Thanks to that, the world has been made a better place through their gifts.

There Are Too Many Holes in Our Net

But what about all of those students who slipped past the narrow focus of our net? What of the students who gave up after being cut from the team, who stopped writing or who hated math after getting discouraging grades, whose passion fell outside those subjects we place at the top of the hierarchy? While we're focusing so heavily on standardized testing, how many seeds of brilliance never had a chance to take root?

I'm convinced that for every student who made it out the other side, there are several young adults walking around who have little to no idea what they're good at, what they're passionate about, or even what would make them happy. They don't think of themselves as being innovative or brilliant. What inventions, medical cures, new ways of doing things, mentoring, peace brokering, and laughter and joy, has the world missed out on?

> *"You should not be teaching what to think, you should be teaching how to think."*
> *–Jasper*

Jasper's insights on evaluation

When I gave a presentation to a group of Grade 12 students and asked how they would reimagine learning environments, this is how one student, Jasper, responded:

1. *First, you should not be teaching what to think, you should be teaching how to think, because if you just teach one thing, you just know that one thing, but if you know how to learn and how to go about doing something, then you can know as many things as you want.*

2. *Second, your understanding of a subject is more important than your performance on it because a test is not really the best measure because you can be stressed out and things can happen. But if you can have some way to judge how much they (a student) really understand it and what they understand, then that's a better assessment of what the student knows.*

3. *And third, you should be able to choose what you want to learn, and be able to go about, to some degree, how you learn as well. Because everyone learns differently. Although you can't always learn something in a certain way.*

But you should be able to learn how it best suits you. And if you can choose what you want to learn earlier on in your life, then you can kinda get to know [the] *what* more *and be better at what you're going to do earlier on.*

To hear Jasper himself, use the QR code for Video 12.1.

Video 12.1

Jasper: A Student's Insight on Evaluation

Jasper provides his ideas on how schools should be reimagined and why tests are not really the best tool for evaluation.

You Can't Teach Brilliance or Test It, and That Scares People

I've found the same individuals who get nervous about loosening our death grip on standardized tests start to sweat even more profusely when I say you can't teach innovation, creativity, or brilliance, nor can you measure, test, or grade it. You can't wrap innovation up in a nice, neat box. It's messy. It involves making mistakes, or what we like to call experiments. And attempting to grade it, to say this is right and that is wrong, can cut off the branches of future thoughts and ideas. I don't mean to worry people, so I try to explain there are a few reasons behind my thinking.

First, by its very nature, innovation is something new; it's the next step *beyond* what has been learned in the classroom. Knowledge is based on what we know, but innovation is based on "what can be." You can teach someone how to spell and construct sentences, but these are merely tools. It's the innovation within a person, their seed of brilliance, that takes the knowledge a step beyond to write the award-winning screenplay or a novel or a speech that spurs people to action. You can teach kids to memorize multiplication tables and divide fractions, but innovation is fueled by imagination and curiosity that leads to the next step, the spark to make several attempts and failures in designing a new type of city. As we learned from Boyan Slat in Chapter 3, it was not his math scores that drove him to design technology that cleans the oceans but his unwavering curiosity to research and to use his math knowledge to figure out how it could be done. We can reach proficiencies, but after that, it's curiosity and innovation that takes us to the next level.

Second, a seed of brilliance rarely manifests to its full potential within a school term. As we're seen, students whose abilities were graded as mediocre or poor sometimes went on to do great things in the same subject area. Grading brilliance is like grading a seedling for the size of the pumpkin that it hasn't yet grown.

Last but not least, I strongly believe that trying to grade brilliance is just plain wrong. It damages and harms students to attempt to assess and evaluate their seed of brilliance, or the things they are passionate or curious about. Imagine how a student feels when they become engaged in an emerging passion, something that really begins to spark their interest and their desire to learn more, only to be told that's the "wrong answer."

We Need to Wean Ourselves Off Our Addiction to Analytics

There's another reason why our inability to measure brilliance can be quite frightening to some people. It's because in our Age of Complexity, with so many competing factors and variables, figuring things out is very hard, and knowing the best decision to make or the right course of action to take is even harder.

I believe that's often the appeal of a multiple-choice test, given to everyone, marked by a machine, used as the same scorecard for all. It appears to simplify the whole process, to make the required next steps seem more obvious. For some, it even feels soothing, and that's not imaginary—some people can actually become addicted to checking their analytics and metrics, as doing so supplies the same shots of dopamine one gets from seeing upvotes on their social media posts (Weinschenk, 2012).

To be clear, we're not saying test analytics are a bad thing, but they need to be taken in context and the results used judiciously.

(Although I must say, I oppose the public posting of standardized test scores. Likewise, the pressure to maintain or raise home values in the surrounding community should have no place in educational decision-making.)

Evaluate the Learning Environment, Not the Students

So where do we start with assessing a student's creativity? By not doing it!

We've included a chapter on evaluation because we think it is essential that educators evaluate the learning environment (not the students!). In our misguided *upside-downity*, as we speak of creativity, some seek to impose some contrived hierarchy, testing children and placing them in rank order of how creative they are. It wouldn't surprise me if we next see remedial classes for the uncreative, with step-by-step guided learning on how to be creative.

So it is not the children's creativity that we measure. That is a travesty to be avoided. Instead, it's our job to identify, explore, play with, and assess the critical elements that contribute to cultures of possibility—cultures of creativity.

The goal is to evaluate the learning culture, to ensure the environment meets the imperatives, the conditions, and the characteristics that will enable creativity to take hold. These categories are those that will guide our assessment of possibility.

Strategies for Getting Buy-In from Stakeholders

Don't expect your cultural shift to an innovative learning environment to be easy. Your leaders and decision-makers may understand the benefits that creativity and innovation bring, they may say they want those things, but the bottom line is that you will get pushback. This final chapter will help you find common ground and buy-in within your spheres of influence, and to deal with pushback in a productive way.

And if someone whose support you need is still very reluctant to move beyond the narrow two-subject focus and standardized tests and embrace creativity, you can tell them that studies show students' math and language scores increase if they're encouraged to be curious in the classroom, and this influence was even greater for children from impoverished backgrounds (Shad et al., 2018).

In *The Wonder Wall*, we explored the four common fears that leaders and team members may have and how you, as an innovation or creativity leader, could help them overcome these. Briefly, these are shown in Figure 12.1.

Figure 12.1 Strategies for Helping Colleagues Overcome Their Fears

Fear	Your task as an innovation leader
The unknown	Demystify the concept. Demonstrate how this cultural shift will bring benefits for all.
Losing control/lost productivity	Demonstrate that creativity follows a process, has rigor, involves weighing pros and cons and, rather than disrupting entrenched processes, helps them expand and grow.
Losing autonomy or earned benefits through flattened hierarchies	Show how supporting informal leadership at all levels exponentially expands innovation that will benefit the organization and all members.
Being left behind/no seed of brilliance to offer	Create the conditions that draw out seeds of brilliance through fostering a culture of belonging and a strength-based approach. Emphasize all viewpoints, knowledge and experiences are needed at the table.

Start Creating Your Evaluation Framework

Creativity and innovation are fundamentally messy pursuits, so we shouldn't expect our assessments to come in nice, neat packages. There's overlap and dependency, and every child, every situation, every district, and the situation and goals of every organization are different. The questions one school asks to cultivate their students' seeds of brilliance will never be exactly the same as another school's.

To give you some examples of what you might start asking yourself, your team, and your leadership, we've given some sample questions here. Bear in mind that this is a thinking exercise, not a box-ticking exercise. You can find more ideas in *The Wonder Wall* and on my website.

Figure 12.2 Assessment of Environments Supporting Leadership Characteristics

Metric	How is it defined?	How is it experienced?	Notes
Leadership Leadership capability is believed to exist in every person, at all levels of the organization.	Who are considered leaders in the organization? Are informal leaders included in the definition of leadership? How is leadership defined? What are the qualities, actions, and values of an ideal leader? Does leadership mean taking a strength-based perspective?	Is there trust among the senior team? Is the culture of trust established throughout the organization? How is this communicated and brought to life? Provide specific examples. Are hierarchies flattened? Does the leadership team embrace uncertainty, risk-taking, and messiness in the pursuit of learning and innovation? What are some examples? How does leadership ensure ideas and feedback are invited and accepted from all levels? How is informal leadership encouraged and embraced? Are decision-making or planning sessions inclusive of employees from across all job categories and levels? Are parents and external business and community leaders included whenever possible?	
Curiosity Curiosity is recognized as the driving force for learning and embedded into the learning culture.	How do people define curiosity and imagination in your organization? Does curiosity mean the same thing to everyone? How do you create the diverse learning spaces to allow for the curiosity within everyone to ignite?	How is curiosity modeled throughout the organization? How is curiosity infused into the learning culture? Are partnerships, both internal and external, used to provide real-world project experiences? Does the culture foster curiosity and wonder for the individual, group and organization?	
Challenging of assumptions—and the assumptions on which the assumptions are based	From passive to active learning, is critical interaction with the inquiry encouraged? Do individuals and teams have a voice? How is having a voice defined?	How do you model and encourage the challenging of assumptions? Are students and adults allowed to question and challenge what at first appears to be nonnegotiable truths? Are people comfortable stating their own insights, or does everyone just agree with the most senior person in the room?	

Metric	How is it defined?	How is it experienced?	Notes
Challenging or questioning the status quo and ingrained beliefs is viewed as the lifeblood of innovation, and is not something to be feared.	How do you define a culture of questioning rigorous inquiry? What does it look like?	Are there discussions and learnings of how to research, to debate respectfully, to weigh evidence, to actively listen to different viewpoints with a goal to learn, accept new ideas, and to find common ground on which to work toward solutions? Are formal structures set up to ensure all voices are heard? Is there a formal structure to give individuals and teams the opportunity to think and to provide input about how things might be done differently?	
Collision of ideas A trusting and open learning culture encourages people to be curious and to challenge assumptions, which in turn allows for the collision of ideas and a pathway forward to new ideas, new futures, and innovation.	What does social responsibility mean? What might happen if two individuals or groups disagree? How is the concept of differing beliefs or values viewed? For example, is it fighting, or is it about dancing together with ideas? Are pathways to learning expected to be beautiful all the time? Can learning be sometimes painful?	Are structures developed through which people's voices can be heard? Are students encouraged to think of themselves as change makers? Do students and teachers have the opportunity for choice? Is emotional intelligence and empathy taught and modeled? Are differences between people, cultures, organizations, and viewpoints embraced? Are people who disagree with leadership or decisions invited to share their insight? Are they seen as a nuisance or is their insight valued? Do you engage diverse multiple perspectives and points of view as an integral part of your decision-making, learning, and work culture? Is your organization culturally diverse? Do you engage a broad range of people with different thinking and learning styles? Do you invite people in from other industry sectors and ask for their ideas?	
Shift from a culture of one right answer to embracing the messiness and complexity of learning	How do you define the shift from teaching students to answer the questions to encouraging them to question the answers?	How do you model this? How do you encourage this? What are the safeguards in place to allow people to experiment while mitigating the risks? Do the leadership say it's okay to experiment but react negatively when failure occurs?	

209

Characteristics of a Reimagined Learning Culture

During our Renfrew district road trip (Chapter 8), many of the participants were moved by other characteristics of imaginative and supportive learning cultures.

Here are some of the major themes that inspired our visitors, and their takeaways.

Leadership support is a key indicator

Leadership arose as perhaps the most essential component creating innovative environments. Without the cooperation and support of leaders, virtually nothing can move forward.

This involves leadership not only within the district but also on a broader scale. The concept of leadership needs to be broadened and redefined.

"We need all the voices, but we also need leaders with different perspectives to step forward and share their thoughts and ideas," Lynn said. "And it can't always just be the person who gets paid the most or has the biggest office."

Savannah also saw the value of multiple leadership levels, with different backgrounds, collaborating. "I love being a part of this (road trip) group because there are people from so many different levels and backgrounds of education, coming together to discuss creativity and innovation in the classroom. I'm wondering about the ways in which different levels can contribute within the field of education. Where can you contribute the most? What types of impact are greatest for student and adult organizations? I'm excited to see different levels here, to talk with superintendents, teachers, and consultants in the field."

Flatten the hierarchies

For Brianna, flattened hierarchies provide another means to strengthen and empower leadership. "I love that theme of breaking down barriers and for me, one of the foundational aspects of that is flattening hierarchies. Leadership lies in the informal leaders because they're the heart and the soul of the organization. If you can unleash leadership, it's very powerful. Unfortunately, all too often, people in an organization with hierarchically framed leaders feel stifled."

Betty built on that point. "You need a person with authority to say I'm going to enable you to bring ideas forward. I really loved the leadership clubs (in Renfrew) where we saw leadership at all levels, where the teachers enabled the kids to be leaders. The teachers were enabled first by the structure to be comfortable doing that. It's a domino effect."

Tawana sees leadership as a pathway to sustainable, systemic change. "I've been looking at how to transform organizations. How do you understand the organizational culture and use that knowledge to implement systemic change that is long lasting, permanent, and sustainable?"

Personalize learning

Tim, a Renfrew teacher, says, "If you give students an opportunity to do something a bit different and use some practical skills when they're learning, they just thrive. We saw an opportunity and a real need for kids to learn some things our normal curricular courses don't provide. We started bundling credits together and having them work all day in the outdoors and inside. It's worked better than we possibly could have imagined."

Emma noted that project-based learning ought to be the norm, and we need to push back on the stereotype that such learning is noisy, without structure, and chaotic.

Instill an attitude of celebration and positivity— especially in building relationships

Savannah was struck by the overall mood of the teaching environment. "In addition to the intentionality of relationship building was the intentionality of positivity, is how everyone talks about everything going on in their district. It goes a long way when you intentionally adopt a rhetoric of positivity; it trickles down and extends to everyone."

Betty agreed. "It struck me how the theater teacher spoke so positively about the students, about how wonderful they were, how creative they were, and what a joy it was to work with them. It was striking the way in which he talked."

Value teacher voice

Throughout our road trip journey, the TeachHouse and TLFP fellows emphasized the importance of your own teacher voice—how the ability to use it and to have it respected is essential to teacher well-being. This is something that both institutions foster within their fellows, so seeing how teacher voice is supported in the Renfrew schools was therefore of keen interest to them.

It's not just giving students and teachers a voice to check off a box, there's an openness to that feedback. They're interested in feedback

A reimagined learning culture is . . . "accepting, it's inclusive. It's a place where learning happens without being forced or being imposed on anybody . . . . It's a space where people can be themselves, their best selves."

–Jen Barnes

and ideas from everyone in their organization—even from a group of visitors. They believe they're going to learn something valuable.

In closing, I'd like to share with you a quote from Jen Barnes, Renfrew's superintendent of Business and Corporate Services. When I asked her what her reimagined a learning culture would look like and sound like, she responded, "It would be a happy hum. It's an energy. It's a feeling, it's when you walk into a school, whether it's a noisy or a quiet classroom, it's people, it's accepting, it's inclusive. It's a place where learning happens without being forced or being imposed on anybody, but rather it's a space where people can be themselves, their best selves."

I don't think truer words have ever been spoken.

CHAPTER 12

Key Takeaways

▶ If we are to have innovative, imaginative minds to be able to flourish in an Age of Complexity, then we must reimagine our schools instead of doing the same thing over and over again.

▶ We cannot measure or assess brilliance, but we can and should assess our classroom and students to ensure they have the imperatives and conditions for healthy, innovative learning environments. Evaluate the environment, not the brilliance.

▶ Leadership support is critical to igniting and transforming the transformational cultural shift required to bring out the seeds of brilliance in every individual.

Reflective Questions

1. How comfortable are you with undertaking transformative change? How will you model confidence and help others get excited and motivated for the changes ahead?

2. How comfortable are you with taking risks? How does your district react when mistakes happen, or failures occur? In what ways can teachers and students see failures as a learning opportunity on the way to success?

3. Transformative change doesn't happen overnight. What milestones do you expect to see on your journey? How will you celebrate each one?

Try This!

Get Ready for Your One-of-a-Kind Journey

Whether you're now bursting with ideas and itching to go or you're just contemplating that first important step, you're about to embark on the journey of a lifetime. And what makes that trip all the more fascinating is that it will be totally unique—no other school or district in the world has exactly the same students, teachers, staff, location, parents, community, potential partnerships, challenges, or opportunities that yours does. So while we're on the subject of evaluation, why not begin assessing all the unique aspects and highlights that will make the journey exciting?

- Start with a kickoff "Bon Voyage" celebration at your next team meeting. Pick up some dollar-store sun hats, flowered necklaces, and sunglasses to make it fun, and bring in a giant suitcase. Arrange charts around the room and sticky notes and ask your teams to start off by envisioning all the unique things about your school or district and posting them on the charts with sticky notes. Assure them that should include the bad things as well as the good. Other charts can include areas they want to explore, such as new teaching techniques, different ways to organize classrooms, or a new structure for professional development.

- Next, tell your team it's time to pack for the trip. They need to figure out which unique aspects they want to take on the journey—and what they might want to leave behind. For example, they might want to take flattened hierarchies on the trip but less testing. Anyone can take a sticky note and toss it into the suitcase. Whatever is left on the charts are the things to be left behind for now, while you have a whole suitcase of things to pack for your journey.

Good luck! Send us a postcard!

References

ABC7 Eyewitness News. (2021). 12-year-old prodigy set to attend college, says she plans to land job at NASA. March 14, 2021 edition.

Berman, M. G., Jonides, J., & Kaplan, S. (2009). The cognitive benefits of interacting with nature. ResearchGate. From https://www .researchgate.net/. doi: 10.1111/j.1467-9280.2008.02225.x ISBN: 1467-9280

Bezzina, A. (2016). A mathematician who nearly failed maths. *Cosmos Magazine, 16* September, 2016. Cosmosmagazine.com.

Bloomberg School of Public Health staff report. (2020, March 25). *Study finds increases in anxiety, depression, suicidal thinking among U.S. adolescents seeking mental health care.* Baltimore, MD: John Hopkins.

Boyanslat.com. (2020). *Big problems require big solutions.* ©The Ocean Cleanup.

Bridgeland, J. M., Dilulio Jr., J. J., & Burke Morison, K. (2006). *The silent epidemic: Perspectives of high school dropouts.* Seattle, WA: Bill & Melinda Gates Foundation.

California Academy of Sciences. (2011, August 24). How many species on Earth? *Science News.* From Calacademcy.org.

Clark, D., & Shang, P. (2021). *A guide to gem-cutting styles: An introduction to gemology.* International Gem Society. From gem-society.org

Copland, A., & Ryan, J. (1942). *Fanfare for the common man* [Music].

Dawson, M. R. W., & Medler, D. A. (2010). Sympathetic resonance. *Dictionary of Cognitive Science.* Edmonton, Canada: University of Alberta.

Dodgson, L. (2017, May 16). 15 successful people who didn't do well at school. *Insider.* From Businessinsider.com.

Dunckley, V. L. (2013, June 13). Nature's RX: Green-time's effects on ADHD. *Psychology Today.* From Psychologytoday.com.

Ellucian. (2019). *Course correction: Helping students find a path to success—A survey of U.S. students.* ellucian.com

Fitzgerald, R. (2020). *10 Takeaways: How schools impact home values.* Raleigh Realty Homes. From Raleighrealtyhomes.com

Frank, R., & Livingston, K. E. (2002). *The secret life of the dyslexic child.* Emmau, PA: Rodale Books.

Gadye, L. (2021, June 7). *The past and future of the IQ test.* Brainfacts/SfN. From Brain facts.org

Gamwell, P. (2002). *Learning through the arts: An investigation of intermediate students as they explore and construct their understandings of language and literature through artistic activities* (pp. 206–231). Ontario, Canada: University of Ottawa.

Gamwell, P., & Daly, J. (2017). *The wonder wall: Leading creative schools and organizations in an age of complexity.* Thousand Oaks, CA: Corwin.

Gardiner, F., Fox, A., Knowles, F., & Jeffrey, D. (1996, May 23). Learning improved by arts training. *Nature journal.* From Nature.com

Glasser, H. (2016). *Transforming the difficult child.* Nurtured Heart Approach™. From Howardglasser.com

Geocaching.com. (n.d.). *3 steps to begin your adventure.* From www.geocaching.com/play

Greenberg, M. T. (2016). *Teachers stress and health: Effects on teachers, students and schools.* Princeton, NJ: Robert Wood Johnson Foundation. From Academia.edu.

Harmon-Jones, E. (2004, October). Contributions from research on anger and cognitive dissonance to understanding the motivational functions of asymmetrical frontal brain activity. *Biological Psychology.* [Special Issue: Frontal EEG asymmetry, emotion, and psychopathology], *67*(1), pp. 51–76. doi: PMID 15130525. S2CID 81 37723

Huxley, A. (1962). *Island.* New York, NY: Harper & Row.

Johnson, C. (2007, June). 2007 Study. *Journal for Research in Music Education* [Study funded by NAMM Foundation under its Sounds of Learning initiative].

Kaplan, R., & Kaplan, S. (1989). *The experience of nature: A psychological perspective.* Cambridge, MA: Cambridge University Press [ISBN 978-0-521-34139-4].

Kappes, A., & Sharot, T. (2019). Here's what happens in the brain when we disagree. *The Conversation.* From Theconversation.com

Kopestinsky, A. (2021). What is the average American income in 2021? *Policy Advice.* From Policyadvice.net

Kuo, M., Barnes, M., & Jordan, C. (2019, February). Do experiences with nature promote learning? Converging evidence of a cause-and-effect relationship. *Frontiers in Psychology, 19.* doi10.3389/fpsyg.2019.00305

Kuo, M., Browning, M. H. E. M., & Penner, M. L. (2018, January 4). Do lessons in nature boost subsequent classroom engagement? Refueling students in flight. *Frontiers in Psychology.* doi.org/10.3389/fpsyg.2017.02253

Lloyd-Strovas, J. (2018). Nature increases student performance on standardized tests. *Nature Matters with Dr. Jenny.* From jennylloydstrovas.com

Lund, D. (2018, June). Top 5 benefits of children playing outside. *Sandford Health.* From https://news.sanfordhealth.org/childrens/play-outside/

McKinley, M. B. (2006). *Hockey: A people's history* [TV series]. Canada: Canadian Broadcasting Corporation (CBC), Documentary Unit.

Michael. (n.d.). Using a Socratic wheel for assessment. *Ecology of Design in Human Systems.* From Ecologyofdesigninhumansystems.com

Michon, H. (2018). *The other Mozart prodigy: The life of Maria Anna, Mozart's sister.* From Liveabout.com. August 6, 2018 edition.

Military.com. (2020). *Why UFO sightings are up in 2020* [Video]. From https://www.military.com/video/why-ufo-sightings-are-2020

Milligan, F. (2017). *Dyslexic Daisy.* From https://www.downrightdyslexic.com/about

Milligan, F. (2019). Downrightdyslexic.com.

Morjaria, D. (2019). Boyan Slat's Ocean Cleanup project successfully retrieves plastic from the Great Pacific Garbage Patch. *DOGOnews,* October 7, 2019. From DOGOnews.com

Murphy Jr., B. (2015). *14 inspiring people who found crazy success later in life.* From Inc.com.

NAMM Foundation. (2007). *New study reveals strong relationship between quality music education programs and higher standardized test scores: Making music helps make the grade* [News Press Release]. From Nam.org

National Center for Educational Statistics. (2012). *Schools and staffing survery (SASS).* From Nces.ed.gov

Nield, D. (2018). Scientists show the effect quitting Facebook has on your body and stress levels. *ScienceAlert.* From Sciencealert.com

Oommen, A. (2014). Factors influencing intelligence quotient. *J Neurol Stroke 1*(4): 00023. doi: 10.15406/jnsk.2014.01.00023

Orlowski, J., Coombe, D., & Curtis, V. (2020). *The social dilemma.* [Documentary]. From Netflix.

Ottawa Carleton District School Board. (2012). *Unleashing potential, harnessing possibilities: An odyssey of creativity, innovation and critical thinking* [Report]. Ottawa, Canada: Ottawa Carleton District School Board.

Perkins School for the Blind. (2021, February 11). Q&A: A factual look at Helen Keller's accomplishments. (2021). *Perkins School for the Blind, Stories.* From perkins.org

Quaglia, R. (2014). *Teacher Voice Report 2010–2014.* Quaglia Institute for Student Aspirations and Teacher Voice and Aspirations International Center. In partnership with Corwin and Southern New Hampshire University.

Rice, T., Eckford, R., Webber, A. L., & Stimpson, P. (1972). *Jesus Christ superstar: The authorized version.* London, UK: Pan Books.

Schafer, M. (1993). *Our sonic environment and soundscape: The tuning of the world.* Detroit, MI: Destiny Books.

Shah, P. E., Weeks, H. M., Richards, B., & Kaciroti, N. (2018, April). Early childhood curiosity and kindergarten reading and math academic achievement. *Pediatric Research, 84*(3), 380–386. From nature.

com, April 26, 2018. doi.org/10.1038/s41390-018-0039-3

Sharot, T., Kappes, A., Harvey, A. H., & Lohrenz, T. (2019, December 16). Confirmation bias in the utilization of others' opinion strength. *Nature Neuroscience 23,* 130–137. From https://neuroscience-news.com/neuroscience-disagree-15351/doi:10.1038/s41593 -019-0549-2

Sparks, S. D. (2017). How teachers' stress affects students: A research roundup. *Education Week.* From edweek.org

Stainburn, S. (2014). Finland's latest export: A novel approach to recess. *Education Week.* From edweek.org

Svalbard Global Seed Vault. (2021). From seedvault.no

Wicker, E. (2021). About. From Thebrownstemgirl .com

Theoceancleanup.com. (2021). *How it all began.* ©The Ocean Cleanup.

Tornio, S. (2019). 12 powerful statistics that prove why teachers matter. *We Are Teachers,* From weareteachers.com

Uncapher, M. (2016, October 14). The science of effective learning spaces. From edutopia .org

University of Kentucky. (2016). Study finds our desire for "like-minded others" is hard-wired. *KU News Service, Lawrence.*

University of Michigan. (2010). Empathy: College students don't have as much as they used to. *Michigan News.*

University of Sydney, Australian Government, Australia Council for the Arts. (2014). *Arts participation and students' academic outcomes.* From YouTube: ACARA.

Walsh, C. (2021, February 17). Young adults hit by loneliness during pandemic. *The Harvard Gazette.* Cambridge, MA.

Weinschenk, S., & Wise, B. (2012, September). Why we're all addicted to texts, Twitter and Google. *Psychology Today.* From psychologytoday.com

Worrall, S. (2012, February 17). We are wired to be outside. *National Geographic.* From nationalgeopraphic.com

Index

A SAGE Publishing Company

CORWIN HAS ONE MISSION: to enhance education through intentional professional learning.

We build long-term relationships with our authors, educators, clients, and associations who partner with us to develop and continuously improve the best evidence-based practices that establish and support lifelong learning.

Keep learning...

Also from Peter Gamwell and Jane Daly

THE WONDER WALL

PETER **GAMWELL**

JANE **DALY**

FOREWORD BY SIR KEN ROBINSON

LEADING CREATIVE SCHOOLS & ORGANIZATIONS IN AN AGE OF COMPLEXITY

The philosophy behind **Peter Gamwell** Consulting is simple: the health and prosperity of any organization is directly proportional to the manner in which it values its people; affords them autonomy to make decisions; and allows them creative rein. Visit petergamwell.com to learn more.

Jane Daly knows how you can make your business more innovative. Visit janedaly.ca for webinars, workshops, and more to help your company make the extraordinary happen.

Peter Gamwell

CULTIVATING INNOVATION

Check out the Cultivating Innovation YouTube page!

CORWIN

LDN22370